DATE DUE

JUN 7 '89			

Spanish-Speaking Children
of the Southwest

Spanish-Speaking Children
of the Southwest

Their Education and the Public Welfare

by **HERSCHEL T. MANUEL**

UNIVERSITY OF TEXAS PRESS AUSTIN

International Standard Book Number 0-292-73385-2
Library of Congress Catalog Card No. 65–13516
Copyright © 1965 by Herschel T. Manuel
All Rights Reserved

Third Printing, 1971
Manufactured in the United States of America

To
Parents, Teachers,
and
Friends of Children

PREFACE

My initial interest in the Spanish-speaking children of the Southwest grew in part out of a course which I taught about a third of a century ago dealing with individual differences and exceptional children. I had spent my early life in the Midwest and had come to The University of Texas from a teaching position in a Colorado college. With the assistance of the University Fund for Research in the Social Sciences, I completed a study which was published by the University in 1930 under the title *The Education of Mexican and Spanish-Speaking Children in Texas.* During the intervening years I have had a keen interest in this area, and my experience with linguistic and cultural problems has been enriched in various ways, notably by contacts with education in Puerto Rico. A number of my students have contributed research studies.

In 1958, with the generous support of the Hogg Foundation for Mental Health, the opportunity came for me to return actively to the research which had been initiated many years earlier. In this latest study my primary objective has been to produce a volume addressed to the general public but useful also to teachers and others who are professionally interested in Spanish-speaking children. Information from many sources is related to the education of Spanish-speaking children, but the materials are scattered. In this book some of the existing materials and certain new data are brought together and discussed.

I have been puzzled by the problem of crediting source material, both to acknowledge my indebtedness and to introduce the reader to additional information. To make the text more readable I have avoided footnotes and have reduced parenthetical references to a minimum. Compensating in a degree for this lack, I have listed a number of references to related materials under References.

I deeply regret that I am unable to give adequate credit to the host of persons from whom I have received help of one kind or another.

My indebtedness runs back through the years. In this most recent study I have visited schools in five states and have conferred with many persons in school and out. I have had the benefit not only of printed materials but also of outlines, reports, and personal letters. Many persons have helped in other ways. I could not possibly give the personal credit which I should like to give without overburdening the discussion with names. I have given a few names in the text, but I am conscious that in listing some persons I have neglected others of equal or perhaps greater merit. I am extremely grateful for the help which I have received.

For helpful comments at various stages in the preparation of the manuscript, I am indebted to Mrs. Anita Brewer, journalist, staff of *Austin-American Statesman*; Dr. Ralph B. Long, professor of English, University of Puerto Rico; Dr. William Madsen, associate professor of anthropology, The University of Texas; Dr. Thomas F. McGann, professor of history, The University of Texas; Mrs. Bert Kruger Smith, mental health education specialist, Hogg Foundation for Mental Health; Dr. Wayne H. Holtzman, professor of psychology, The University of Texas, and associate director, Hogg Foundation for Mental Health; Dr. Robert L. Sutherland, professor of sociology, The University of Texas, and Director, Hogg Foundation for Mental Health.

I am especially indebted to the Hogg Foundation for Mental Health for the financial support which made the study possible. But it goes without saying that neither the Hogg Foundation for Mental Health nor any of the persons who have assisted me are responsible for the point of view, the choice of materials, or the opinions which I have expressed. This responsibility is mine alone.

HERSCHEL T. MANUEL

Austin, Texas

CONTENTS

ILLUSTRATIONS

(following page 98)

Reading Groups—El Paso, Texas
Library and Laboratory—Austin, Texas
School and Community Cooperate—Tempe, Arizona
Language-Learning Center—Los Angeles, California
Happy Birthday—El Paso, Texas
A Contrast in Housing
Halloween—Alamosa, Colorado
"Have we not all one father?"
Kindergarten—Denver, Colorado

FIGURES

TABLES

Spanish-Speaking Children
of the Southwest

1. A Problem of Education
and the Public Welfare

We of the Southwest—Arizona, California, Colorado, New Mexico, and Texas—are more than thirty million people, and a varied lot. We are descendants of southern Europeans, northern Europeans, native Americans, Asians, and Africans. Among us are wide differences in ancestry, physical appearance, historical background, language, beliefs, attitudes, values, and living patterns. Out of these different people we are trying to build an effective democratic society. We are struggling with the age-old and world-wide problem of learning to live together and to bring the benefits of cooperative action to all our people.

In the kind of society which we are trying to build and maintain, education is a basic necessity. Of this we are certain. But the pressures of other demands are so great that we need periodically to review our commitment to education and to seek ways of doing a better job.

The Southwest has sufficient resources to give a higher priority to education, but ability to educate is not enough. The will of a people to educate its children—all of them—is of equal importance with the resources at hand for providing that education. In fact, if there is a failure to provide adequate educational opportunities, the cause of failure is more likely to be in the will to educate than anywhere else. The quality of the schools of a community is in large part a measure of the community's interest. The priority or lack of priority of educational needs is clearly reflected in the kind of schools which it provides.

Old Articles of Faith

Statesmen and others have many times pointed out the two-sided relation of education to a democratic society—first the right of every child to an education, and second the necessity of education for such a society. The community has not only an obligation to educate its children but also a self-interest in their education. More than a hundred years ago, Horace Mann wrote (his Annual Report of 1846):

I believe in the existence of a great, immortal, immutable principle of natural law, or natural ethics—a principle antecedent to all human institutions, and incapable of being abrogated by any ordinance of man—a principle of divine origin, clearly legible in the ways of Providence as those ways are manifested in the order of Nature and in the history of the race, which proves the *absolute right* to an education of every human being that comes into the world, and which, of course, proves the correlative duty of every government to see that the means of that education are provided for all.

In regard to the application of this principle of natural law—that is, in regard to the extent of the education to be provided for all at the public expense—some differences of opinion may fairly exist under different political organizations; but, under our republican government, it seems clear that the minimum of this education can never be less than such as is sufficient to qualify each citizen for the civil and social duties he will be called to discharge—such an education as teaches the individual the great laws of bodily health, as qualifies for the fulfilment of parental duties, as is indispensable for the civil functions of a witness or a juror, as is necessary for the voter in municipal and in national affairs, and, finally, as is requisite for the faithful and conscientious discharge of all those duties which devolve upon the inheritor of a portion of the sovereignty of this great Republic.

Educational Demands of a Modern World

The eloquent statement of Horace Mann is still valid, but it now understates the need of formal education. In this century we have moved into an urban, industrial, scientific, and small-world society in which the needs of formal education are multiplied over and over. Times have changed, and our people must be prepared for citizenship in a different world and for participation in a different economy. Large numbers of our people are longing for greater security and for higher standards of living. Automation is remaking industry. To meet the needs of this new day, to compete successfully, and perhaps even to survive, we must conserve and develop our human resources to the highest possible level. The number at the top from whom we must draw our scientists, inventors, artists, engineers, writers, and other leaders is limited. We must find them wherever they are. At the other end of the scale we have a constantly diminishing need for unskilled labor. The community needs the maximum contribution which every person can make, and the individual needs the opportunity to make that contribution.

The waste of a human life through lack of appropriate education and guidance is always a double tragedy, and frequently a triple tragedy. The person lacking education and guidance loses a vital part of the life which he might have lived, and society loses a part of its most valuable resource—human capacity. If in addition the person becomes antisocial, the loss is not only a failure to receive the positive contribution which he might have made, but also a subtraction from the common welfare.

A recent study of high school drop-outs (*Research Bulletin*, National Education Association, 1960) points out that "one in every three ninth-graders fails to finish high school," that "schooling is closely related to job level," that persons who lack a high school diploma are at a "disadvantage in periods of high unemployment," and that "juvenile delinquency is 10 times more frequent among drop-outs than among high school graduates."

The President's Committee on Youth Employment discusses the problem of finding jobs for young men and young women in its report *The Challenge of Jobless Youth* (Government Printing Office, 1963). In the opening paragraph the Committee points to the increased need of education and training for finding a place in the labor force:

Today's youth are tomorrow's adults—production and service workers, technicians, professionals, clerks and managers—parents or other heads of families. For most, their admission to this adult world, their badge of belonging, is a job. But it is much harder today for a boy or girl with limited education and training to get a job. The numbers of young people between 16 and 21 have increased greatly over the last generation because of the rise in the birth rate starting in the 1940's. The kinds of jobs they used to be able to fill are disappearing, and many of the jobs that are available demand much more skill and training than they now can offer.

Later the Committee expresses the need in greater detail:

In the 1960's, while the labor force is growing so rapidly, employment needs for unskilled workers will remain about the same and for farmworkers will drop about 20 per cent. These occupations have always been an important source of beginning jobs for young men coming out of school. By contrast, jobs will rise by about 40 per cent for professional and technical workers, and 20 per cent for sales workers and for managers and proprietors.

At the same time, more education and training is now required. The average professional or technical worker now has more than 4 years of college; clerical workers have more than a high school education.

The world confronting young people today is different from the world of their grandparents or parents. Old answers are outdated.

Before 1910 and even in the 1920's, many jobs were open to young people. Youths were needed on farms, were employed in local distribution and service trades, in factories, shops, and even mines. Nearly everyone could count on finding a job he could do with relatively little schooling.

These conditions no longer prevail. Our living and working standards as well as our job requirements now impose greater demands .

Automation, mechanization, and scientific advances are causing many unskilled jobs to disappear. Today's and tomorrow's jobs require higher skills, more maturity and judgment, and more experience.

The Committee recognizes the special problems of the unemployed youth who live in congested city areas:

Many of the unemployed youth live in congested city areas, surrounded by social disorganization, poverty, and despair. Their families usually occupy most inadequate housing. They are surrounded by other disadvantaged people, many of whom are unemployed or intermittently employed at low wages. Without successful examples among their elders to guide them, the youth of such families are unlikely to succeed.

The Education of Spanish-Speaking Children

Spanish-speaking people, the second largest of our population groups, are known variously as Mexican, Mexican-American, Latin, Latin-American, Spanish, Spanish-surname, Spanish-American, Spanish-speaking, and the like. Wide differences exist within the group, and none of these names is entirely satisfactory, but because Spanish is the home language of most (but not all) of the group and because language is a factor of major importance in the school and the community, the term "Spanish-speaking" will be used in this book.

Again emphasizing language rather than national origin, the largest of our population groups, often called Anglos, will be called

"English-speaking." At the risk of oversimplifying, little will be said of other groups.

The educative process is much the same for all children. Many children in the Spanish-speaking group have no greater difficulties than do English-speaking children. This favorable condition of many Spanish-speaking children we must constantly keep in mind. In large proportion, however, Spanish-speaking children are seriously handicapped by difficulties not shared equally by English-speaking children.

The first source of difficulty is one that really affects us all—the division of the community into contrasting groups, English-speaking and Spanish-speaking, each with a lack of understanding of the other and with a degree of hostility toward the other. After more than a century of living together, in many respects we are still a divided people. As suggested in the first paragraph, this division is itself a major problem—the problem of bringing the members of different population groups into a fully cooperative relationship from which original group lines have disappeared. A failure to understand each other and a hostile attitude between groups make it difficult for a community to plan its educational activities wisely and create problems within the school itself.

Differences in culture are a second source of difficulty in the education of Spanish-speaking children. These differences demand a corresponding adjustment of learning opportunities. They discourage free association and thus tend to perpetuate the isolation of one group from the other. It is often difficult for a Spanish-speaking child to become a full member of the community as a whole. Indeed many a youth is caught between his parental group and the rest of the community and is in part rejected by both.

A third difficulty is language, a cultural difference but listed separately because of its importance. Typically, the Spanish-speaking child has to learn English as a second language and then to use this second language in his school work while his out-of-school language is mainly Spanish. The result for a large number of children is lack of sufficient mastery of any language. This makes learning more difficult and tends toward further isolation.

As if these three difficulties were not enough, a large proportion of the Spanish-speaking children of the Southwest suffer the privations of low family income, often indeed of long-continued poverty. These privations have a direct bearing on the amount of education which the child is likely to receive and the kind of opportunity which the school finds it necessary to provide.

The purpose of this book is to present in perspective the difficulties of these children, to point out basic relationships and trends, and to consider possible ways of meeting specific needs.

2. The Background

If men could learn from history, what lessons
it might teach us! But passion and party
blind our eyes, and the light which experi-
ence gives is a lantern on the stern, which
shines only on the waves behind us!

—Samuel Taylor Coleridge

The present is but a scene in a never ending drama. The conditions and events which come and go with the passing of time are continuous with those which precede and those which follow. Persons who wish to exercise any control over the future would be well advised to know not only what the present is but also how it came to be.

Elements of the past of special importance to this study are: (1) the migration of two different peoples into the Southwest—groups representing the highest civilizations of Western Europe, but of different language and culture; (2) the background of intergroup strife from which these peoples came and the continuing of that strife in the American setting; (3) the reversal of the majority-minority status and the governmental role of the two groups; (4) the later migration into and out of the area; and (5) the more recent developments related to the problems of education. The first three of these will be reviewed briefly in this chapter.

Geographical Influences

The geography of the Southwest is an essential part of the picture. The location of the area between but somewhat distant from the earliest settlements of the English and Spanish invited both groups to come, but delayed their coming. The continuity of the Southwest with the territory north and south without serious natural barriers such as seas and mountains has made it easy to migrate into and out of the area. Its vast extent, now shared by five states, has given distinctive characteristics to its problems.

The Southwest is a huge area extending north and west of the Rio Grande from the Sabine River to the Pacific Ocean (see Figure 1). The border between the United States and Mexico—roughly from Brownsville, Texas, to San Diego, California—stretches for more than 1,500 miles. The state of Texas alone has an area greater than that of Massachusetts, New York, New Jersey, Pennsylvania, Ohio, Indiana, and Illinois together. New Mexico, Colorado, Arizona, and California have a combined area greater than that of Texas.

The low altitude, the soil fertility, and the mild temperature of East Texas invited farmers from the north and east and made this section a part of the Old South with a large Negro population. The arid plains of West Texas, which are continuous with those of northern Mexico, discouraged migration and limited the population which could be supported by agriculture in that area. Water courses were determiners of early settlements, and later became important sources of vast irrigation projects. Irrigation, in turn, has developed a type of agriculture which demands the seasonal labor provided in large measure by the Spanish-speaking population.

Mineral deposits also have influenced the development of the Southwest. The movement northward by the early Spanish explorers was determined in part by their search for precious metals, but their failure to find attractive sources of gold and silver in what is now called the Southwest discouraged large-scale migration. Generations later, the discovery of gold in California (1848) and in Colorado (1858) stimulated a heavy stream of migrants, but these were in large proportion English-speaking people. Still more recently the discovery of petroleum deposits at various points has led to increased industrialization.

A Heritage of High Culture

The English-speaking and Spanish-speaking people who came into the Southwest represented two great divisions of the culture of Western Europe, but they had much in common. Both England and Spain were among the leading powers of Europe. Both shared the learning inherited from Greece and Rome, and each had developed a language of its own. Both had provisions for education at the university level—

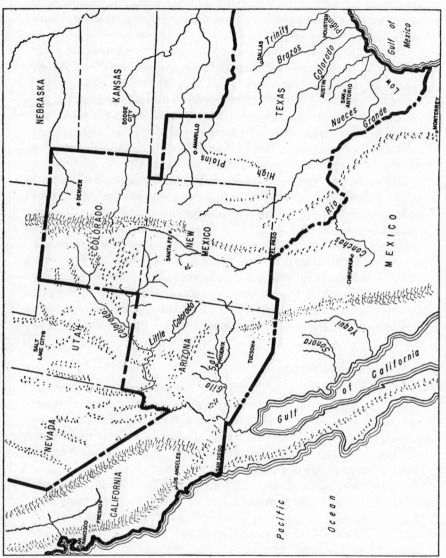

Fig. 1—The southwestern United States and northern Mexico.

Oxford and Cambridge in England and Salamanca in Spain. Both professed the Christian religion. Both had a vigorous trade, and both had ships sailing the seas.

The English-speaking people came to the Southwest from the north and east little changed by the native Indian population. The Spanish-speaking people, on the other hand, came through Mexico, where they had conquered the native people and in part mingled their blood with that of the natives. Intermarriage was approved by royal decree in 1514. The result was a Mexican population predominantly of mestizos (primarily a mixture of Spanish and Indian), with a smaller number of descendants of each of the original stocks.

The natives of Mexico, though isolated for centuries, had reached a high cultural level. Long before the Spanish conquest the Mayans had developed a calendar, hieroglyphic writing, and a number system including a symbol for zero. At the time of the coming of the Spaniards in 1519, the Aztecs then dominant had built a great Venice-like city, Tenochtitlán, approached by causeways, protected by drawbridges, and provided with palaces, market places, and temples. The native culture left its mark on the Spanish culture with which it came into conflict, but the culture emerging from this conflict was primarily Spanish—in language, religion, social relations, and political organization.

Differences and Intergroup Conflicts

Common elements in the heritage of the English-speaking and the Spanish-speaking people of the Southwest tend to bind them together, but differences tend to push them apart. Both are Christian, to be sure, but, typically, Protestant and Catholic. In general they speak different languages, have different traditions, and see the same events from different points of view.

The divisive effect of these differences is aggravated by a heritage of conflict. Throughout modern history the English-speaking and Spanish-speaking people have often been on opposing sides in armed conflict. First it was England against Spain: the battle of the English fleet with the Spanish Armada in 1588 was only the forerunner of many clashes during the next two centuries. Later it was the English-speaking people and the Spanish-speaking people of the New World who were in conflict—in 1836 Texas with Mexico, and ten years later the United States with Mexico.

Religious Differences

The heritage of conflict has centered in part around differences in religion. In the Middle Ages and well into the modern period church and state were closely related, and force was long a method of dealing with religious differences.

As early as the eleventh century, after much strife most of Europe was firmly Christian. The Roman Catholic Church prevailed in the West and the Greek Orthodox Church in the East, notably in Greece and Russia. The Moslems held the Near East, North Africa, and a part of Spain. In 1492 the Moslems lost their foothold in Spain, and in the same year the Jews were expelled from Spain. Two centuries earlier the Jews had been expelled from England (1290) and France (1306).

The forces of Christianity, already divided into East and West, were to suffer a further division, one which has never been overcome. Before the end of the Middle Ages both the doctrines and the authority of the Roman Church were being seriously questioned from within. John Wyclif (1320–1384) at the University of Oxford and John Hus (1369–1415) at the University of Prague appeared as forerunners of the religious upheaval known as the Protestant Reformation. The feelings aroused in centuries of mutual intolerance are illustrated in the fact that Hus was burned at the stake as a heretic and that the remains of Wyclif, who had died naturally, were disinterred and burned thirty years after his death.

The sixteenth century—a period when European nations were struggling for positions of influence in the Americas—was marked by the rise of Protestantism and the beginning of a Protestant-Catholic struggle which profoundly influenced the course of events for many years, and which, though changed in form, still lingers to divide people in the modern world. North Germany and the Scandinavian countries became Lutheran. England by action of Parliament established the Church of England, substituting the King for the Pope as the head of the Church. From Geneva Calvinism spread to various countries, notably to Scotland, where the Calvinistic Presbyterian Church became the state church. The French Huguenots also were Calvinists. The governments of Spain, France, and Italy remained Catholic.

In one way or another religious differences played a large part in civil wars and wars between nations until the end of the Thirty Years' War in 1648. Within both Protestant and Catholic countries, church and state cooperated to force people to accept the established religion. In Spain and Rome the Inquisition was a ruthless enemy of those who departed from the Catholic faith. In Protestant England laws were passed against recusants who refused to attend the established church. Elsewhere persecution, sometimes extreme, was a common method of dealing with those who dared to disagree.

Movement into the Southwest

Toward the Southwest, inhabited only sparsely by a native population, moved two peoples—the Spanish-speaking from the south and the English-speaking from the north and east. Into the Southwest they came and are still coming, streams flowing from immense reservoirs and intermingling like interlacing fingers which never lose their identity.

The Spanish-speaking were first. The dates of many of the early settlements are shown in Figure 2. The conquest of Mexico by the Spanish (1519–1521) was followed by a gradual movement northward. "New Spain" became a viceroyalty in 1535, and a settlement was established as far north as Saltillo in 1586. Santa Fe was founded in 1609, only two years after the first English settlement far to the east in Virginia. By 1680 there were some 2,500 settlers in New Mexico. A permanent settlement was established at San Antonio in 1718, and a mission and presidio were placed at San Diego in 1769. San Francisco was founded and a presidio was established at Tucson in 1776. According to the 1932 *Report of the Committee on Linguistic and National Stocks in the Population of the United States,* representing the American Council of Learned Societies, the white population of the Southwest in 1790 was practically all Spanish, an estimated 23,000 distributed as follows in areas which later became the states of Arizona, 1,000; California, 1,000; New Mexico, 15,000; and Texas, 6,000.

In the meantime the English-speaking people, with smaller numbers of others, had established the thirteen original colonies of the United States along the eastern coast, and these colonies had declared their independence. In 1803, by the purchase of Louisiana, the territory of the United States came in direct contact with the territory of Spain, and the population moving westward was soon to enter Spanish territory. By 1821, the year of Mexico's independence, the Eng-

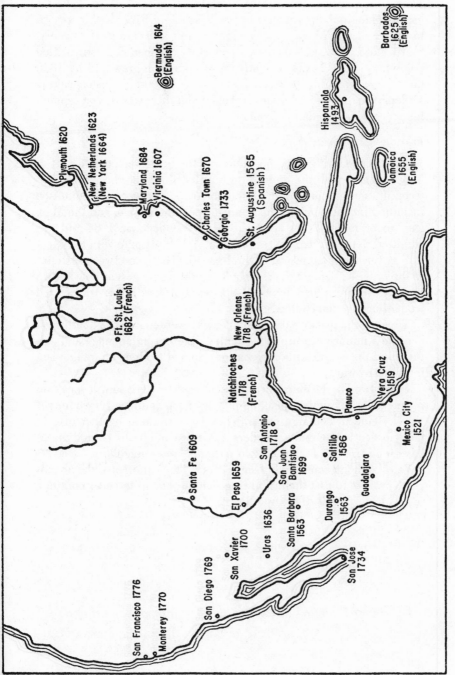

Fig. 2—Early settlements in North America.

lish-speaking population west of the Mississippi River had increased
to the point that Missouri was admitted to the Union as the twenty-
fourth state. This also was the year in which Stephen F. Austin settled
a colony in East Texas. The stream of migration grew and by 1835
there were probably between 25,000 and 35,000 English-speaking
settlers from the United States in Texas. But there was no corresponding increase in population from Mexico.

Transfer of Authority

Most of the foreigners who came into the Southwest, then a part of
Mexico, came with the understanding that they were becoming subjects of a new country. But trouble developed between the colonists,
including indeed some of the Spanish-speaking people, and the Mexican government. Texas achieved its independence in 1836 and was
admitted to the United States in 1845. A U.S. dispute with the Mexican government led to war with Mexico in 1846, and two years later
in the peace settlement the remainder of the Southwest as now known
(except a strip added by the Gadsden Purchase) was transferred
from Mexico to the United States.

Thus the Spanish-speaking people, who were first in the Southwest,
became a minority group in a country different in language and culture, and the two neighboring nations nursed feelings of antagonism
inflamed by war.

In the two World Wars of the present century the Spanish-speaking
people and the English-speaking people of the Southwest have fought
side by side in common cause. They have worked together also in
many peacetime pursuits. Leaders in Mexico and in the United States
have long tried to make the two nations "good neighbors." Yet despite what "men could learn from history," the enmities of the distant
past continue to cast their blighting shadow, and differences continue
to divide the people of the Southwest.

3. Spanish-Speaking Population
of the Southwest

In 1790 there were some 23,000 Spanish-speaking people in the Southwest. Changes in the population since that date are the result of the same factors that influence all populations—increase through births and migration into the area and decrease through deaths and migration out of the area. The movement into the Southwest from Mexico has been a major factor in increasing the number of Spanish-speaking people from the 23,000 of 1790 to the 3.8 million of 1960, and the movement continues.

Migration across the Border

Reports of the U.S. Immigration and Naturalization Service are the primary source of information on immigration and emigration. An indirect source of information is the United States census, which records at intervals the number of foreign-born and their country of origin. The balance between immigration and emigration is reflected in the number of foreign-born enumerated in the census.

Immigration to the United States from Mexico was relatively small before the present century. The number of immigrants by decades, beginning with 1861–1870 and continuing until 1951–1960, with the exception of two decades for which data are incomplete, is shown in Table 1. The peak was reached in 1921–1930 with almost a half million. The years of the depression then brought a sharp decrease in the number, but since that time the flow has again increased, reaching nearly 300,000 in the decade 1951–1960. During the decade 1952–1961 immigrants with Mexico as the country of birth num-

TABLE 1

Immigration to the United States from Mexico

Decade	Number	Decade	Number
		1911–1920	219,004
1861–1870	2,191	1921–1930	459,287
1871–1880	5,162	1931–1940	22,319
1881–1900	Records incomplete	1941–1950	60,589
1901–1910	49,642	1951–1960	299,811

bered 354,572. (There are minor differences in statistics based upon immigration "by country" and "by country of birth.")

Recent trends are shown by statistics not included in the table. The records for 1927 show approximately 68,000 immigrants from Mexico and about 3,000 emigrants to Mexico. By 1932 there was only a small flow of recorded immigrants but 37,000 emigrants. In 1945 the situation had become fairly stable, with a net recorded immigration of 5,500. A sharp upturn began about 1953, and the number of immigrants reached 61,300 in 1956, in contrast with some 200 emigrants, but as unfavorable economic conditions developed, immigration then declined for three years. When conditions improved, it again began an upward swing, to some 41,500 in 1961.

Of 41,632 immigrants admitted to the United States from Mexico as the country of birth during the year ended June 30, 1961, a total of 36,941 (nearly 89 per cent) gave one of the five states of the Southwest as the place of intended future permanent residence. But many were also going to Illinois. The distribution among the five states of the Southwest and of Illinois is shown in Table 2. To give an idea of what this immigration means in relation to the resident population, the table shows also the ratio of the number of immigrants to the number of white Spanish-surname persons enumerated in the U.S. census of 1960. In the Southwest as a whole this ratio is 1.1 per cent. (Not included in the census enumeration were Negro persons with Spanish surname, Oriental persons with Spanish surname, etc., but the number in such groups is negligible.) The ratio of immigrants (1961) to the white Spanish-surname population (1960) is greatest in California (1.6 per cent) and least in Colorado (0.1 per cent) and New Mexico (0.3 per cent).

The movement of Spanish-speaking people in significant numbers

TABLE 2

Immigrants of 1960–1961 Who Were Born in Mexico

State of Intended Future Residence	Number		Ratio to Spanish-Surname Persons Listed in 1960 Census
Arizona	2,274		1.2 %
California	22,484		1.6
Colorado	177		0.1
New Mexico	903		0.3
Texas	11,103		0.8
Southwest states		36,941	1.1 %
Illinois	2,463		
All other states	2,228		
Non-Southwest states		4,691	
All states		41,632	

across the Mexican border will undoubtedly continue, as will the pattern of immigration exceeding emigration, except for brief periods.

The year-by-year addition of an immigrant population to the resident Spanish-speaking population, together with the geographical continuity of the Southwest and Mexico, is a condition of great significance to education and the public welfare. For an indefinite future this area will have a large first generation and second generation of Spanish-speaking immigrants.

In round numbers, the foreign-born population from Mexico in the United States was 13,300 in 1850 and a little more than double that number in 1860. Of these totals 92 per cent and 96 per cent, respectively, were in the Southwest. The increase in numbers was especially rapid from 1900 to 1930. Here are the numbers in the Southwest alone for successive ten-year periods beginning in 1890:

Year		Year	
1890	75,400	1930	543,500
1900	100,200	1940	333,700
1910	201,600	1950	398,200
1920	427,400	1960	502,300

The half-million foreign-born persons from Mexico in 1960 were about 1.7 per cent of the total population, including all classes. In the five states the percentage varied from 0.3 per cent in Colorado to 2.8 per cent in Arizona.

The number of foreign-born persons and of native persons of

foreign or mixed parentage with Mexico as the country of origin is shown in Table 3. The statistics reveal a Southwest native-born population of foreign or mixed parentage about twice the number of Mexican foreign-born.

TABLE 3

*Southwest Population of Foreign Stock from Mexico as Country of Origin
(Census of 1960)*

	Foreign-Born	Native-Born of Foreign or Mixed Parentage	Total
Arizona	35,834	69,508	105,342
California	248,542	447,101	695,643
Colorado	4,882	15,209	20,091
New Mexico	10,725	23,734	34,459
Texas	202,315	453,208	655,523
Southwest	502,298	1,008,760	1,511,058

A percentage distribution of native and foreign stock in the 1960 population of white persons of Spanish surname is given in Table 4. In the Southwest as a whole, 15.4 per cent of the Spanish-surname population were foreign-born and another 29.7 per cent were of foreign or mixed parentage. The percentage of foreign stock was much lower in Colorado and New Mexico than in the other three states.

TABLE 4

*Percentage of Native and Foreign Stock in
Spanish-Surname White Population in the Southwest
(Census of 1960)*

	Native-Born		Foreign-Born
	Native Parentage	Foreign or Mixed Parentage	
Arizona	49.3	33.1	17.6
California	46.0	34.0	20.0
Colorado	86.1	10.4	3.5
New Mexico	87.4	8.6	3.9
Texas	54.8	31.2	14.0
Southwest	54.8	29.7	15.4

Spanish-Speaking Population in Relation to Total Population

The U.S. census of 1930 carried a racial classification of "Mexican." Enumerators were instructed to put into this classification "all persons of Mexican origin who were not definitely white, Negro, Indian, or Japanese." In the census of 1940, on the basis of a 5-percent sample, the population was classified on the question of "mother tongue, or language other than English spoken in the home in earliest childhood," and from this count statistics were tabulated on persons whose mother tongue was Spanish. In the census of 1950 and again in 1960 white persons of Spanish surname were identified on the schedules returned from the five states included in this study, and certain characteristics of this population were determined by a systematic sampling.

For a study of Spanish-speaking children the 1930 census is least useful. The creation of a racial classification of "Mexican" outside the white group was misleading, and accurate enumeration on this basis was impossible. On the other hand, the 1940 classification on the basis of home language was a very significant one from the standpoint of education and cultural assimilation. For example, it was shown that in the United States as a whole, only about 7 per cent of the native population with Mexican parentage reported English as their mother tongue. This percentage is undoubtedly increasing, and it would be helpful to know the rate of change. It was shown also that, at that time, more than four-fifths of all persons of Spanish home language lived in the five Southwestern states. Unfortunately the home-language basis of enumeration was abandoned in later censuses.

Although the names of people are a factor of minor significance in studying cultural problems, the count of Spanish surnames as used in the census of 1950 and the census of 1960 gives a useful estimate of the size of the cultural and linguistic group called Spanish-speaking. The figures are far from accurate, probably underestimating the number by 7 to 12 per cent. Intermarriage has brought non-Spanish names into the group and has taken some Spanish names out of the group culturally and linguistically. Moreover, names are not always distinctive—Abel and Martin, for example. In the census of 1960, of a group of foreign-born white persons identified by their Spanish surname or Mexican birth or both, 5.6 per cent were of Mexican birth without Spanish surname, and for that reason would not be included in a count of Spanish-surname persons. In the present study a count in four schools of 1,725 pupils whose home language was Spanish revealed approximately 11 per cent with non-Spanish names.

Population Statistics

The total population, the white Spanish-surname population, and the non-white population enumerated in the census of 1960 and the percentages of increase from 1950 to 1960 are shown in Table 5.

TABLE 5

Population of the Southwest in 1960
and Percentage of Increase in Population from 1950 to 1960

| | Total Population | | White Population | | | | Nonwhite Population[a] | |
| | | | Non-Spanish Surname | | Spanish[b] Surname | | | |
	No.	% of Increase	No.	% of Increase	No.	% of Increase	No.	% of Increase
Arizona	1,302,161	73.7	975,161	85.3	194,356	51.5	132,644	39.5
California	15,717,204	48.5	13,028,692	42.3	1,426,538	87.6	1,261,974	88.1
Colorado	1,753,947	32.4	1,543,527	31.0	157,173	33.0	53,247	87.3
New Mexico	951,023	39.6	606,641	59.1	269,122	8.1	75,260	47.6
Texas	9,579,677	24.2	6,957,020	22.2	1,417,811	37.1	1,202,846	22.4
Southwest	29,304,012	39.2	23,111,041	36.5	3,465,000	51.3	2,727,971	49.1

[a] The largest nonwhite population in Arizona and New Mexico is Indian and in each of the other three states is Negro.

[b] For a rough estimate of the number of Spanish-speaking persons, as the term is used here, add to each number 10 per cent of itself.

Applying a rough correction of 10 per cent to the Spanish-surname statistics of Table 5, an estimate is obtained of 3.8 million Spanish-speaking persons in the Southwest out of the 29.3 million enumerated in the census of 1960. By 1964 the number probably exceeded four million, and the nonwhite group was probably about three million. In 1960 California and Texas had nearly the same number of Spanish-surname people, and together the two states had more than four-fifths of the entire number. These states had about the same number of non-white persons also, and together had nearly nine-tenths of the total population of all classes.

The total population of the Southwest increased 39 per cent from 1950 to 1960, but the percentage of increase of both the Spanish-surname white population and the nonwhite population was much greater (51.3 per cent and 49.1 per cent, respectively). The percentage of increase in the total population was greatest in Arizona (73.7 per cent), next highest in California (48.5 per cent), and lowest in Texas (24.2 per cent). In the percentage of increase of the Spanish-surname population and the nonwhite population, California led with 87.6 and 88.1 per cent, respectively. The percentage of increase of the nonwhite population was almost as high (87.3 per cent) in Colorado, but the increase in the Spanish-surname population of the state was only 33 per cent. In the percentage of increase of the Spanish-surname population, New Mexico was lowest (8.1 per cent), and in the percentage of increase in the nonwhite population, Texas was lowest (22.4 per cent).

The ratio of the Spanish-surname white population to the total population in 1950 and 1960 is shown in Table 6; for comparison, the ratio of the Spanish–mother-tongue population to the total population in 1940 is also presented. Although surname data and mother-tongue data are not directly comparable and although the ratios are probably too low to represent accurately the Spanish-speaking population, the general trends shown by the table are probably correct—a decrease in the ratio of the Spanish-speaking population to the total population in Arizona and New Mexico, and an increase in the other three states. The decrease in New Mexico is particularly striking.

TABLE 6

*Ratio of Spanish-Surname Population of 1950 and 1960 to
Total Population, and Ratio of Spanish–Mother-Tongue
Population of 1940 to Total Population*

	Arizona	California	Colorado	New Mexico	Texas	Southwest
1940	20.4	6.0	8.2	41.7	11.5	10.1
1950	17.1	7.2	8.9	36.5	13.4	10.9
1960	14.9	9.1	9.0	28.3	14.8	11.8

In Table 7 estimates are made of the composition of the total population in 1950 and 1960: non–Spanish-speaking white persons, Spanish-speaking white persons, nonwhite persons (Negroes and persons of other races). Percentages of the nonwhite population were computed from census data. The estimates of the Spanish-speaking

group are the ratios which are recorded in Table 6, each increased
by one-tenth of itself, to compensate for the omission of persons
whose surnames were not Spanish. The percentages of the non–Spanish-speaking group are those which are necessary to bring the totals to
100 per cent. In California and Colorado approximately one person
in ten is Spanish-speaking; in Arizona and Texas, one in six; and in
New Mexico, one in three. Thus in each of the states the Spanish-
speaking people are a minority group by a wide margin, but they
are the largest of the minorities.

TABLE 7

*Estimates of Composition of the Population
in the Southwest in 1950 and 1960
(In percentages of the total population)*

| | White Population | | | | Nonwhite Population | | | |
| | Non–Spanish-Speaking | | Spanish-Speaking | | Negro | | Other Races | |
	1950	1960	1950	1960	1950	1960	1950	1960
Arizona	68.5	73.4	18.8	16.4	3.5	3.3	9.2	6.9
California	85.7	82.0	7.9	10.0	4.4	5.6	2.0	2.4
Colorado	88.1	87.0	9.8	9.9	1.5	2.3	0.6	0.8
New Mexico	52.3	61.0	40.2	31.1	1.2	1.8	6.3	6.1
Texas	72.5	71.1	14.7	16.3	12.7	12.4	0.1	0.2
Southwest	79.3	77.7	12.0	13.0	7.1	7.4	1.6	1.9

Distribution of Population within the States

The population of each of the states is increasingly an urban population, as is shown in Table 8. In 1960 in the Southwest as a whole, approximately four of every five persons of the total population and also
of the white Spanish-surname population lived in an urban area. The
percentage of urban dwellers was greatest in California (86.4 per
cent) and least in New Mexico (65.9 per cent). From 1950 to 1960
the urban population increased in each of the five states, the increases
ranging from 48.6 per cent in Texas to 133.3 per cent in Arizona for
the population of all classes and ranging from 52.3 per cent in New
Mexico to 114.4 per cent in California for the white population of
Spanish surname. On the other hand, the rural population decreased
in each of the five states except California, but the percentages of decrease in the rural areas were much smaller than were the percentages

TABLE 8

Urban and Rural Population in the Southwest in 1960

	All Population Groups				White Spanish-Surname Population			
	% of Total Population 1960		% of Increase or Decrease 1950 to 1960		% of Total Population 1960		% of Increase or Decrease 1950 to 1960	
	Urban	Rural	Urban	Rural	Urban	Rural	Urban	Rural
Arizona	74.5	25.5	133.3	— 0.6	74.9	25.1	84.9	— 1.6
California	86.4	13.6	58.9	4.8	85.4	14.6	114.4	13.2
Colorado	73.7	26.3	55.5	— 6.6	68.7	31.3	84.0	—17.3
New Mexico	65.9	34.1	83.2	— 4.3	57.7	42.3	52.3	—22.5
Texas	75.0	25.0	48.6	—16.7	78.6	21.4	58.2	— 7.9
Southwest	80.7	19.3	58.0	— 7.1	79.1	20.9	80.3	— 5.9

of increase in the urban areas. In the area as a whole the rate of decrease for the ten-year period was 7.1 per cent in the population of all classes and 5.9 per cent in the Spanish-surname population.

A study of population by counties gives a more detailed picture of the distribution of major population groups. Using 1960 census reports, tables were prepared showing the total population, the number of white Spanish-surname persons, and the number of nonwhite persons in each of the 421 counties of the five states of the Southwest. From these tables an Appendix was prepared to show the number of white persons of Spanish surname, the number of nonwhite persons, and the ratio of each of these numbers to the total population in each county. Figures 3 and 4 are maps showing the distribution of the Spanish-surname population in the 421 counties—Figure 3 in terms of numbers and Figure 4 in terms of the ratio of the numbers to the total population. A third map, Figure 5, shows the ratio of the nonwhite population to the total population in the 421 counties.

In each of the states the number of Spanish-surname persons is highly variable from county to county. As would be expected, the number tends to be greatest in the counties in which large cities are located. The cities of the five states having white, Spanish-surname populations over 35,000 in 1960 are listed in Table 9. Some counties which do not include the cities listed in the table have very large numbers—for example, in California: Alameda (67,866), Fresno (61,-418), Orange (52,576), San Bernardino (60,177), and Santa Clara

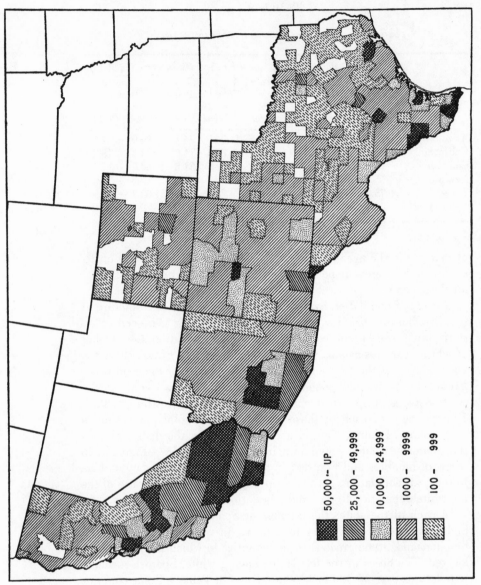

50,000 – UP

25,000 – 49,999

10,000 – 24,999

1000 – 9999

100 – 999

Fig. 3—Number of white persons of Spanish surname in the Southwest.

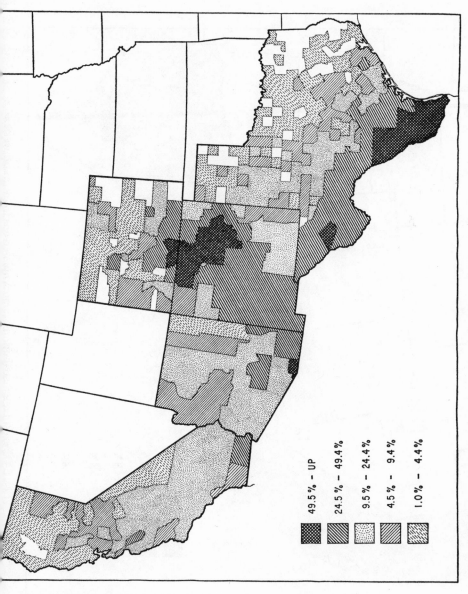

49.5 % - UP
24.5 % — 49.4%
9.5 % — 24.4%
4.5 % — 9.4%
1.0 % — 4.4%

Fig. 4—Percentage distribution of white persons of Spanish surname in the Southwest.

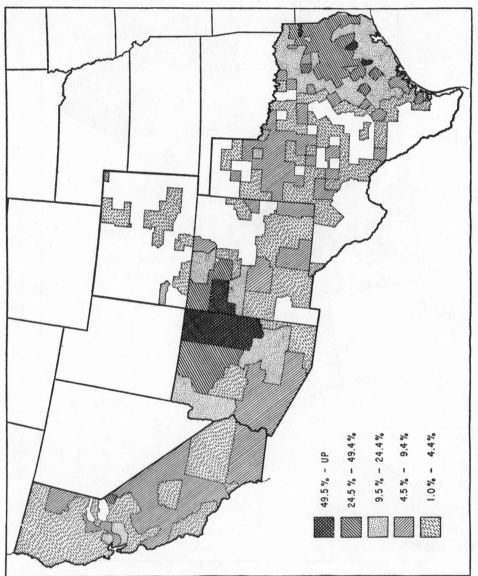

Fig. 5—Percentage distribution of nonwhite persons in the Southwest.

49.5% – UP

24.5% – 49.4%

9.5% – 24.4%

4.5% – 9.4%

1.0% – 4.4%

TABLE 9

Southwestern Cities Having Largest Spanish-Surname Populations
(Census of 1960)

	Total Population	Spanish-Surname Population	Percentage of Total Population
Arizona			
Phoenix	439,170	40,241	9.2
Tucson	212,892	35,722	16.8
California			
Los Angeles	2,479,015	260,389	10.5
East Los Angeles			
(unincorporated)	104,270	70,802	67.9
San Francisco	740,316	51,602	7.0
San Diego	573,224	38,043	6.6
Colorado			
Denver	493,887	43,147	8.7
New Mexico			
Albuquerque	201,189	43,790	21.8
Texas			
Brownsville	48,040	35,440	73.8
Corpus Christi	167,690	59,859	35.7
El Paso	276,687	125,745	45.4
Houston	938,219	63,372	6.8
Laredo	60,678	49,819	82.1
San Antonio	587,718	243,627	41.4

(77,755); and in Texas: Hidalgo (129,092). On the other hand, in some counties few or no white Spanish-surname persons are found.

Not only the number of Spanish-speaking persons but also the ratio of this number to the total population varies from place to place within each state. A large number of Spanish-speaking persons in a community may be only a small percentage of the total, or a small number may be a large percentage. For example, only 9.2 per cent of the population in Phoenix have Spanish surnames, only 10.5 per cent in Los Angeles, only 8.7 per cent in Denver, and only 6.8 per cent in Houston. On the other hand, 57.6 per cent of the population in Santa Cruz County (Arizona) have Spanish surnames, 33.1 per cent in Imperial County (California), 85.4 per cent in Mora County (New Mexico), 72.6 per cent in Costilla County (Colorado), and 88.7 per cent in Starr County (Texas). In the Southwest as a whole the percentage of the population having Spanish surnames tends to decrease with distance from the Mexican border.

A significant generalization from this study of the population is that the Spanish-speaking people are distributed among English-speaking people throughout the Southwest and are not concentrated in an area which could be set off as a Spanish-speaking state. There is no large area in the five Southwestern states which is occupied almost exclusively by Spanish-speaking people; except in small areas the Spanish-speaking people are a minority group among a larger English-speaking population. This intermingling of the two groups has an important bearing on linguistic and other problems to be discussed.

Distribution of Spanish-Speaking Persons within a Community

Although no large areas of the Southwest are occupied by Spanish-speaking people alone, within large communities there are small communities and "islands" which are almost entirely Spanish-speaking. Even when both English-speaking and Spanish-speaking people live in the same community, there is a strong tendency for them to occupy different residential sections. This is quite natural. People are drawn together by similarity of language, culture, and economic level, and they are pushed apart by differences.

But living in different residential sections creates problems. The geographical isolation of the Spanish-speaking people within a community must be listed as a major handicap of the Spanish-speaking children of the Southwest. At first thought this separation may seem unimportant, for a degree of isolation is a common characteristic of all persons who occupy different sections of a community. Obviously, not everyone can live in the same limited area. The separation geographically becomes a source of difficulty, however, when it reinforces other divisive factors such as a difference in language. The isolation of Spanish-speaking children tends to defeat their attempts to learn English; it weakens motivation and decreases opportunity. It tends also to support historic hostilities of the groups, and it lessens the chances of improving understanding through association. It retards the development of a common culture. The track, the street, or the river which lies between the groups is a symbol of a much greater barrier, and the processes of democracy run into serious difficulty because of this division. Although the group which is less powerful economically suffers most, the loss extends to the community as a whole.

4. A Conflict of Cultures

The meeting of Spanish-speaking and English-speaking people in the Southwest has brought two historical cultures into contact and, insofar as they are different, into conflict. To assess properly the meaning of this conflict we may start with three or four generalizations. First, the underlying culture of a people is the product of a long past. Second, the culture of a people changes at varying rates as a result of forces within the group and of contacts with other cultures. Third, cultures which develop in isolation from each other and in different environments tend to diverge in important respects—in language, for example—and cultures in contact tend to develop common elements. Finally, when two peoples are brought together geographically, cultural differences tend to keep them apart and cultural likenesses to bring them together.

Describing a Culture

It is difficult to give an adequate description of the culture of a group, first, because the term is so broad. How people live, what houses they build, what foods they eat, what recreations they enjoy, what institutions they develop, what knowledge they have, what art and literature they possess, what customs they observe, what language they speak, what religion they profess, what they value—in brief, the life characteristics of a people are their culture.

A second difficulty in describing the culture of a group arises from the fact that cultures change. A condition which may well have been typical at an earlier time may no longer be so. This is particularly true of a people whose culture was developed within a rural-village environment and who are suddenly transplanted into a modern urban culture.

A third reason why the description of the culture of a people is difficult is that there are extreme differences among persons who are within the same group. Within many large groups there are sub-groups markedly different from each other, and the differences among individual members of the group are even more extreme. It should be emphasized that a kind of central tendency—or, in statistical terms, the mode of a population—is just that: the average of a series of conditions which vary along a continuous scale, or a condition which is characteristic of a fraction of the group sufficiently large to have significance. Thus, although the 1960 U.S. census report states that the average (median) number of school years completed by Spanish-surname persons twenty-five years old and over in El Paso County, Texas, was 6.6 years, this figure is only a middle point in a series of values ranging from no schooling to the completion of graduate and professional work. In like manner, characterizing a group as "Spanish-speaking" expresses only a "usual" condition to which there are many exceptions, and even "Spanish-speaking" varies in degree.

Mexico, the geographical area in which most of the Spanish-speaking population of the Southwest has had its origin, is itself a country of the widest extremes in the degree of education of its people, in their beliefs and customs, in the way they live, in their socioeconomic status, and in their material environment. The country is both old and new. It is still a vast reservoir from which unskilled and semiskilled labor is drawn to the United States, but this is only part of a varied picture. The Mexican which the tourist visualizes may be an agricultural laborer wearing traditional peasant garments and working with primitive tools, or a person gaily clothed in holiday costume, or a skilled worker in handicrafts, or even a haughty *patrón*; but in increasing proportion he is something different—a laborer modern in dress and skilled in the use of machines, a person of middle socioeconomic status in an industrialized society, an artist, a musician, or a member of the learned professions.

Arthur L. Campa, in the Fall, 1958, number of the *Denver Public Library News*, describes some of the characteristics of modern Mexico. Among other things, he says:

The peón on a sleepy little burro is now a symbol of the past, an interesting design for the artist. Surfaced roads have replaced the dusty trails, and the trailer truck has taken the load off the little donkey's back. Wooden plows have been largely replaced by tractors, dams have reclaimed millions of acres through irrigation, and ballots have replaced bullets as instruments of public office.

Today we like to look south at a democracy which all North Americans are happy to have as a neighbor. . . . It is not only artifacts and curiosities that the traveler seeks today, for Mexico without sacrificing its artistic past has entered into the present era producing necessities which make life more pleasant and practical.

. . . In the last three years, 1,600,000 acres of land have been reclaimed and put under cultivation. . . . In the last four years, there has been a 50% increase in agriculture.

It is no longer only souvenirs that Mexico exports, important though they are, but a diversification of products which produce jobs and income for large sectors of the population.

The significant fact is that each year marks an improvement over the preceding one.

The economic development of the country is not being emphasized at the expense of its cultural and educational efforts.

Individual Differences and Group Trends

The statement that there are wide subgroup differences and wide individual differences is made over and over in this book because it is crucial. The process of generalization for the purpose of finding averages and trends is not reversible. The status of an individual cannot safely be inferred from the average or trend of the group. The only way to find the real characteristics of any person is to study him individually.

Although one must constantly be aware of individual differences, it is important too to know group trends, the conditions which are frequently found within a group. This is important for two very practical reasons. First, knowing the conditions which are frequently found, general measures can be taken to meet these conditions. If little knowledge of English, for example, is a frequent source of difficulty, the problem presented is very different from the problem presented when it is only the occasional child who knows little English. In the second place, a knowledge of conditions often found in the group is helpful in dealing with individual cases. The investigator is alerted to conditions which *may* be important in individual diagnosis; some of the points are known where difficulties are most likely to be found.

But general group characteristics merely alert one to conditions which *may* be found in an individual case. Group membership can never be safely depended upon as a basis for understanding a person. Yet such reliance is a common error. Spanish-speaking people form an opinion from their own experiences or other sources of what an "Anglo" is, and, however wrong the opinion may be, they tend to think of all Anglos in the same way. In like manner, English-speaking people build up an idea of "the Mexican," often from contact with only culture-deprived persons or from distorted information from other sources, and they too tend to think of all Spanish-speaking people in the same way.

One is reminded of the Puerto Rican boy of Spanish descent who was brought to the States by well-meaning people for an education soon after the American occupation of that island. To what school did they bring him? The Carlisle Indian School! Was he not from the West Indies, and who but Indians would be living there? To come closer to the problem, the case has been recorded of a Spanish-speaking child in the Southwest who for teaching purposes was segregated with other children who knew no English, although he could read both Spanish and English when he entered the first grade. Many a clean child has been called dirty because some others have been dirty. On the other side, many a kind and friendly person has been considered an enemy because some others have been unkind and unfriendly.

Descriptions of Spanish-American Culture

The culture of the Spanish-speaking people of New Mexico has been discussed by many writers. In 1940 George I. Sánchez presented a study of the descendants of the Spanish colonials under the title *Forgotten People*. Although he recognized that some members of the group had "adapted themselves to the new environment," it was his conclusion that "the great masses of the people constitute a severely handicapped social and economic minority." "Generally speaking," he said, "their status is one of privation and want, of cultural inadequacy and of bewilderment."

In 1943 Lloyd S. Tireman and Mary Watson gave a vivid description of Nambé, a village near Santa Fe, in their *La Comunidad*, reporting on an experiment with a community school. This village was in a period of transition between the old ways of cooperative living in an agricultural community to life in a modern industrial world. The lands on which the people lived were no longer adequate; they were "bewildered" and were living at a low economic level.

Kluckhohn's Study of Values

Florence Kluckhohn, a student of Spanish-American culture in New Mexico since 1936, contrasts sharply the "value" orientations of the old Spanish-American culture and the dominant "American" culture at four points, stating that one orientation is virtually a "mirror image" of the other (Florence R. Kluckhohn and Fred L. Strodtbeck, *Variations in Value Orientations*, 1961). In the Spanish-American culture she finds a "subjugation-to-nature" orientation, in contrast to a "mastery-over-nature" orientation in the dominant American culture. Thus in one culture there is a kind of fatalism in attitudes toward illness and death, with acceptance of these misfortunes as the "Lord's will," but in the other culture there is a strong effort to control illness and prolong life. In "time" orientation the Spanish-American tends to value the present over the past or the future, but the American continually looks toward a better future. The Spanish-American, for example, is less interested than is the American in accumulating property for future use or for handing down to future generations. A third difference is in "activity" values. The Spanish-American values "being" more than "doing"; his activity is more likely to be a spontaneous expression of his impulses and desires. The American, on the other hand, values activity on the basis of what it will accomplish; he wants to get things done. A fourth difference is in a "relational" orientation. The Spanish-American traditionally accepts and depends upon the guidance and support of a father or older brother, a *patrón*, or other person in authority. The American is more individualistic and assumes more responsibility for himself.

Kluckhohn recognizes wide individual variations within these cultural patterns, and also a tendency to change. The *patrón*, for example, was much more individualistic than were the persons dependent upon him. Change in the usual pattern is illustrated by the shift toward individualism already apparent in the Spanish-American population. In a statement summarizing a study of the Spanish-Americans of a New Mexican village, she foresees much greater changes than those which have occurred in their value orientations:

. . . basic changes in the total value system are to be expected. There can be no turning back by these people, given the facts that they are firmly held within the borders of the United States and are increasingly subjected to dominant Anglo-American culture as one by one the small villages like Atrisco decay and the inhabitants of them move off to urban centers.

Cultural Differences Described by Saunders

One of the detailed and readily available summaries of differences in culture of the Spanish-speaking people and the English-speaking people of the Southwest is that of Lyle Saunders in his *Cultural Difference and Medical Care: The Case of the Spanish-Speaking People of the Southwest* (Russell Sage Foundation, 1954). Saunders recognizes three major subgroups with certain similarities within each group and with recognizable differences among the groups. The first is the Spanish-American group of New Mexico and southern Colorado, members of which have descended from the early colonists who came from Spain and New Spain and to some extent from a mixture of the early colonists with the native Indian population. These people developed relatively isolated village communities whose economy was based upon farming, sheep, and cattle in a semiarid environment. The family group was an "extended" family of different generations living together. There was a great deal of sharing of labor and the products of labor in the community. The Catholic Church provided a strong unifying force and a center for various activities. Within this simple social structure leadership was provided by a *patrón*—a man of wealth or position, possibly a large landowner—who helped the people and in turn received their support. Most of the people of the community needed little formal education. In recent years this early pattern of community life has changed rapidly, though unevenly, with the coming of other cultural influences, but many of the characteristics of the early village culture survive.

The second group Saunders calls "Mexican-Americans." In contrast with the Spanish-Americans, who knew no allegiance to Mexico except for the period from the independence of Mexico in 1821 to the treaty of 1848 between the United States and Mexico, the Mexican-Americans are immigrants or descendants of immigrants from Mexico, to which they feel ties of varying strength. Both the Spanish-Americans and the Mexican-Americans came from an economy based upon agriculture and both were accustomed to a village life of which the *patrón* system, the Catholic Church, and the extended family group were characteristic. In the Spanish-American group there has been a kind of stability through family ownership of ancestral lands, and there has been less breaking of familial ties than among the Mexican immigrants. Although the Mexican-Americans have some cultural ties with the homeland, through living near the border or in a district peopled by others like themselves, as a group they are more widely dispersed than the Spanish-American group and feel a greater pressure from the culture of English-speaking people.

Both Spanish-Americans and Mexican-Americans, Saunders points out, have to make a double transition: (1) from a way of life developed in southern Europe and modified by Indian influences to a way of life developed primarily in northwestern Europe and modified by many cultural streams, (2) from a "rural folk way of life . . . to that of an urban-industrial society in which nearly everything . . . is very different." Some, he says, have made the transition so well that they can hardly be distinguished from the "Anglos" among whom they live, but others have hardly begun. A growing number are "at ease in both cultures."

The third group, called "Mexicans" by Saunders, is made up of more recent comers, most of them, he says, illegal entrants or workers on temporary permits, who intend generally to return to Mexico.

Recognizing that group characteristics may or may not be found in a given individual, Saunders lists "characteristics in which there is considerable variation between the Anglo and Spanish-speaking ideal." Four of the differences are similar to the differences in value orientations described by Kluckhohn. According to Saunders:

(1) "Unlike the Anglo, the Spanish-American or Mexican-American is likely to be strongly oriented toward the present or the immediate past." Anglos are oriented toward change and progress. The Spanish-speaking people, having had until recently little contact with change, find the old and tried more attractive than the new and unfamiliar.

(2) "Anglos are doers" and are preoccupied with success. Spanish-speaking people want "to be" rather than "to do." Life in the villages did not stimulate a drive toward success.

(3) The Spanish-speaking people are more inclined than the Anglo toward acceptance of and resignation to whatever may come to them.

(4) The Anglo has a greater preference for independence. In harmony with relations in the village culture, the Spanish-speaking people accept the role of dependency as a quite natural relation.

Saunders finds that the difference in language of Spanish-speaking and Anglo groups "is both a cause and an effect of isolation, and as such exerts a strong influence in the perpetuation of other cultural

traits of Spanish-speaking people and in retarding their integration
into the Anglo group."

Ulibarri's Comments

A critical summary of modern cultural conditions among the
Spanish-speaking people of New Mexico is contributed by Horacio
Ulibarri in an unpublished report on "The Effect of Cultural Difference in the Education of Spanish Americans" (1958), a report growing out of a research study directed by Miles V. Zintz at the University
of New Mexico. The author makes two important points relative to
the generalizations of others concerning the characteristics of
Spanish-Americans. One is to call attention to the danger of thinking
that all of a group conform to a certain generalization which is true of
some only. "It is prudent," he says, ". . . to treat each individual on
an individual basis and use the backlog of cultural knowledge only as
a possibility for explanation of the individual's behavior." Second, he
points out that conditions are changing rapidly "and what was true
ten years ago may no longer be true today." Commenting on the
"broad gap" between the Spanish-American and the Anglo he notes
that Spanish-Americans are spread over a long cultural continuum—
"a great number of unacculturated," a number who "exist in a half-
Spanish half-Anglo world," and others who "have lost all the Spanish
values, practically speaking." Some are "highly acculturated in one
or two fields but still quite traditional in others."

Ulibarri's comments on time orientation are interesting. He says
that Anglo culture has three classes and three time orientations. The
upper class looks far back into the past and plans for generations
ahead. The middle class looks back one generation and plans for one
future generation. The lower class seeks more immediate rewards. In
the traditional Spanish-American culture there were only the upper
and lower classes—*patrón* (about 10 per cent) and *peón*—and their
time orientations corresponded to those of the extremes of the Anglo
culture. Now, he points out, there is a rising middle class among
Spanish-Americans.

According to Ulibarri, the alleged fatalistic attitude of the Spanish-
American toward his environment is a misinterpretation of his behavior. Actually, Ulibarri thinks, the Spanish-American does what he
can within the limits of his knowledge and "as a matter of mental-
hygiene therapy" exclaims, "God wills it," only after he has "ex-
hausted all the possibilities at his disposal."

The transition from the traditional culture, says Ulibarri, has brought, among other changes, an increase in addiction to alcoholism and an increase in the number of divorces.

Mexican Immigrants

In his *Mexican Immigration to the United States* (University of Chicago Press, 1930) Manuel Gamio contrasts the culture of the upper minority in Mexico with that of the lower majority, from which most immigration to the United States has come. In the first instance the Mexican culture has developed along European lines, he thinks, and in the second toward a very different "markedly personal and national" culture. Mexican immigrants from the latter culture, in contrast with the English-speaking people of the United States whose background is scientific, tend to interpret events in terms of convention and of magic and supernatural powers. Their culture, he says, is a "folk culture." In such a thing as a mental test, for example, a child from this culture is confused by "inexpressible and vague tendencies" so that the result cannot represent his real abilities in comparison with the abilities of those who approach the task without such mental conflict.

Ralph L. Beals and Norman S. Humphrey in *No Frontier to Learning: The Mexican Student in the United States* (University of Minnesota Press, 1957) turn attention from the lower socioeconomic levels to the Mexican urban upper class and parts of the middle class. Among the traditional values of these groups they find a first loyalty to the extended family, which includes family groups having a common ancestry and often also the so-called *compadres*, who have a kind of godfather relationship to the family. Men are regarded as superior to women, and it is felt that they must have more freedom in their sex life. The home centers in the mother, whose major fields of activity are the kitchen, the church, and the children.

According to Beals and Humphrey, status rests largely upon race, caste, and class. Indian blood is often an unfavorable factor in attaining status. Loyalty to *la raza* (literally, "the race"), to Latin culture as opposed to Anglo-Saxon culture, provides a kind of spiritual unity. Society and morality are based upon religion, and there is a feeling that all things happen as God wills. If one would lead the good life, he must have nonmaterial goals and put spiritual and intellectual matters first.

The same writers find that most interpersonal and economic rela-

tionships have an authoritarian structure. Yet the individual personality is valued highly. The people are highly sensitive to criticism, and
face-saving has great value for them. Within these classes manual
labor is considered degrading and is associated with low social status.
The person is successful who achieves economic security without effort and who acquires prestige and status symbols such as position
and land ownership.

Other Comments

Various writers have commented on the organization of the
Spanish-speaking family, in which the father is the dominant figure
with much less sharing of authority with the mother than is found in
the English-speaking family. In the absence of the father the oldest
son frequently takes the authoritarian role. Typically, it is said, the
Spanish-speaking father spends less time in the home in family activities. Typically also, the mother and the daughters have much less freedom in social contacts than is found in English-speaking families.
Women are said to attend religious services much more than men.

Ruth D. Tuck provides an interesting description of "Mexican-
Americans in a southwest city" in her book, *Not With the Fist*, published in 1946. The title is taken from a quotation indicating that
social wrongs are more often by-products than results of a direct will
to produce them, that they "are done . . . with the elbows rather than
the fists." In general, this is her point of view with reference to the
difficulties of Spanish-speaking people in the Southwest. She traces in
an interesting way the development of a small California city from its
earliest days. She tells of the relations of the old Spanish settlers and
the "Americans" and the changes which came with immigration, particularly the flood of Mexican immigrants between 1910 and 1930.
These immigrants were predominantly from an agricultural economy
and possessed rather generalized skills adapted to that kind of life.
They came from towns "along the pathways of travel and trade," not
from isolated Indian villages. They came in part because of unsettled
conditions in Mexico, but primarily to improve their economic condition. Most of them became laborers on railroads, in shops, and on
farms.

Mexican-American life in the United States is characterized by
Tuck as a subculture of the civilization of this country. She enumer-
ates many changes from the native culture brought to this country by
Mexican immigrants. They share the material culture of the com-

munity, and even in areas in which cultural survival seems strongest —language, food habits, and family life—they show a continuous trend toward the American style of life.

The Best of Both Cultures

At least a measure of control over changes in the cultures of the Southwest is an enticing possibility. But accepting the possibility of control, thoughtful persons may disagree on the direction which changes should take. One possibility is an effort to preserve the cultures as they are, having one group representative of Spanish-American culture and the other of Anglo-American culture. The effort in such a solution would be to build a community in which the two groups could have maximum differences but would cooperate effectively for the common good.

The goal, however, of preserving distinct cultures in two groups which are in contact in the same community as are the Spanish-speaking people and the English-speaking people of the Southwest seems quite unrealistic. Cultures in such contacts inevitably change. Not only that, but differences increase the difficulties of effective cooperation. A more reasonable goal is probably that of developing a common culture which includes the best of both cultures and yet permits wide individual variations.

Differences in Language

A common language is a necessary first step toward complete participation in the life of a community. The necessity of a common language in any large cooperative enterprise is impressively illustrated in the Bible story of the tower of Babel. All went well as long as the people could communicate, but the whole project went to pieces when the builders began to speak different languages.

Since English is the language of the state and nation, the primary adjustment in the Southwest must necessarily be the learning of English by the Spanish-speaking group. A sound language policy cannot be based upon a sentimental attachment to one language or another. Inevitably the language of the government and of the majority in business and industry will be the prevailing language. This is the stern reality faced by the Spanish-speaking child. If he wishes to be effective outside his Spanish-speaking subcommunity, he must know English.

The language problem cuts more deeply than appears on the surface. Language is used in thinking as well as in communicating with others. It is not enough to be able to buy and sell, to talk to the employer, to understand street signs, and to read laboriously the morning paper—unless, of course, that is the extent of one's capacity. There must be a mastery of language sufficient to interpret experience and to extend knowledge in ever widening circles and at progressively higher levels. This is precisely the mastery which many Spanish-speaking children fail to achieve, in either English or Spanish. They are handicapped both in their own thought processes and in communication. The result is that the individual fails to attain his full possibilities, and the community loses human resources which it greatly needs.

There is no easy solution to the language problem of the Spanish-speaking people along the border. Contacts across the border and the continuous migration to and from Mexico make it necessary as well as natural for a large number of persons to know Spanish. Moreover, even if they desired, the thousands of adults who know Spanish and little or nothing of another language could not possibly be given a command of English in a short period of time. In the Southwest the day cannot be foreseen when there will be only a few homes in which Spanish is the mother tongue. For a long time there will continue to be a large number of children who must learn English as a *second* language, either in the home, in the community, or later in the school. They will come to school with varying degrees of mastery of English, from none to excellent.

But acceptance of the need for Spanish-speaking children to learn English does not dispose of the language problem. The initial knowledge of Spanish which these children have acquired in the home is an asset to be cultivated rather than neglected. Experience in the home and market place is not enough to develop ability in the use of the Spanish of literature and science and to raise the ability the child already has to the level of greatest usefulness to the individual and the community. Formal education is necessary to carry the language skills forward. In fact, our common culture would be greatly enriched by giving formal training in Spanish to both Spanish-speaking and English-speaking children.

Differences in Religion

Another difference, far from universal, is in religion. The Spanish-speaking people are predominantly Catholic and the English-speaking predominantly Protestant. There has been some shift among the Spanish-speaking people of the Southwest toward Protestantism. Without giving statistics, Ulibarri comments that there are a great number of Protestants among the Spanish-Americans. On the other hand, many English-speaking people are Catholic. As the groups become more alike through membership in the same religious organizations, religion will be less a divisive factor. Then, too, there are encouraging signs of increasing tolerance and cooperation among different religious groups and among individuals of different faiths.

Mutual Distrust

Another frequently found difference between the Spanish-speaking and English-speaking peoples of the Southwest is their feeling of oneness with a different part of the community. Each has a kind of latent suspicion of and antagonism toward the other. This is partly a residue of the past centuries in which English-speaking and Spanish-speaking people were bitter rivals and sometimes enemies in armed conflict. It is partly a lingering resentment on the part of the defeated and an attitude of superiority on the part of the victorious. It is partly a difference in values. It is partly a difference in economic level. On both sides it is partly a matter of underrating those who are different and not well known. It is partly a matter of building up one's own importance by depreciating the importance of others. It is partly the result of a lack of common ground in literature, in art, in traditions, in heroic figures, and in other cultural products which bind people together.

Dislike and antagonism are nourished by clumsy ways of expressing loyalty to a people's past and to heroic parts of their own history. In Texas, for example, one of the historic places is the Alamo, which of course Texans cannot and do not want to forget. The question is whether they can learn to remember it in such a way that the child of Mexican descent who wants to be a good Texan will not be made to feel inferior and resentful. Similarly, when events of great importance to Mexicans are celebrated, the question is whether they can be seen by others as milestones important to all human beings in their struggle toward a better life.

Family Organization

In family organization the change is likely to be largely in the direction of the dominant culture. The Spanish structure—the authoritarian father, the mother devoted largely to home and church duties, the extended family including different generations and even unrelated persons, the close supervision of the girls and relative freedom of the boys—was developed in a social and economic setting which no longer exists, or at least is rapidly disappearing. As this structure changes in adaptation to its new setting, one may well wish that some of the loyalties which it cultivates will be saved to enrich the common culture.

The Fine Arts

There can be little question that the best of Spanish and Mexican cultural products in art, music, and literature should be preserved for all people. They are part of the heritage of civilization which should be limited by no group barriers but known and enjoyed by Spanish-speaking people and English-speaking people alike. Too, the community needs the unifying influence of having all its people view many of the same artistic creations, sing many of the same songs, listen to many of the same symphonies, and read many of the same literary masterpieces.

Value Orientations

Differences in the traditional values of the Spanish-speaking people and the English-speaking people have been listed as major divisive factors. They hinder full cooperation in the community at large, and they increase the difficulties of children who are trying to find a secure place in the larger community. If the differences are to be decreased, obviously one set of values must move toward the other or else both must find some common ground. It is likely that the movement will be chiefly toward the Anglo-American values, both because of the weight of numbers in the dominant group and because of better adaptation to an urbanized industrial society. It might be hoped, however, that the "mirror image" of the Anglo-American values could help toward a balance which would be better than either extreme, so that members of both cultures might learn to live more complete lives in the present as well as to strive for a better future.

5. The Handicap of Poverty

To the typical cultural differences which divide the people of the Southwest and create special problems for the Spanish-speaking child must be added differences in social and economic levels. The range, to be sure, in both the Spanish-speaking population and the English-speaking population is from very high to very low, but the proportion of Spanish-speaking persons at the low end of the scale is much greater than the proportion of English-speaking persons. In any group an inferior socioeconomic position finds expression in values, in living patterns, in quality of language, in level of learning, in acquaintance with the fine arts, and in the opportunities open to members of the group.

Inferior Occupational Status

Immigrants from Mexico since the early colonial days have been and still are in large proportion, though by no means exclusively, unskilled or semiskilled laborers. The imbalance between professional and laboring groups is vividly illustrated in a contrast of the occupational classification of immigrants from Canada anu immigrants from Mexico. Table 10, based upon the *Report of Immigration and Naturalization* gives these statistics for the fiscal year 1960–1961. The table includes only the extremes of the classification. In the professional and technical group was approximately one in four of the Canadian immigrant workers but, in sharp contrast, only one in thirty-seven of the Mexican immigrant workers. At the lower extreme was approximately one in five of the Canadian immigrant workers but only three in four of the Mexican immigrant workers.

TABLE 10

Comparison of Occupations of Immigrants from Canada and Mexico, 1960–1961

| | Canada | | Mexico | |
	Number	Per Cent	Number	Per Cent
All persons in classified working groups	14,380	100	19,809	100
Professional, technical, and kindred workers	3,541	24.6	542	2.7
Private household workers, service workers, farm laborers and foremen, and laborers except farm and mine	2,821	19.6	15,073	76.1

Additional evidence of the inferior occupational status of the Spanish-speaking people of the Southwest is provided by the U.S. Census of 1960. Table 11, prepared from census data, presents a classification of occupations and the distribution of employed male persons of ages 14 and over among these occupational groups. The generally inferior economic level of Spanish-surname workers is shown both by the percentage of those persons employed in the higher and lower occupational groups and by the median income. Except in California, where the ratio was more favorable, the ratio of the median income of the general population to that of the Spanish-surname subgroup was roughly three to two. The highest median incomes were in California, the lowest in Texas.

A comparison is shown in Table 12 of the percentage of white families of Spanish surname and of families in the general population of Southwestern states who were in high and low income brackets in 1959. The table gives additional evidence that low incomes are much more frequent and high incomes much less frequent in the white Spanish-surname population than in the general population. More than one-third of the incomes of white Spanish-surname families in the Southwest as a whole were less than $3,000—in Texas more than one-half. It should be noted, however, that there were substantial numbers of white Spanish-surname families whose income was as high as $10,000 or more—in Texas approximately one in thirty-seven, in California one in nine, and in the Southwest as a whole, one in fifteen.

A comparison of two family characteristics related to family in-

TABLE 11

Occupational Grouping of Male Persons of Ages Fourteen and Over in the Southwest among General Population and among White Persons of Spanish Surname (Census of 1960)

	Arizona		California		Colorado		New Mexico		Texas	
	General	Spanish-Surname White	General	Spanish-Surname White	General	Spanish-Surname White	General	Spanish-Surname White	General	Spanish-Surname White
TOTAL NUMBER EMPLOYED										
General Population	297,132		3,858,815		310,411		201,914		2,267,099	
Spanish-Surname, White		44,828		336,609		29,238		48,454		277,639
PERCENTAGE EMPLOYED IN OCCUPATIONAL SUBGROUPS										
a	10.7	2.6	13.5	4.5	14.3	4.2	13.3	6.0	9.6	3.1
b	2.2	.7	2.0	1.9	.5	2.8	4.9	3.5	6.1	2.6
c	12.4	3.8	11.9	4.2	14.1	3.2	12.5	5.2	12.0	4.6
d	5.2	2.7	7.0	4.7	8.0	4.2	5.7	6.3	6.2	4.5
e	7.2	2.7	7.7	3.2	8.5	2.7	5.5	3.7	6.8	3.7
f	20.2	13.5	20.2	16.3	19.8	12.7	19.9	16.6	18.7	15.9
g	16.1	22.0	16.5	24.0	15.9	26.1	17.4	20.0	18.0	21.8
h	.1	.1	.1	.1	.1	.1	.1	.1	.1	.2
i	5.2	6.0	6.4	6.4	7.1	8.5	6.1	11.0	5.8	7.4
j	7.4	28.0	3.3	15.7	.9	11.0	4.1	9.0	4.4	16.2
k	7.6	13.7	6.2	12.8	6.8	20.3	7.3	15.0	7.7	15.8
l	5.1	4.2	5.2	6.2	4.1	4.2	3.2	3.6	4.7	4.3
MEDIAN 1959 INCOME OF OCCUPATIONAL SUBGROUPS										
	$4,069	$2,713	$4,966	$3,849	$4,191	$2,814	$3,941	$2,630	$3,394	$2,029

a) Professional, technical, and kindred workers (engineers, lawyers, physicians, teachers, etc.)

b) Farmers and farm managers (owners, tenants, etc.)

c) Managers, officials, and proprietors, except farm (public officials, buyers, etc.)

d) Clerical and kindred workers (secretaries, stenographers, bookkeepers, etc.)

e) Sales workers (brokers, salesmen, newsboys, etc.)

f) Craftsmen, foremen, and kindred workers (carpenters, mechanics, bakers, etc.)

g) Operatives and kindred workers (bus drivers, dressmakers, railroad brakemen, etc.)

h) Private household workers (housekeepers, laundresses, baby sitters, etc.)

i) Service workers, except private households (police, firemen, barbers, etc.)

j) Farm laborers and foremen (unpaid family and self-employed farm service laborers)

k) Laborers except farm and mine (teamsters, garage laborers, fishermen, etc.)

l) Occupation not reported

TABLE 12

Frequency of Low and High Family Incomes in the Southwest
(Census of 1960)

	Families with Incomes under $1,000		Families with Incomes under $3,000[a]		Families with Incomes of $10,000 or More	
	General Population	White Spanish-Surname Population	General Population	White Spanish-Surname Population	General Population	White Spanish-Surname Population
Arizona	5.9%	7.2%	21.3%	30.8%	14.4%	4.6%
California	3.3	4.5	14.1	19.1	21.8	10.8
Colorado	3.5	6.4	18.3	35.0	14.6	4.8
New Mexico	6.9	11.3	24.4	41.5	14.3	4.5
Texas	7.6	13.6	32.5	51.6	11.8	2.7
Southwest	4.9	8.8	21.0	34.8	17.6	6.6

[a] Incomes under $3,000 include incomes of $1,000. Incomes between $3,000 and $10,000 are omitted from the table.

come is made in Tables 13 and 14. Table 13 shows the ratio of families of two or three members and the ratio of families of seven or more members to the total number of families in the general population and in the white Spanish-surname population. In the general population more than half of the families are small families of two or three persons, but only slightly more than a third of the white Spanish-surname families are as small. On the other hand, the ratio of large families (of seven or more persons) to the total number of families is approximately only one to seventeen in the general population but nearly one to five in the white Spanish-surname population. More of the white Spanish-surname families are larger and more of them have less income than do families in the population as a whole.

A striking contrast in the number of years of school completed by heads of families in the general population and in the white population of Spanish surname in the Southwest is shown in Table 14. In each of the five states a markedly lower percentage of heads of Spanish-surname families has completed at least elementary school. The contrast is even greater at the high school and college levels. Approximately one-third of the heads of white Spanish-surname families in the Southwest as a whole had less than five years of school, and only one in thirty-seven had a college education of four years or more.

Their relatively low educational level is in agreement with their relatively low occupational status and income.

Low Economic Level and Substandard Living Conditions

The low economic level of large numbers of Spanish-speaking fami-

TABLE 13

Frequency of Large and Small Families in the Southwest
(Census of 1960)

	Percentage of Families Having Only 2 or 3 Members[a]		Percentage of Families Having 7 or More Members	
	General Population	White Spanish-Surname Population	General Population	White Spanish-Surname Population
Arizona	50.9	31.7	8.4	21.8
California	56.5	39.8	4.5	13.5
Colorado	53.5	33.7	5.6	20.1
New Mexico	46.3	34.8	10.0	20.5
Texas	53.7	31.2	7.3	24.8
Southwest	54.9	35.4	5.8	19.2

[a] Families of 4-to-6 members are not included in the table.

TABLE 14

Percentage of Heads of Families in General Population and in White
Spanish-Surname Population in the Southwest Who Completed
Designated Years of School
(Census of 1960)

	Less than 5 Years	Elementary School 8 Years or More		High School 4 Years or More		College 4 Years or More	
	White Spanish-Surname Population[a]	General Population	White Spanish-Surname Population	General Population	White Spanish-Surname Population	General Population	White Spanish-Surname Population
Arizona	30.0	80.2	47.7	46.4	16.8	10.6	2.4
California	20.5	86.5	62.1	52.5	26.0	11.9	3.4
Colorado	22.2	87.0	45.0	51.9	19.0	12.7	2.7
New Mexico	27.7	76.5	49.7	45.8	19.5	11.2	3.3
Texas	49.8	70.2	28.7	40.0	12.3	9.5	1.9
Southwest	33.0	80.7	47.1	47.9	19.4	11.1	2.7

[a] No comparable statistics for total population.

lies is reflected in substandard living conditions. Contrasts in the housing of families of different economic levels are illustrated in Figures 6 and 7.

It would be naive to dismiss the living conditions of persons of low economic level with the observation that these people enjoy the kind of living to which they are accustomed, that they want nothing better, and that if they had the opportunity to improve their status they would not take advantage of it. Unfortunately, such statements contain a part-truth, but only a part-truth and a dangerous one at that. It is true that human beings are adaptable and that they learn to live with a degree of satisfaction under most unfavorable conditions. If it were not so, the human race would not have survived. Human beings become accustomed even to slavery and learn to sing to lighten their misery. It is true also that values are moulded by experiences. People who live precariously from hand to mouth develop to some extent the values which grow out of such existence.

Opportunity Brings Improvement

The statement that human beings will not improve the physical conditions under which they live if they have the opportunity is simply not true. That standards of living do rise with a rise in economic level can be seen by anyone who will take the time to look around. In some cases the changes are rapid and dramatic. In Puerto Rico, for example, where the economic level of the masses has risen almost fantastically within a generation, one can find impressive results in improved housing. In a certain slum-clearance project small wooden shacks were moved from a crowded area and put down on lots where there was at least a little breathing space. What happened was like a fairy tale: one by one, the families who lived there began to improve the houses. Some started at the front, perhaps adding a porch and some ornamentation, some at the back, perhaps adding another room. They worked over the shells with which they started until each was a new place, attractive and livable.

A similar transformation of homes can be seen in the States. This kind of evolution takes place at all economic levels and in all groups, and is one thing which makes the opening of new subdivisions so profitable! In a city in which a Spanish-speaking population has been resident for two or three generations, it is interesting to see how with each succeeding generation the rise in economic level is registered by the nature and location of the houses in which the people live.

6. School Population and Enrollment

As provisions for education are extended downward to nursery schools and upward to facilities for adult education, nearly every person after the first few months of life is of "school age," and increasing numbers are enrolling for some kind of formal education. The chief interest in this study, however, is in the graded system of schools from kindergarten through college, including graduate and professional schools, and in the population of ages normally enrolled in these schools.

The U.S. census of 1960 gives statistics on the population and school enrollment of persons from five to thirty-four years of age. "Persons were included as enrolled in school if they were reported as attending or enrolled in a 'regular' school or college at any time between February 1, 1960, and the time of enumeration." The departments of education of three states of the Southwest report a scholastic census—New Mexico and Texas an enumeration of children of ages six through seventeen, and Colorado six through twenty-one. The U.S. census reports both the number of white children of Spanish surname and the number of children in the general population. No state department of education routinely reports a separate enumeration of Spanish-speaking or Spanish-name children, but in Texas some special counts of Spanish-name children have been made from the scholastic census rolls.

Children of Ages Five to Seventeen

Children who enter kindergarten at five and advance one grade each year through high school would enter the fourth year of high school at age seventeen. Some children advance more rapidly, some more slowly, and some because of physical or mental deficiencies

cannot enroll. To a certain extent the number of persons within the
age bracket who are not enrolled is offset by the number of overage
persons who are still enrolled. As a rough estimate, the number of
persons within the age bracket of five to seventeen may be taken to
represent the potential enrollment in the school system below the
college level.

The population of ages five to seventeen in the states of the Southwest in 1960 is shown in Table 15. According to the table about one-
sixth of the children of ages five to seventeen in the Southwest are in
the Spanish-speaking group. In 1964 the number of these children
probably exceeds 1.25 million. The ratio of the number of Spanish-
speaking children to the number of children of all classes (including
the Spanish-speaking) in this area varies from 12 per cent in California to 36 per cent in New Mexico.

TABLE 15

Population of Ages Five to Seventeen in the Southwest
(Census of 1960)

	Population of All Classes		Population of White Persons of Spanish Surname		Population of White Spanish-Speaking Persons[a]
	Number	Per Cent	Number	Per Cent	Per Cent
Arizona	350,978	100	61,479	17.5	19.3
California	3,710,251	100	408,456	11.0	12.1
Colorado	442,203	100	53,962	12.2	13.4
New Mexico	274,457	100	90,826	33.1	36.4
Texas	2,483,733	100	479,232	19.3	21.2
Southwest	7,261,622	100	1,093,955	15.1	16.6

[a] In this column the percentage of white Spanish-surname persons has been increased by one-tenth of itself.

The nativity of the Spanish-surname children, ages five to seventeen, of each state and of the Southwest as a whole is shown in Table
16. Nearly seven of ten children of this age range in the five states are
native born of native parents—that is, are of the third generation or
beyond. Another 25 per cent are native born of foreign or mixed
parentage (second-generation children), and only 5 per cent are
foreign born. In Colorado and New Mexico nine-tenths of the children
are native born of native parents and scarcely 1 or 2 per cent are

TABLE 16

*Nativity of White Persons of Spanish Surname, Ages Five to
Seventeen, in the Southwest
(Census of 1960)*

	Total Number	Native-born Persons Native Parentage		Native-born Persons Foreign or Mixed Parentage		Foreign-born Persons	
		Number	Per Cent	Number	Per Cent	Number	Per Cent
Arizona	61,479	39,626	64.5	18,412	29.9	3,441	5.6
California	408,456	255,037	62.4	123,745	30.3	29,674	7.3
Colorado	53,962	49,157	91.1	4,437	8.2	368	0.7
New Mexico	90,826	82,972	91.4	6,427	7.1	1,427	1.6
Texas	479,232	326,594	68.1	128,553	26.8	24,085	5.0
Southwest	1,093,955	753,386	68.9	281,574	25.7	58,995	5.4

foreign born. Turning the figures around, approximately three of ten children in the Southwest come from homes in which one or both parents were foreign born.

Public and Private Schools

Education in the Southwest is primarily a public activity. Approximately nine-tenths of the enrollment in kindergarten, in elementary grades (1–8), and in high school is in public schools. The percentages are remarkably similar in the several states except at the kindergarten level, as is shown in Table 17.

Statistics in general agreement with these estimates are available

TABLE 17

*Percentage of Total School-Age Population Enrolled in
Public Schools in the Southwest
(Census of 1960)*

	Kindergarten	Elementary School	High School
Arizona	74.1	91.0	93.4
California	96.0	89.3	91.7
Colorado	90.8	89.6	91.9
New Mexico	59.8	89.7	92.3
Texas	65.5	93.3	95.0
Southwest	90.1	90.7	92.8

for Arizona, California, and New Mexico. The *Annual Report* of the Arizona Superintendent of Public Instruction for 1957–1958 lists the public school enrollment for the state and the enrollment in 151 private or parochial schools of the state's 213 known nonpublic schools. The statistics show that the private- and parochial-school enrollment (including kindergarten) was approximately 8.6 per cent of the total enrollment. In California statistics prepared by the State Department of Education on public-school enrollment as of March 31, 1958, and by the California Taxpayers' Association on parochial-school enrollment (including kindergarten) as of June, 1958, show that the parochial-school enrollment was approximately 9.7 per cent of the total enrollment. Computations for New Mexico are based upon statistics taken from the *24th Biennial Report* of the Superintendent of Public Instruction. These computations show that 10.1 per cent of the total enrollment from the pre-first grade to the twelfth grade was in parochial and private schools. There are no corresponding state figures for Colorado and Texas.

A large proportion of the nonpublic schools in the Southwest are Catholic schools. The *Official Catholic Directory* for 1959 reports the enrollment in their diocesan, parochial, and private schools as shown in Table 18. The percentages listed in the table show the approximate relation of the total enrollments to the public school enrollment (grades 1–12) as reported by state departments of education for 1957–1958.

TABLE 18

Enrollment in Catholic Schools in the Southwest

	Elementary Schools	High Schools	Total	Ratio of Total to Public-School Enrollment
Arizona	16,969	3,006	19,975	7.8 %
California	231,423	52,227	283,650	11.1
Colorado	26,439	5,654	32,093	10.5
New Mexico	19,081	2,909	21,990	10.5
Texas	109,063	16,983	126,046	6.6

Population in Relation to School Enrollment

The ratio of the number of persons in the Southwest enrolled in school in 1960 to the total number in the Southwestern population is shown in Table 19 for various age brackets ranging from five to thirty-four years. The table was compiled from figures in the U.S. census of 1960.

In nearly every age bracket the percentage of Spanish-surname persons enrolled in school is less than the percentage of the total population enrolled in school. The percentages for the two groups are closest in New Mexico, where the Spanish-speaking population is a larger part of the total than in the other states. The early drop-out from school of Spanish-surname children begins to be evident at the age bracket fourteen to fifteen and is quite marked at the age bracket sixteen to seventeen. At every age bracket from five to nineteen the lowest enrollment ratio for Spanish-surname children is found in Texas.

TABLE 19

Percentage of Population of Designated Ages Enrolled in School in the Southwest (Census of 1960)

Ages	Arizona Population		California Population		Colorado Population		New Mexico Population		Texas Population	
	Total	Spanish-Surname	Total	Spanish-Surname	Total	Spanish-Surname	Total	Spanish-Surname	Total	Spanish-Surname
5 and 6	57.5	55.0	82.8	79.9	69.3	63.9	50.9	49.6	39.0	34.5
7 to 13	96.9	96.2	98.2	97.6	98.1	97.4	96.8	96.4	96.9	94.5
14 and 15	92.9	90.2	96.3	92.9	95.2	89.4	93.4	93.3	91.6	82.7
16 and 17	79.1	68.3	83.3	73.7	83.5	68.0	81.5	76.3	76.3	58.6
18 and 19	45.4	36.6	40.8	33.1	48.0	34.0	41.6	41.7	41.9	31.1
20 and 21	21.4	10.1	21.5	12.1	26.3	12.4	17.6	14.5	20.2	11.9
22 to 24	11.8	6.0	12.3	7.2	13.1	8.1	11.2	10.0	9.6	5.5
25 to 34	5.7	3.3	6.6	4.4	6.5	4.3	6.4	5.6	4.1	3.3

Enrollment data from Other Sources

With the abandonment of the policy of providing separate schools for Spanish-speaking children, it is increasingly difficult to get accurate statistics on enrollment, attendance, and other characteristics of this group. In 1930 the present writer summarized conditions in Texas in part as follows (*Education of Mexican and Spanish-Speaking Children in Texas*, page 154):

The number of Mexican children enrolled (in the public schools) is only about 50 per cent of the number of Mexican scholastics [then children of ages 7 to 17, later ages 6 to 17]. Parochial and private schools increase the enrollment of Mexican children not more than 10 per cent of the number of scholastics. Only about a third of the number of Mexican scholastics are in average daily attendance in the public schools, in contrast with three-fourths or more of the other whites. Nearly half of the Mexican children who are in school at all are in the first grade, nearly three-fourths in the first three grades, and only 3 or 4 per cent in the high school. In contrast with this, about one-fifth of the enrollment of other whites is found in the high school.

The past three decades have changed this situation radically. Wilson Little's study of Spanish-speaking children for the school year 1942–1943 included enrollment statistics from districts which had some 78 per cent of the scholastic population of Texas. In the districts reporting, the enrollment in the first grade was 27.1 per cent of the total enrollment, in the first three grades 52.3 per cent, and in the high school 10.3 per cent. The total enrollment was 70.1 per cent of the number of children between six and seventeen years of age.

The Texas Education Agency made a special study of the 1955–1956 enrollment and attendance of white Spanish-surname pupils in the public schools, reporting the results in a leaflet dated August, 1957. The report was compiled from statistics recorded in the Superintendents' Annual Reports for that year. Because of the difficulties inherent in a project of this kind, the data must be regarded as only approximate. According to this report 1,745,347 pupils were enrolled in grades 1 to 12 of Texas schools, and of this number 286,292 had Spanish surnames. The ratio of these enrollments to the number of scholastics (discussed earlier in this section) is 94.2 per cent for the total population and 91.6 per cent for the Spanish-surname group. The ratio of the enrollment of Spanish-surname pupils to the total enrollment is 16.4 per cent. No one knows what correction if any should be applied to this figure to arrive at the percentage who would be included in the group of Spanish-speaking children as the term is used here. Using the correction of one-tenth which has been previously suggested, the Spanish-speaking pupils in the total enrollment are found to be approximately 18 per cent. The distribution of all pupils and of Spanish-surname pupils by grades in Texas public schools in 1955–1956 is shown in Table 20. Although the statistics of the table are old, they are the latest available, and they provide a basis for comparison with results of studies which may be made in the future. In

TABLE 20

Percentage Distribution of Pupils in Texas Public Schools, 1955–1956

Grade	All Pupils	Spanish-Surname Pupils
1	13.0	21.5
2	11.4	13.8
3	11.6	12.8
4	9.4	10.5
5	8.7	9.4
6	8.7	8.4
7	8.4	7.3
8	7.4	5.4
Elementary Schools	78.6	89.0
9	6.8	4.0
10	5.9	3.0
11	4.7	2.1
12	4.0	1.8
High Schools	21.4	11.0

this state study, all Spanish-surname pupils, of whatever ethnic group, were included.

The study of the Texas Education Agency pointed out marked differences in the ratio of first-grade enrollment to twelfth-grade enrollment—about 3 to 1 for all pupils and about 12 to 1 for Spanish-surname pupils. The ratio of the enrollments in grade 5 to enrollments in grade 12 were similarly in marked contrast—about 2 to 1 for all pupils and about 5 to 1 for pupils with Spanish surnames.

The average daily attendance, expressed as a percentage of enrollment, was 87.5 per cent for all pupils and 81.0 per cent for Spanish-surname pupils. The percentage of all pupils who withdrew and did not re-enter was 6.9 per cent as compared with 11.3 per cent for Spanish-surname pupils. The concentration of Spanish-surname pupils in the first grade is indicated by the fact that more than one-fifth of the total number enrolled were in that grade. This, however, is a great improvement over the "nearly half" who were in the first grade thirty years earlier.

Enrollment in College

In a study in 1928–1929 data were collected from seventy-three Texas institutions of collegiate rank on the total enrollment of white students of college and graduate rank and the number of these who were Spanish-speaking, as the term is being used here. Of the 38,538 students reported, only 188 were Spanish-speaking, and 34 of these claimed residence in Mexico. In other words, about one-half of 1 per cent of the white college students were Spanish-speaking, although about 16 per cent of the scholastic population of the state were Spanish-speaking.

Slow progress in college enrollment was shown by the survey reported by Ruth Ann Fogartie, who sought to find the number of Texas-born Spanish-name students in Texas colleges and universities (*Inter-American Education Occasional Papers, III*, University of Texas, 1948). Her data represent twenty-nine of thirty-three senior colleges. The percentage of Spanish-name students reported by her varied from zero to 13.2 per cent in the different colleges, with a state average of 1.7 per cent for the colleges reporting. She reports the following percentages of Texas-born Spanish-name students at The University of Texas for a twenty-five year period:

Year	Per Cent
1920	0.64
1930	1.20
1940	1.06
1945	1.25

For a recent study of the enrollment of Spanish-speaking students in colleges of the Southwest the colleges were asked for statistics on the total enrollment of freshmen who entered from high school in the fall of 1958 and on the number of these who had Spanish surnames. Because of the varying quality of replies there are many sources of error in such reporting and statistics resulting from the study must be considered only approximate. Usable materials were secured for 146 of 229 colleges addressed. In each state at least one branch of the state university was represented. The number of colleges to which requests were mailed and the number contributing usable statistics were as follows:

States	Requests Mailed	Usable Statistics
Arizona	6	3
California	100	50
Colorado	18	16
New Mexico	9	9
Texas	96	68
Total	229	146

TABLE 21

Freshmen Entering 146 Colleges of the Southwest from High School, Fall, 1958

	Male			Female			Male and Female[a]			Percentage of 1960 Population Having Spanish Surnames[b]
		White Spanish-Surname			White Spanish-Surname			White Spanish-Surname		
	All Freshmen	No.	% of All Freshmen	All Freshmen	No.	% of All Freshmen	All Freshmen	No.	% of All Freshmen	
Arizona (3 colleges)	2,065	154	7.5	1,249	56	4.5	3,314	210	6.3	14.9
California (50 colleges)	19,756	683	3.5	14,691	399	2.7	35,884	1,872	5.2	9.1
Colorado (16 colleges)	5,306	179	3.4	3,524	106	3.0	9,730	285	2.9	9.0
New Mexico (9 colleges)	2,759	454	16.5	1,153	161	14.0	4,173	732	17.5	28.3
Texas (68 colleges)	19,538	1,158	5.9	11,880	602	5.1	32,467	1,760	5.4	14.8
Southwest (146 colleges)	49,424	2,628	5.3	32,497	1,324	4.1	85,568	4,859	5.7	11.8

[a] Since some reports give only totals, the combined group is not necessarily the sum of the other two groups.
[b] Table 6.

The results of this inquiry on college enrollment are shown in Table 21.

Because of the lack of full coverage and because of the way in which the data were assembled, the statistics of Table 21 must be interpreted with a great deal of caution. Two summary statements may be made from the table:

(1) The ratio of men to women in the group as a whole is approximately 3 to 2, in the Spanish-speaking group 2 to 1. Apparently Spanish-speaking women go on to college in smaller proportion than do women in the general population.

(2) The Spanish-surname freshmen are about 5.7 per cent of all freshmen reported, but the total Spanish-surname population is much larger in proportion to the total population (11.8 per cent in 1960). If the figures may be taken at their face value, the percentage of Spanish-speaking persons entering college in 1958 was little more than half of the percentage of the Spanish-speaking group in the general population.

The percentage of freshmen who have Spanish surnames varies from zero to 77.5 per cent in the individual colleges from which reports were received. In general the higher percentages are found in colleges which are located in centers having a relatively large proportion of Spanish-speaking population. It is not true, however, that all colleges in these centers have large enrollments of Spanish-name students. One Texas college, for example, has only 3.9 per cent of Spanish-name freshmen although it is located in a county in which 34.4 per cent of the population in 1950 had Spanish surnames.

A count was made of Spanish-surname students enrolled in The University of Texas at Austin for the years 1928–1929, 1938–1939, 1948–1949, 1958–1959—a thirty-year period. The results are shown in Table 22.

During the thirty-year period from 1928 to 1958 the percentage of Spanish-surname students at The University of Texas increased from 1.0 per cent to 3.2 per cent. Except for the year 1958–1959 the students who came from Latin American countries cannot be subtracted from the number of Spanish-surname students. In the first semester of this year 139 students were enrolled from Latin America. Subtracting the 139 foreign students in the first semester of 1958–1959 from the total number of Spanish-surname students that semester leaves 428 as an estimate of the Spanish-surname students from this country, or 2.4 per cent of the total enrollment for that semester.

TABLE 22

Enrollment of White Spanish-Surname Students Compared to
Total Enrollment in The University of Texas

Year	Undergraduate			Graduate			Graduate and Undergraduate		
	Total Students Enrolled	White Spanish-Surname Students No.	%	Total Students Enrolled	White Spanish-Surname Students No.	%	Total Students Enrolled	White Spanish-Surname Students No.	%
1928–1929	5,390	57	1.1	465	1	0.2	5,855	58	1.0
1938–1939	10,103	152	1.5	818	3	0.3	10,921	155	1.4
1948–1949	16,356	395	2.4	2,177	37	1.7	18,533	432	2.3
1958–1959[a]	15,533	518	3.3	2,229	49	2.2	17,762	567[b]	3.2

[a] Early in fall semester only.

[b] During this semester 139 students from Latin American countries were enrolled; most of them are probably included in the Spanish-surname count. There is no count available of the foreign students who may have been included in the figures for previous years.

Corrected for underenumeration, an estimate can be made that about 2.6 per cent of the University enrollment were members of the Spanish-speaking group with which this study is concerned. This small percentage contrasts sharply with the ratio of approximately 16 per cent of Spanish-speaking persons to the total population of the state.

Decreasing Enrollment at Upper Levels

In a paper read before the Seattle meeting of the American Sociological Society in 1958, Paul M. Sheldon reported a study of the records of 2,062 students who left three Los Angeles public senior high schools in 1955–1956. He reported that "the socio-economic status of Mexican-American families was lower than that of non-Mexicans attending the same school," that "the drop-out rate for the Mexican-American population was higher . . . than that of any other ethnic group," that "areas of low socio-economic status furnished a disproportionately high number of students who dropped out," that there was no significant differences in the drop-outs of male and female students, that drop-outs tended to have unsatisfactory behavior ratings, and that "Mexican-Americans were more likely to stay in school in the areas where other groups represented a majority."

A few examples of information gathered in visits to individual schools will illustrate varying conditions of enrollment and attendance. In general, there was testimony of definite improvement over earlier conditions. In one Texas junior high school with an enrollment of approximately 2,000 pupils, 40 per cent of whom were Spanish-speaking, the enrollment dropped rapidly from the seventh to the ninth grades (42 per cent, 32 per cent, and 24 per cent, respectively, with a small enrollment of special students). In the low-eighth grade the average chronological age was seven months higher than the median for the city. Approximately one-third of the Spanish-speaking students went on to the senior high school.

In another Texas city one of the high schools, in which nearly all of the students were Spanish-speaking, reported a heavy drop-out in enrollment at the end of the eighth and tenth grades. From 20 to 25 per cent of the graduates of this high school were going on to college.

Without giving statistics, another school system reported an increase in the number continuing through high school and entering college. In a village school in which three-eighths of the total enrollment were Spanish-speaking, only one-sixth of the high school graduates were Spanish-speaking. A Colorado high school with an enrollment of approximately 2,900 students had from 500 to 700 Spanish-speaking students. An elementary school in the same city illustrated improvement by the fact that five years earlier only 3 Spanish-speaking pupils from the area served by the school graduated from high school but that in the preceding year (1957) 18 Spanish-speaking pupils graduated.

In Los Angeles the comparison over a thirty-year period was dramatically expressed in the statement that the percentage of the Spanish-speaking population who were completing the *junior college* in 1957 was as large as the percentage who were completing the *eighth grade* in 1927. With the guidance of Professor Helen Bailey a Mexican-American Club at East Los Angeles Junior College has had a special project of encouraging pupils in the junior high schools of the area to continue in school.

7. Ability and Achievement

Many studies made with commonly used tests of ability and achievement have yielded lower average scores for Spanish-speaking children than for English-speaking children in the same school or school system. In a 1930 monograph it was reported that the intelligence and achievement of Spanish-speaking children in Texas, as measured by the tests used, were on the average below the intelligence and achievement of other white children of the same age and grade. This is still true of children who are similarly handicapped in home background and language.

Studies of Achievement

A study of school achievement in grades 2 to 8 of a number of schools in the Lower Rio Grande Valley in the early 1930's pointed out the serious overage condition of Spanish-speaking pupils and their lower standing, age for age, on tests of reading and arithmetic. A comparison of chronological ages and "subject ages" showed the English-speaking children on the average about one-third of a year below the norms, but the Spanish-speaking children were on the average about 3.6 years below the norms in reading and about 2.6 years in arithmetic. As age increased, the Spanish-speaking pupils fell farther and farther behind. In both groups a comparison of scores by occupations of the parents gave evidence that school achievement is related to economic level.

Data obtained in 1959 from some of the same school systems reveal a similar tendency toward lower scores for Spanish-speaking children than for English-speaking children and toward lower scores in reading than in arithmetic. Although the results are not directly comparable with those of the 1930's, they are interesting in themselves. Table 23 records comparative scores in reading and arithmetic for one school system. They are expressed in terms of grade level as compared with the publisher's reference groups. Thus a score of 5.2 indicates a performance equivalent to that of the fifth grade at the end of the second month. The statistics are for grades 4, 5, and 6, but the report states that "scores for the first three grades give a similar picture." Note that the differences in the scores are greater in reading than in arithmetic.

TABLE 23

Average Test Scores in Reading and Arithmetic in an Elementary School in the Lower Rio Grande Valley in Texas

		Reading		Arithmetic	
Grade	Total Number of Pupils	English-Speaking Pupils	Spanish-Speaking Pupils	English-Speaking Pupils	Spanish-Speaking Pupils
4	626	5.2	3.3	5.1	4.5
5	687	5.9	4.0	5.9	5.4
6	544	6.5	4.9	6.9	6.3

Another of the school systems reported the test scores of various groups of pupils in grades 6 to 12. The average test score of the Spanish-speaking pupils was distinctly lower than the average test scores of the English-speaking pupils in every comparison: reading in grade 12; a scholarship-qualifying test and a scholastic-aptitude test in grade 11; reading (both word and paragraph meaning) in grade 10; reading (both vocabulary and reading skills) in grade 9; reading (both vocabulary and paragraph meaning) in grade 8; reading (both vocabulary and comprehension) and language in grade 7; and reading (both word and paragraph meaning) in grade 6. In grade 9 there were seventy-one students who had repeated a grade from one to three times, and of these repeaters seventy had Spanish names. Tests administered in grade 7 revealed a greater difference between the scores of English-speaking and Spanish-speaking students in the "verbal" area than in the "quantitative."

Other Studies

In 1951 Mary Anderson reported a comparative study (unpublished thesis, The University of Texas) of the ability and achievement of first-grade children in another of the schools in this area. Using the

Cooperative Inter-American Tests of General Ability (in part a non-verbal test) and Reading, she found that nine-tenths of the Spanish-speaking children made scores no better than the average score of the English-speaking children. Upon applying the Warner scales for socioeconomic status, she found that only 3 or 4 per cent of the Spanish-speaking children were in the middle and upper ranks as contrasted with almost two-thirds of the English-speaking children.

A recent study of first-grade children in a city outside the area in which the studies just cited were made supports the finding that low ability and low socioeconomic status are related (Yvonne Ratliff's unpublished thesis, The University of Texas, 1960). The measuring instrument which was used was the Goodenough test of intelligence, in which intellectual level is estimated from the child's drawing of a man. At the age of a first-grade pupil a child reveals his concepts in his drawings. In addition to the evidence on general mental maturity as revealed by this test, teachers' ratings of school achievement were collected, and a careful rating of socioeconomic status was made, using the Warner scale. The Spanish-speaking children were on the average eight months older than the English-speaking children. In spite of this advantage in age, their average level of intelligence, as measured by this nonverbal test, was four months lower than that of the English-speaking children. The obtained average intelligence quotients of the two groups were 93 and 107, respectively. The Spanish-speaking children were found to be not only significantly lower than the English-speaking children in school achievement but also of lower socioeconomic status. When the results of both groups were thrown together there was a marked tendency (correlation .42) for high intelligence quotients to go with high socioeconomic status and low intelligence quotients to go with low socioeconomic status, although there were high and low intelligence and achievement scores in both groups, an illustration of the individual differences previously emphasized. The average socioeconomic rating of the Spanish-speaking children was within the lower-lower rank, and half of the Spanish-speaking children had ratings below the lowest rating received by any English-speaking child. The difference in average socioeconomic status was much greater than was the difference in intelligence or achievement.

Under the supervision of R. J. Waddell, Tests of General Ability, Level 1, of the Inter-American Series were administered in the fall of 1961 to groups of first-grade English-speaking and Spanish-speaking children in the city in which Mrs. Ratliff made her study. These tests, developed in an interlanguage research supported by the U.S. Office of Education, are of special interest because they are constructed in parallel English and Spanish editions. For every test in English there is a test in Spanish with the same content except for the language used. Thus the English-speaking children were tested in English and the Spanish-speaking children in Spanish. In these groups fewer than 10 per cent of the Spanish-speaking children reached or exceeded the median (average) of the English-speaking children. Tests of the same series, however, administered in a Colorado city under the supervision of Helen K. Bailey gave a more favorable showing: slightly more than one-fourth of the Spanish-speaking children scored above the mean of the English-speaking children. Still more favorable results were obtained from tests of the Spanish edition administered to first-grade children in a school having a somewhat selected enrollment in a city of the Republic of Mexico. The median score of these Spanish-speaking children was *higher* than the median score of the English-speaking children of either of the groups just discussed. The main point to be made by these comparisons is that the standing on comparable tests varies greatly from group to group as well as from child to child.

An Arizona Study

An intensive study of first-grade and second-grade Spanish-speaking children in three schools has recently been completed at Arizona State University (*Investigation of Mental Retardation and Pseudo Mental Retardation in Relation to Bilingual and Sub-cultural Factors*). "School communities were chosen which normally had nearly total enrollments consisting of children of Mexican-American and Indian bilingual home backgrounds." Psychological and educational tests were administered, and with the assistance of the teachers and a social worker, extensive observational information was gathered. The low average socioeconomic status and the low average scores on tests of mental ability and achievement are reflected in the following quotation from the report (p. 155):

The children, as a whole, come from economically deprived families where the father has had little formal education and there are many mouths to feed. By and large, these children are older in a given grade than are children from other groups, and they perform less well on tests of all sorts. The median performances on most tests of mental ability were about one standard deviation below average of Anglo groups. On achievement tests the apparent retardation varied from one subject area to another, showing a progressive retardation in reading with advancing grade, but no clear trend in arithmetic or English language.

Although in average annual family income the families were in the lowest quarter nationally, the range within the group was from $900 to $8,000. Even in the better two of the three communities which were included in the research about one-fourth of the families studied depended on welfare aid for economic support. Yet in these two communities almost all of the families had electricity, half had both hot and cold water, nine out of ten had television, and two out of three had telephones. In the third community, living conditions were much worse: miserable housing, almost no paved streets, few recreational facilities, water usually from a cold-water tap in the back yard, generally outside toilets, and so on.

Generalizations concerning living conditions fail to tell what these conditions mean in the lives of individual children. The meaning of the struggle against the conditions imposed by poverty and poor living conditions can be seen in all its stark realism only by looking at the child who suffers these deprivations.

The fact that the average ability and average achievement as measured by tests were low should not obscure the fact that there were also high test scores. It is significant that higher scores "in both performance and verbal tests of [mental ability] were found for children who, as a group, represented the top socioeconomic families among those studied." There can be no doubt that the mental development of children in their early years is profoundly influenced by the home environment. The central importance of language is emphasized also by the finding of a "progressive retardation in reading with advancing grade."

Commenting on conditions in New Mexico, W. H. Sininger, of the New Mexico Highlands University in a personal letter refers to the large numbers of Spanish-speaking college freshmen with low scores on tests of reading, English, and intelligence. In the elementary schools, he says, pupils start falling below the norms in the fourth grade and lose ground in each of the succeeding grades. This, he thinks, results from language difficulties—inadequate development of meanings and vocabularies. In Volume 2, Number 7, of "Sharing Ideas," a series of memoranda edited by Mrs. Mamie Sizemore, classroom specialist in Indian education (Arizona State Department of

Public Instruction), Mrs. Grace Blossom makes a similar point relative to Indian children. She points out that in the first two school grades and most of the third, the classroom work is based on a spoken vocabulary, but that beginning with the second half of the third grade the emphasis shifts to a comprehension vocabulary and to reading in which there is much less help from pictures. The result is frustration for the child and a special teaching problem for the teacher.

Evidence from Visits to Schools

Visits to schools in the different states provided additional evidence of the scholastic difficulties of many Spanish-speaking children as well as evidence of encouraging and even outstanding records of others. A few illustrations are given here. In the low-eighth grade of a large Texas junior high school with an enrollment which was approximately 40 per cent Spanish-speaking, the average intelligence quotient as measured by a group test administered in English was 92, in comparison with an average of 103 for the city. Pupils of the same grade reached an average score in reading equivalent to that of grade 7.2, compared with a city-wide average equivalent to that of grade 9.3. The language handicap was shown also by the fact that many Spanish-speaking girls seeking employment with the telephone company failed because of their speech. On the other hand, at least one boy played football and at the same time made all *A* grades. In a Colorado senior high school approximately 5 per cent of the students whose intelligence quotients were 115 and above (as measured by tests administered in English) were Spanish-speaking. It was estimated that from 17 to 24 per cent of the total enrollment were Spanish-speaking.

Difficulties of beginning children were illustrated over and over. A keen observer in California commented that school people like to hold Spanish-speaking children two years in the first grade and remarked that the beginners felt more secure with other Spanish-speaking children. In two New Mexico schools, one a mountain school and the other a city school, approximately only one-third of the beginners were able to go on to the second grade in one year. In a Texas school where the children had no kindergarten or preschool training, 80 per cent of the first-grade children went forward to the second grade, but only about one-half of that number were actually qualified for ordinary second-grade work. In one border city it was estimated that not over 5 or 6 per cent of the Spanish-speaking children knew enough English to go forward with other children at school entrance. But in a town school, about one-fourth of the beginning children were going directly into the first grade, though ten years ago none were qualified. It was estimated that an eight-weeks summer school could probably prepare another 25 per cent for first-grade work. And in another city it was estimated that 80 to 85 per cent of the Spanish-speaking six-year-olds knew English when they entered school.

Intelligence and Achievement

The relatively low average achievement of many groups of Spanish-speaking children on commonly used tests of intelligence and achievement is precisely what one would expect. More of the Spanish-speaking children than of the English-speaking children come from "culture-disadvantaged" homes, more of them have little or no knowledge of the language of the school when they enroll, more of them must continue their education in a language different from their home language, more of them lack a background of experience and incentive favoring high educational achievement. Lack of comparable opportunity is a sufficient reason for their lower average scores on tests. There is no reason to doubt their basic learning capacity.

Intelligence is a word frequently used and often misunderstood. The word is properly used to refer to a person's ability to do mental work in general and includes abilities in specific kinds of intellectual activity. The intelligence of a child is inferred from his performance on a test. The test, in turn, is a series of tasks requiring mental work of one kind and another. The intelligence quotient (IQ) is a device for expressing the standing of a child in relation to others of his age group—60 is low, 100 is average, and 140 is high. But one should not accept the result of a single test as an adequate measure of ability. The performance of a child varies from time to time, and different tests commonly give somewhat different results. The IQ registered on a given test should be considered only an *estimate* based on a specific test administered at a specific time. Even repeated tests may fail to give an adequate measure of intelligence.

Various factors in addition to the ability which is being measured influence a test score—the testing situation, acquaintance with testing procedures, the condition and motivation of the person tested, acquaintance with the language of the test, ability to give sustained attention, and the like. When factors other than the ability being tested affect the test score of one person more than another, the interpretation of the scores is especially difficult. One child's score may be influenced more than that of another, and to an unknown degree, by irrelevant factors and thus fail to represent adequately the ability which the tester is trying to measure.

One other thing should be kept in mind. A test measures performance (and ability only by inference) *at the time of the test.* Any statement as to what the ability in question might have been under different circumstances or how it may yet be developed must also depend upon inference, and such an inference requires information beyond that which is revealed by the test. If a child's development has been seriously handicapped for even the first six years of his life, this handicap cannot be easily and quickly overcome. Every year of poor cultural and educational advantages adds its blighting influence to future development and contributes to an appalling waste of human resources.

The typical language experiences of Spanish-speaking children in the Southwest create special problems for the tester. Mainly using spoken Spanish at home and in their community outside of school, having little opportunity to develop a reading knowledge of Spanish and ability in that language at a high conceptual level, and using English in their school work, the children are handicapped by lack of sufficient mastery of any language. This handicap is a factor in test performance as in school work in general.

Teachers are continually seeking tests which will be "fair" to Spanish-speaking children. If children know only Spanish—as may be the case at school entrance or on transfer from a school conducted in Spanish—the obvious procedure is to test in Spanish. When these children enter an English-language school, however, the situation changes rapidly. Even in the second grade most of the children will do about as well when directions for a group test of general ability are given in English as when the directions are given in Spanish. Typically, in the higher elementary grades, since the children know very little written Spanish, tests requiring reading will have to be given in English—unless, of course, the objective is to test ability to understand Spanish. Another reason for using English in achievement testing is that school achievement can usually be tested best in the language in which the learning has occurred.

There are occasions in which ability in English, the language of the school, is a significant part of the ability which the teacher wishes to measure, not a factor disturbing the test results. It is important to know what the children can do in the language in which they are being taught. If a school has a supply of tests in parallel English and Spanish editions—such as the Inter-American Series—the teacher can administer a test in the language which seems most appropriate. On the other hand, many of the tests used with English-speaking children are quite appropriate for Spanish-speaking children, if the results are correctly interpreted. The "unfairness," if any, is more likely to be in the interpretation than in the test itself.

Again Individual Differences

As in the case of adults, individual differences among children must constantly be emphasized. It is easy to get lost in a discussion of averages and forget that the differences within a group are far greater than the differences in group averages. Like children of other groups, Spanish-speaking children have abilities ranging all the way from feeblemindedness to genius. Even at the same level of general ability, some children are stronger in one type of activity and some in another. The same thing holds for the individual child; in some fields his abilities are above and in some fields below the average level at which he operates.

Wide differences in physical appearance are obvious, but differences in the physical organism run far deeper to basic differences in internal structure, in metabolism, and in general physiological functions. Children are very different also in the way they do things, in what they want to do, and in how they feel. They have characteristically different styles of action. Some move slowly, others more rapidly. Some prefer one type of activity, some another. Some have a wealth of energy, others less. Some are nervous, sensitive, fearful, or aggressive. Some feel inferior or insecure. On the other hand, there are those with exceptional poise, confidence, courage, and self-control.

Heredity itself sets the stage for many differences, and environment complicates the situation still further. Children are different in part because of the germ plasm which they received from their parents at the beginning of life. They are different also because of differences in the conditions under which they develop. Some have much more favorable conditions for development than do others, and in any case the conditions are different from child to child. Some are handicapped by disease or accident in infancy or even before birth. Some live in a shack, others in a mansion. Some grow up through severe hardships; others come from homes of luxury. Some are hungry and ill-clothed much of their lives; others always have more than enough. Some have little love; others are over-protected. There are significant differences even among children in the same home.

Accent on Talent

In one way or another it is often said that the school should try to adjust its learning opportunities to the unique characteristics and needs of each child. But this is no easy task under any circumstances and is especially difficult when a teacher has to deal with a number of children. Children at the extremes may be neglected in the vain attempt to teach all of a varied group at the same grade level. It is easy to see that the less able need special help, but not so easy to appreciate the needs of the most able. In general the most able will make a good record with a minimum of attention, but the danger is that they will fall far below their possibilities.

Adjusting to the deficiencies of Spanish-speaking children and other children is only part of the task of the home, the community, and the school. The gifted—the potential leaders in government, science, engineering, the fine arts, and the professions—need encouragement, stimulus, and direction. Failure with these children means an especially great loss of human resources.

8. Problems as Seen by Parents
and Teachers

A sampling of the opinions of parents relative to the problems of their children was secured with the assistance of the principals of a few schools. A letter addressed to the parents invited their comments; the form enclosed for their reply was entitled "The Education of Spanish-Speaking Children—Experiences and Opinions of Parents." Two questions asked were:

"As a parent what do you find to be the special problems of Spanish-speaking children?"

"What should I tell teachers and the public about schools for these children?"

A Common Goal for All Children

We desire for our children, said some, the same things that other parents desire for their children. One of the Denver parents stated it this way:

We like to enjoy the better things in life. We want our children to be well educated and successful. We want them to lead good, clean, moral lives.—Like any other parent I want what is best for my children.

An Arizona parent voiced the same feeling:

I believe every parent wants the same things for his children—no matter what race or color.

There was evident also a strong desire to be accepted, to belong, to be a full member of the community. The not-belonging feeling of their children was a matter of deep concern. A California parent

showed a keen perception of the effect of rejection and the significance of the attitudes generated by rejection:

My husband and I many times feel we do not fit in certain groups or
are not accepted because we are of Mexican origin. We realize most of
the time we are wrong. Yet, I'm afraid they [the children] will begin to
feel the same way.

Her concern was further expressed:

The one thing I wish [is that] my children would grow up to feel more
true loyalty for our country. To feel they are actually a part of this nation, not just a Mexican that happened to be born on this side of the
border. To be proud of their origin, but to keep it in its place.

Another parent showed her attempt to guard her children against
the effect of prejudice toward them:

I've always told my children, "You are only what *you* make of yourself.
Nobody is better than you, and you are no better than anybody." . . . Spanish children should be proud of what they are.

Another, remembering her childhood in a little town where prejudice was shown toward the Spanish-speaking people, noted her own
good fortune:

I have been very lucky because I had red hair, freckles, and a light
complexion.

She offered no suggestions on the special educational treatment of
Spanish-speaking children. Instead:

All I can say is, Teach the children; we are all God's children, no matter
what we look like or who we are.

An Arizona father expressed a strong view against segregation of
Spanish-speaking children in separate schools, rooms, or even groups,
adding:

I believe that every Spanish-speaking [child] knows he is different and
does not need reminding.

Economic Conditions

Lack of money was said to be a source of difficulty. A Texas mother
expressed the opinion that "the economic conditions of the Spanish-
speaking have a direct bearing on the ability of their children to learn

English." Another expressed two unfavorable results of insufficient income: lack of educational materials at home and having to withdraw children from school so the parents may find work in another community:

With six children I am unable to provide educational toys, records, or books for them. . . . More jobs are needed in our hometown for Spanish-speaking people so we could become permanent residents of this or any community. So many times we must withdraw the children from school in order to look for jobs elsewhere.

Another parent expressed the point of view that lack of money or failure to use it for education is a serious problem:

The most important problem is money. Many of the Spanish-speaking Americans don't have enough money to help their children through school. Some people do acquire enough money but will rather use it on some-thing of less importance, ignoring their children's education.

The complicated relation of prejudice and economic conditions is suggested in the remarks of one parent:

If a Spanish kid gets into some mischief with the law, the reaction is usually, "Well, what can you expect; he's Spanish, isn't he?" The public should be educated to the fact that many times these kids get into trouble because of family financial troubles or environment. Many times their parents cannot get higher paying jobs because of their nationality. Society rather than the individual is more often than not responsible for poverty.

I think that the Spanish group has come a long way in the way of improvement, but it has a long way to go yet. Establishing anything like economic equality with other groups will mean increasing their number in skilled trades and professional and clerical work.

The responsibility of parents for an active part in the education of their children was recognized in various statements. Some felt that teaching English to their children at home was a parental responsibility. One expressed regret that she had done so little to contribute to the language development of her children:

I see the mistake I have made now, because my children are not progressing as fast as I thought they would. I have started to speak English to my five-year-old hoping that by the time he enters school, he will be better prepared than the others.

One parent expressed the need for team-work on the part of parents and teachers in these words:

Most teachers will not help children because the parents do not coop-erate, and most of the Spanish people are not interested in school activities. I think that the parents need to help more and encourage the children better.

Another expressed the need for cooperation in these words:

We cannot expect the teacher to do our job for us. They are wonderful to try to understand them, but the foundation is the home; the next step is the school.

Language Difficulties

The problem of language was recognized in various comments, some of which have already been given. Individual differences among children on this point were clearly evident. A Denver mother wrote that her husband and her children did not speak Spanish. In fact, at the time of writing, her husband and one son were "taking Spanish" by television. Another parent expressed the opinion that if people would speak English to their children at home, their children would be more confident. She commented that her little son was taught English first and now can express himself much better in English than in Spanish.

Some parents expressed the need for a school program for five-year-old children. A father said that one year of kindergarten or pre-school education is worth as much as three years later on:

I believe that one year at the start for a Spanish-speaking child will be as effective—if not more so—as about three years at the age when a child loses interest in school (ages 13 to 16). I believe that, if a Spanish child at this age had the kindergarten background, he would very likely con-tinue through high school and possibly college.

The problem of keeping children in school was recognized by an-other parent in these words:

The number-one problem with the Spanish-speaking children is [that] they go as far as the eleventh grade, and then they quit. They lose all in-terest with only a year or two to go.

She feels that schools should make it "almost impossible" for a child to leave school.

That different children have different needs is evident from various comments. One parent remarked:

I have ten children, among them a set of twins, and not even the twins are alike in any of their habits or ways of thinking.

One way in which children are different, it is pointed out, is in their feeling of security or insecurity, of trust or timidity.

It is obvious that the parents who made the comments quoted here are of an economic and cultural level above that of a large number of less fortunate people who have children in the schools. In general, however, the problems listed are problems also of the children from poverty-stricken and culture-deprived homes. Some of the problems, such as achieving status, acquiring a new language, and finding money to support children in the schools, are frightfully magnified in groups of lower economic levels. In these homes there is often a lack of understanding and a resulting lack of an aggressive interest in the education of their children. There is a certain hopelessness and lack of ambition fostered by continued poverty and frustration. On the other hand, there are many very poor people who have a vision of better days for their children and who are struggling forward, perhaps groping from lack of direction.

Problems as Seen by Teachers

In general, teachers emphasize problems related to their work. The principal of an Arizona elementary school presented a group of problems as a summary of questions listed by his teachers. Naturally, some of the questions dealt with policies and methods of teaching. For example, should Spanish-speaking children be allowed to speak Spanish to one another in class? Do teachers tend to make class work easier for Spanish-speaking children? Should drill be used to correct the speech errors of the five-year-old, or should he be encouraged to speak the best English he can by simply listening to other children and to the teacher? When an older child enters without any knowledge of English, how should he be taught? Should he be enrolled in grade 1 and work through grade-by-grade to the grade in which he otherwise belongs? What is the best procedure to use when a child has shown no desire and made no effort to talk?

Some of the questions were directed toward an understanding of cultural difficulties and the ways to deal with them. One teacher expressed the opinion that "there is a strong pressure in each class to keep all individuals at the same level of achievement. Slow learners are not especially looked down upon, but fast learners must be careful not to achieve beyond the group as a whole. Humor is often used to keep an individual in line."

Emotional difficulties, perhaps related to cultural background in the thinking of the teachers, were suggested by some of the comments and questions. What cultural or other factors, excluding the language barrier, tend to influence Spanish-speaking children to be timid and withdrawn in learning situations? How can greater self-expression be developed? One teacher pointed to feuds among girls in the upper grades, remarking that in her opinion girls fight worse than boys. In two comments the opinion was expressed that Spanish-speaking children tend to be either extremely shy or very bold. If this observation is true, it was asked, what kinds of activities and room atmosphere should be planned to meet the situation?

One question pointed to an emotional conflict which seems to stem from a difference in school procedures and home culture. The school, it was said, teaches children to care for themselves, but the home teaches the older children to look after the younger. The result: fourth-graders "beat up" first-graders! Another suggested that the families have a "strange defeatist attitude" toward the behavior problems of the children, accepting the difficulties as a "cross they have to bear" rather than attempting to understand and help the children.

A few questions related to special characteristics or handicaps of Spanish-speaking children. Do the bilingual children at a given grade level learn at the same rate as do other children of the same socioeconomic status? Are Spanish-speaking children more or less creative than are other children of the same socioeconomic level? How does the physical and mental maturity of these children compare with that of other children? How can horizons be expanded for children of very limited experience?

Another List of Problems

A number of Texas teachers, responding to an invitation to list "problems in the education of Spanish-speaking pupils," took the opportunity to stress the techniques of language teaching. For one thing, they called attention to difficulties arising from differences in Spanish and English. Illustrations of differences include pronunciation of the vowel *i*; verb-subject sentence order; inflection of words to show tense, gender, and number; and stress, rhythm, and intonation in sentences. Other problems of teaching technique which occur in teaching Spanish-speaking children, they reported, include building vocabulary, teaching silent reading without vocalization, teaching abstract words, timing progress from one stage of learning to another (for example, from oral work to reading), providing reading materials of appropriate difficulty, stimulating effort toward accomplishment, finding the right amount of drill, using music in language teaching, using Spanish in teaching English.

Three types of factors were pointed out as adding to the difficulties of teaching Spanish-speaking pupils. The first was a group of practices in the schools themselves: promoting pupils, for social reasons, to grades beyond their levels of ability, holding Spanish-speaking pupils to a speed established for English-speaking pupils, enrolling in the same class pupils of very different ability in the use of English, failing to allow time for teachers to give individual help, not providing opportunity for practice in English at school outside the class.

The attitudes and abilities of pupils were considered another source of difficulty. In many cases there seemed to be a lack of motivation for school work. Many seemed to have a feeling of insecurity in the use of English and in dealing with the English-speaking environment. Another depressing factor was said to be the lack of concepts, not only in English but in Spanish as well, and the lack of experience on which concepts must be built. Pupils tended to learn words without grasping the ideas which the words should suggest.

Finally, it was thought that home and community conditions were often a hindering factor. Teachers pointed to a frequent lack of parental cooperation and to difficulty in trying to confer with parents. Many pupils come from homes of poor cultural background, and looming large in the difficulties was the lack of practice in English. Sometimes the use of English is resisted by the child's parents and even by his peers. Continuing immigration of Spanish-speaking persons tends to perpetuate the use of Spanish as the language of the community and of large numbers of children. On the positive side, television was pointed to as being of significant assistance in the teaching of English.

Two Individual Comments

Here are the comments of two teachers of Spanish-speaking children. The first speaker is a person transplanted to the Southwest from another section of the country; the second is herself a person of Spanish name.

1) Being a—, I was quite unprepared for what I assumed was a "foreign accent." And more shocking to my system was the fact that these children speak Spanish as a colloquial language!

Almost all of the children in my class have a pronounced accent which in *this* classroom situation bothers no one but me. However, I have had the experience of teaching in a school for military dependents [elsewhere]. I had the privilege of having in my class a boy born in [the Southwest] and who had spent most of his life here. T– was considered to be extremely dull and of course was a discipline problem. Closer observation (at the *end* of the school year) proved that T– was in fact not dull but that he could not "speak English." Rather than have his classmates laugh at him, T– refused to speak! I realize now, that T– was a boy I could have found *right here*, but never having been in Texas, I was not aware of this problem. Unfortunately, none of his other teachers were aware of it either. These children—here—can "get by," but taken out of this "border land" they are just as much foreigners—on first observation—as DP's. My sympathy is with these children who once having left their own safe little "world" [here], find that they are looked upon with amazement, if not downright ridicule!

2) Personally, I think that the greatest problem encountered by teachers of Spanish-speaking children in the first grade is that of the language handicap. A great number of our children in the southside schools have recently come from Mexico, and, naturally, have never been exposed to the English language. As we all know, oral language is a prerequisite to reading as well as to other subjects taught in the first grade. Here is where our problem lies—teaching them sufficient oral English in as short a time as possible in order that they will be able to cover all the first grade work in one year. The problem of these children can be justified by the mere fact that their parents are Mexican citizens, do not know the language and therefore cannot help them.

However, we have a number of children whose parents were born in the United States, have lived here all or most of their lives, and can speak the English language fluently. Yet these children do not speak a word of English when they first come to school. I don't think there is any excuse whatsoever for these parents' not teaching their children at least a few words of English so that they will not feel lost when first they come to school. Other teachers and I have talked to some of these parents about this but they all give us the same answer—because of social reasons.

It seems that they live in a neighborhood that is strictly Latin American —many of their neighbors do not speak English. When these people hear them speaking English to their children, they regard them as pretentious and conceited and will cease speaking to them. Therefore, in order to maintain friendly relations with their neighbors, these parents refrain from speaking English to their children. I hope this problem of jealousy on the part of neighbors will be solved some day.

The Problem List

The problems of Spanish-speaking children are many and serious, whether enumerated by their parents or by their teachers. The parents were eager that their children receive a good education, and they were keenly aware of their own responsibilities and limitations. They regarded acceptance in the community and the learning of English as major problems. The teachers were struggling with detailed problems of teaching and guidance. They were concerned with techniques of teaching language, with the learning difficulties of the children, with their emotional development, and with parental cooperation. Like the parents, they saw language as a major problem of the Spanish-speaking group as a whole.

9. How High School Students
View Their Problems

How do Spanish-speaking children themselves view their problems? This question will be answered in part by the replies of a number of high school students to a letter which invited a free expression of their ideas and feelings. The letter was placed in their hands with the assistance of principals, teachers, and other staff members in local school systems. The students have written with such clarity and interest that they will be quoted with a minimum of comment or editing.

Invitation to Students

This is the letter which invited the assistance of students.

Dear Student:

You have been selected as one who could give important help in a study of the education of Spanish-speaking boys and girls. I have visited schools in five states and have learned a great deal from teachers. I need now to know how the students themselves feel, what they see as their special problems, and what they think can be done to improve conditions. I want to be able to write something which will be helpful to teachers, to parents (both English-speaking and Spanish-speaking), and to the public. As you know, understanding is a first step toward improvement.

I do hope that you will be willing to write something of your own ideas. An autobiography starting with early childhood would be especially helpful in giving an account of the problems which you and others have met in getting an education. The good and the not-so-good, the things that are funny and the things that are serious or even sad—all will help to get a clearer picture.

You may write very freely. I shall not use your name in any way to embarrass you. In fact, if you prefer, you need not write your name. The only thing is that I should like to be able to write a thank-you letter for your help.

Reply sheets and a stamped return envelope are inclosed for your convenience. You may return your reply directly to me, and I shall be grateful for your help.

The students from whom replies were received were those who had been successful in their school work, at least to the point of high school enrollment. It would be interesting to know what those who have been less successful think and how they feel. In any case, it is certain that many of the basic problems are the same for the successful and the unsuccessful student.

An attempt was made both in the wording of the letter and in the way the replies were to be written and delivered, to get expressions of the opinions and feelings of the students themselves. The success of the attempt cannot be known, for there are no means of determining the extent to which the replies were influenced by teachers, parents, or others. Perhaps in arriving at a list of problems it does not matter much whose list it is. Yet one finds in the replies support for the assumption that they do represent the ideas and feelings of the students.

No statistical summary of the replies will be made. Instead, the replies themselves will be quoted at length, with only brief comments to provide a framework for the presentation. Lengthy quotations from the replies are made to preserve the interest and point of view of the original statements and to make it more likely that these students will be seen as living boys and girls. There will be repetitions but in different contexts, and a repetition will reinforce what someone else has said. The objective at this point is not to evaluate but to understand. As counselors well know, the first step in dealing with a situation is to find out how it looks to those who are most concerned.

How Students View Their Problems

The first letter is from a fifteen-year-old high school sophomore who knew how to read and write a little English before entering the first grade. The naturalness and sincerity of her story, even to the postscript, leads to hope that she may find a way to go to college.

In my opinion, the chief problems in the education of Spanish-speaking boys and girls are that we are not taught to read English in the first grade. Children memorize, not read, the simple lines of their readers. Also, the learning of our own tongue is not emphasized enough. Oh, we know how to speak, but we mix Spanish and English, and create a language of our own.

My schooling started when I was two and a half years old. I was enrolled in a Spanish Catholic convent; consequently I learned to read and write Spanish long before I entered public schools. I have always gotten good grades and I think it was my early discipline that taught me not to be lazy or to avoid work. I enjoy homework and try to get all I possibly can out of school.

Before I entered public schools, Mom sent me to a sort of private school run by a lady who taught me some English. I was five then; so before I entered primer, I knew how to read and write a little English. This gave me a head-start and advantage over many children my age. When I finally entered my first public school, I stayed one week in primer and was promoted to second grade. From then on, it was easy coasting, for we had nothing new or hard until we got to fourth grade. I don't know why, but I immensely disliked social studies. All my other grades were above 93, but I went as low as 85 in geography.

In fifth grade I learned absolutely nothing, except my time tables. I'm sure I would not have learned them had we not had to state them before the class. My fifth-grade teacher was forever telling us of his experiences with oil wells; therefore we learned all about the field of oil, but no knowledge was really acquired. The only milestone of my sixth grade was my joining the band, an organization which gives me much pleasure. I bought a clarinet and felt proud because I was a member of the Jr. Band, though I didn't learn to play until I was in the eighth.

Seventh grade was a different story. Then was when I acquired real interest in my studies. That year a new teacher was to teach English and everyone was anxiously waiting for him. Mr. P— was his name, and it's a name I will never forget. Honestly, sir, he was brilliant! He taught me everything I know about English grammar, and it's surprising how he made me want to learn more. Mr. P— showed me the value of being neat and how it pays to study. That year I was among the few Spanish-speaking students who were given a chance to study Spanish. Seventh grade is a year long to be remembered because of all the fun we had. Mr. P— gave us a party every six weeks and we went on two hayrides, too. The year was gone before I realized it and so I soon found myself in the eighth grade.

From the fourth to the eighth grade I had made the honor roll (average over 92) consecutively every six weeks; so I graduated from Jr. High as salutatorian, losing the position of valedictorian for less than a point.

When I entered high school, I was caught off guard and because I hadn't studied, I couldn't make the honor roll. Our grading system was changed from numbers to letters, and for a while it was confusing. I was greatly disappointed with high school, for I expected something entirely different. I thought life would be a whirl of dances and all. But high school is not that. No one can fool around and expect to pass. That year I made the honor roll only three times, but they were not consecutive. I took Algebra I and this tended to make me study more. My yearly average was an *A* in everything, except algebra.

Now I am fifteen and a sophomore. Being a sophomore is quite an honor, for we aren't at the bottom of the list. I was elected vice-president of the sophomore class, an office which I proudly hold. I made a straight-*A* average this semester and achieved a goal I longed for, the National Honor Society.

Well, here I am, almost through with high school, and I hope and pray I can go to college. I just wish the years would fly because I want to help my parents as soon as possible. My mother works, but Dad cannot take just any job. He was disabled during the War. . . . I want to be a history teacher and relieve my mother of the responsibility of maintaining the household. It's going to be a long time before I go through college and I just pray that my parents can wait, though I don't know how I'm going to do it. I just know I'll find a way to go because I want to badly enough.

P. S. Like all teen-agers, I lead quite a social life. I date, go steady, and enjoy life.

Lack of English

Next is the reply of a high school senior who lives in another state and who knew no English before entering school. This student also emphasizes the language problem but lists with it the problems of money and moving from place to place. As in the preceding case, she remembers one teacher as outstanding.

I think one of the major problems of Spanish boys and girls is not knowing any English when we begin school, or else knowing very little. The [English] we do know is poor English.

Once we have started school and begin speaking English it is very hard to get rid of Spanish accent. It is especially hard on us in grade school. For example, we get in front of the classroom to read, or give a report; then we make a mistake in our English and all the boys and girls laugh. Later on as we continue school we hate to speak in a classroom where everyone seems to know good English. We are very self-conscious.

Yet another problem is a lack of money. Most Spanish people don't have very much money to spend on school for their children. The child therefore hates to go to school wearing the same outfit every day. Children want to feel equal with everyone in school. They want to have enough money for lunch and also a little spending money.

I was almost six years old when I started school. I was afraid to enter

school, because I did not know any English. I knew simply things such as
"yes," "shut the door," and a few other phrases. My lack of English
caused me to remain in the first grade two years. I was very lucky to have
a very nice teacher in the first grade. She was understanding and kind.
She tried real hard to be patient with me. I shall never forget that teacher.
I still visit her when I go to R—.

One of my main problems was the changing of schools. I started school
in R— and attended school there for three years. Then we moved to a
small community a few miles away. There I went to school two years.
Back to R— we went, and I went to school there for a year and a half.
From there we went to L— where I went to school for half a year. I had
two years of junior high in R—; then we moved to D—. One of my
happiest times in school was my junior high days. I had a lot of fun while
I believe I accomplished something. I was very well liked by the teachers
and students alike. I participated in many activities.

I plan to go to business college later on when I graduate, working at the
same time because otherwise I can't make it. I want to get a good business
job some day.

Whenever I get married and have children I want to help them get as
much education as possible. Also I want them to learn English before they
start school, but I also want them to learn to speak, and write, and read
Spanish. I want them to be proud they are Spanish because I am.

The bearing of a knowledge of English upon acceptance by other
students and upon progress through the grades is clearly shown in
the comments of a high school student who knew both Spanish and
English when he entered school. His experience should be of special
interest to Spanish-speaking parents.

I was born in a small town in South Texas where two-thirds of the people
are Spanish-speaking. I learned to speak both English and Spanish at
about the same time. I do not think I have ever had trouble with my school-
work. I believe my being bilingual has helped me much in school. My only
trouble is not being able to pronounce some words correctly.

When I was in the sixth grade my family moved to L—. In my class,
here in L—, there was only one Spanish-speaking student besides me. My
parents had told me how it would be, and soon I had many friends. There
were two younger boys in this school that were always speaking Spanish.
These two boys had no friends because they would speak as little English
as they could get by with. I do not think either one of these boys ever got
past the ninth grade.

The Junior High School I went to had about twenty Spanish-speaking
students. I was the only one that was the same age as our classmates. The

rest were at least three years older than the other students. Out of all the Spanish-speaking students I knew in Junior High School, I know of only three [who went] to high school besides me. I am going to graduate from high school this May, and I plan to go to college.

The parents of Spanish-speaking students are the people that could help the most. It should be explained to these parents what their children go through. The parents should be told to speak more English. Since some children hear only Spanish at home, they only speak Spanish. These children have a very hard time in school. Many parents will not send their children to school until they are eight or nine years old. This throws the child out of his age group, and soon he quits school. Something should be done to force the parents to send their children to school. I think that some of the older Spanish-speaking students do not know the importance of education. I believe the parents and teachers should try to encourage these students.

I hope my letter will help you somehow. Thank you for caring about us.

It may be surprising to some readers that there are children in the Spanish-speaking group who speak no Spanish. Freedom from a language handicap opens the way to normal progress according to ability, but, as in the case of many other children, there may be other difficulties to overcome.

I started school at the age of five. I'm not sure, but I think I skipped part of the 2nd and 3rd grades. My father said they wanted to put me up farther.

I've never really had much trouble with my studies. There are six children in our family; so there is always the thought of money. Many of our clothes get passed down from one to the other because there are five of us girls. School fees and supplies have to be thought about early so we can have the money for them.

My parents didn't have much of an education; so my father doesn't have a real good job. Before my sister married, she worked and gave my parents money.

Last summer I started working in a hospital as an "aide." I bought my own things and many for the kids. Now I work part-time and go to school. I would very much like to become a nurse, but I think I'll work for a while so I can help my parents with schooling the rest of the kids. My parents can't afford to pay for four years of school, and I'm not going to really decide on anything yet.

Need of Language Contacts

The following comments are those of a high school senior who had no knowledge of English at school entrance. The need of contacts with English in school and outside is suggested.

Spanish students should be forced to speak English during school hours; thus will they develop fluency in speaking and correctness in writing English. Their parents should see to it that the children become familiar with the English language before they start school so as to make advancement in school a greater possibility for them.

During my first years of school it was very difficult for me to get used to the language. My slowness in learning English was due to the fact that my playmates in school were mostly Spanish children and speaking Spanish was more common than speaking English. When I entered junior high, my grades in English were very low. This was because I couldn't understand English phraseology. Then, I enrolled in a school in Indiana; since I was the only Spanish student there, I had to speak English constantly. My English, of course, improved considerably.

Since English is a hard language to learn, especially if you have never been introduced to it, I would advise Spanish parents who are planning to educate their children the American way to teach them to speak as early and as fluently as they can.

The fact that many children in the Southwest use only a poor kind of Spanish is illustrated in the comments of a high school student who had no knowledge of English at school entrance.

I think that a great problem a Spanish-speaking child has is the learning of his first words in English. This is because we are used to pronouncing words in the Spanish language and with a Spanish accent. Sometimes we mix the words in English with those in Spanish.

I remember that before I had taken Spanish lessons in high school, I spoke a kind of Spanish that now I am ashamed to hear. I used to mix my words saying half of a word in Spanish and the other half in English. Now that I have taken two years of Spanish and I am in my third year, I recognize the terrible mistakes I used to make. About 90 per cent of the Spanish-speaking boys and girls speak in the manner I once spoke.

Next are the comments of a high school boy who has lived, he says, "in the center of a 'Tex-Mex' district, where both English- and Spanish-speaking peoples have contaminated their respective languages with false derivations from the other." He believes that "lack of practice in speaking English is . . . the chief problem [in] the education of Spanish-speaking students." Note the misinterpretation by his first-grade teacher of his inability to speak English.

I was born in E–, but at the age of five moved with my parents to L–. When I entered the elementary school, I knew no more than ten words in English. Boy, was I lost! I cried the first few days because I could not understand what my teacher said. Eventually, through constant practice of the language, I learned to speak English enough to make myself understood. On one occasion I was sent to an ear specialist by my first-grade teacher who thought I was a bit deaf.

Here is a high school sophomore who has had to struggle with stuttering as well as with learning English.

My childhood was a very happy one. My only trouble was that I stuttered, and at first I would never talk so that I wouldn't be embarrassed. In school it was also my problem, and my learning English was the hardest. My teachers were all very nice and understanding. But one of my teachers was the nicest of all and very understanding; she gave most of her time in teaching me to speak good English. At home my parents were very wonderful. They would tell me when I was wrong and how to pronounce the words, both in English and in Spanish. My teacher, Mrs. W–, rest her soul, did everything to help. I would go to her house every Sunday, and she would get me to go over the words and pronounce them. As the years went on my stuttering became less noticeable and I would pronounce English better.

One of my happiest days was when my art teacher told me that I received a Certificate of Merit from the International Poster Contest. I also received the "over-all prize" on a black and white picture which I did in ink. I may say I was very proud of myself, that is until I had to go to a banquet where the prizes were to be given and had to thank them. I was scared that I wouldn't say the right words or would not pronounce them right. But I spoke without having to think of the words, and my mother was very proud of me.

Emphasis on Motivation

Helping a pupil to feel a need for English is an important step in teaching. Sometimes the need grows out of a situation which students themselves help to create. An emphasis upon motivation can be seen in the following comments.

I was seven years old when I came to E– to attend St. I– School in the first grade. I didn't have trouble at all trying to understand what they said because they would translate it into Spanish. From the second grade I was double-promoted to the fourth grade. The sister in the fourth grade didn't know a word in Spanish. So in this year I knew English a little better. Then the sister of the fifth grade was a very good teacher to me.

She was always correcting my English and pronunciation. I am very grateful to all the sisters that helped me, but specially her. Then when I was ready for the sixth grade, I went to A–. In this school none of my teachers would speak the Spanish language. And so in the year and half that I was in A–, I understood and spoke English better. In November of 1955, we were transferred to B–.

I am working hard trying to improve my English to speak it clearly and distinctly. A few weeks ago we organized a club by the name of (SOS) Stop Our Spanish. By forming and joining the club mentioned above we made the spontaneous proposition of always speaking English while in school and on the campus. We are to influence our classmates and friends to join the club or continue speaking to them in English until they answer us in the same manner.

Students from Mexico

A considerable number of Spanish-speaking children come into this country from Mexico and start their schooling in English after several years in Mexican schools. One such student tells her experiences. Note her analysis of the situation and the sources from which most help came.

I'm writing to you briefly on how I began to speak and understand English and the troubles that I'm having now in order to continue speaking English.

[We] lived twelve and one-half years [in Mexico] and then came to E– to live as residents in the fall of 1955. At first when I went to school I couldn't speak a bit of English, and I would be embarrassed every time that my English-speaking friends would try to talk or make me understand what they were saying. I was in this school for a few months and during that time, I was one of the smartest girls in math, or on tests which I would understand.

I had friends that spoke Spanish and they would tell me in Spanish what the teacher was telling me in English and I would just listen with my head down.

Then, my parents decided to go to C–, and there I went again to the fifth grade. I couldn't understand English yet and in this school there was not a single friend that could help me understand. All of the students of this school spoke English only, and I had trouble. But it just happened that my teacher every day after school helped me as she spoke and understood a little Spanish and every day with the dictionary in Spanish-English she would help me little by little. She taught me all she could, and soon I was beginning to understand English, but still I couldn't hold a conversation with other students. But I'll say that it did me good to be among people that just spoke English and in that way I would listen to them talking. I could understand some of the words as all day long I would hear nothing but English. After school I would do my homework with the help of my cousins and then I would watch television, and I think that helped me a lot.

In the summer of 1965 I did nothing but study English with a Spanish-to-English book that my father had bought for me and my sister. My sister was a year younger than I, and we would practice by little English talks with each other correcting ourselves.

In the fall of the same year, we came back to E— and I started in the seventh grade. Here [where nearly all students are Spanish-speaking] I didn't like it at first because I would hear people speaking Spanish all around school, and I couldn't understand why this was, as I would say that we were here in the United States to learn English and not to continue speaking Spanish. So my first days I just couldn't see how I would become accustomed to this school and I dreamed of the day that I would go back to C—.

Now, I've been here in this school since then, and I don't think that I have extended my knowledge of English as I would have done in C— by now. I will say that I owe all of the English that I know now to that wonderful teacher back in C— that stayed with me every day after school, and slowly I was beginning to understand some words with her wonderful help. She helped me with my first English words and if it hadn't been for her, I'll say that I would still be having trouble to understand English.

I'm now in my sophomore year in the same school and I'm trying to learn all of the English that I can, but sometimes I forget to speak English and I find myself conversing in Spanish. I'm trying hard but sometimes as I said before, you just can't speak English all of the time. My friends and I start to speak Spanish, and we do it almost all of the time except when we are speaking with our teachers or giving reports.

I wish that we all would speak English all of the time. That is the only thing that is holding us back now. Also, most of the time, my friends mix the two languages and I'm speaking like that too and I wish I wouldn't. The thing that is missing is our will, our own will, to continue speaking English all of the time. And now I'm looking toward the day that I'll overcome all of my speaking Spanish except when necessary. I know that I can do it if I will just stop and think that whenever I shall want a job, I will have to speak English all of the time.

A Backward Look by a Graduate

The next comments were written by a high school senior in the summer following her graduation. When she entered the first grade she spoke only English, "because my parents never made me learn Spanish." Now she speaks Spanish, but thinks that her English is better.

I was born in a coal mining camp. I attended the . . . County grade school for one year. This was my kindergarten. I was much older than the rest of my schoolmates, but in county schools they don't mind if you are younger or older, just as long as you go to school. In 1948 my father was run over by a train. I was 7 at the time, and I have never forgotten it. We came to D– and I started school. I was much older than my school-mates; so the principal transferred me to the second grade. I adjusted very fast to my schoolmates. I was the only Spanish girl in the whole school, I think, and I found out then that no one cared what color I was.

I made friends all through grade school, and I was a leader in most of my activities. I think that I was very well accepted; in fact, I was chosen or rather elected to be the president of some tree club. I was in student council all through my grade school years, and I was president of my fifth- and sixth-grade class.

When I went to junior high, I didn't like my seventh grade at all. I was very skinny and more Mexican people attended [that school]. Gangs were forming and I didn't know what way to turn. I started to stick around with [English-speaking] girls and boys, and the Spanish people would call me a "Paddie lover." I didn't care because I knew that they were the foolish ones by not mixing.

In the eighth and ninth grades, I was elected to student council. I was president of the Red Cross and editor of the school paper, and I attended leadership camp twice. I held a lot of offices in junior high.

In high school, I was very lost. I kept up my grades, and success followed. I was in Sophomore Council and Junior Council. After I was admitted to the local honor society, I tried for National Honor. After I was in National Honor, I ran for several offices, and I got them. I was chosen the senior of the year, and I was vice-president of the All-Girls Club, vice-president of the Pep Club, and secretary in the Future Teachers of America. I won a scholarship to . . . College for four years.

[Now] I have a very good job as secretary, and there is no racial prejudice at all in the office.

Supplementing the account of her school experiences, she made some interesting comments on the Spanish-speaking population of the city in which she lives. Among the comments are those which suggest the tremendous social pressures under which these young people live.

Many Mexicans are embarrassed by poverty, language difficulty, or the feeling of difference from other pupils, and quit school early. This gives the Mexicans a bad reputation because they are left to wander in the streets or get jobs that no one else would take.

The name "Mexican" has turned into a dirty word for those of that origin. It means "hoodlum," one who is stupid, dope addict, clown, and a drunk. Some movies always have the Mexican play the dumb guy.

I'll never forget the time when someone called me a "Dirty Mexican." Of course, this bothered me to the extent that I began to cry. What was I crying for? Not for the name itself, but for the meaning behind this name.

You are what you are and you have to learn to accept it and be proud of it, whether you are black, brown, fat, thin, tall, short, pretty, or ugly. What can you do about it? With acceptance comes tolerance.

Another thought that is in the minds of Mexicans is, "Everyone is against us." This is not true. If a person would stick around with [English-speaking] people, he would find out that they don't call him down. You are always asked to do what they do. They consider you part of them. You are part of them.

To be Spanish is to be from a "better" country, of lighter complexion, and a nice kid; so, naturally, everyone wants to be "Spanish." If you would ask a Mexican [living here] what he was, he would tell you that he is Spanish. Why are they ashamed to tell you they are from Mexico? One of the reasons might be when the first Mexicans came they worked in beet fields, and when the season was over, they were left with nothing; so they had to steal to exist. People turned this into a "racial" bias, reinforcing the anti-Mexican feeling. If some of the present Mexicans who deny their race were to go back to Mexico, they would find out that Mexico is a "fantablous" nation. [She explains that "fantablous" is a slang expression meaning that something is extra superb.]

I do not think that I was born under a black star, just because my skin is darker than others. I think that if people would live and let live, there would be no racial prejudice at all. All Mexicans should mix and at the same time work together [with other people]. "All Mexicans must stick together"; this shouldn't be true, because in order to make things better, you should do something about the present situation instead of making it worse.

~.~.~.~.~.~.~.~.~.~.~.~

10. More Information from
High School Students

Replying to the invitation, other high school students discussed their problems.

Social Pressure

A student from Mexico who knew no English when she entered an English-speaking third grade at twelve years of age tells her story. She advanced rapidly and entered the junior high school from the fifth grade. The only malice toward her which she recalls was that shown by Spanish-speaking people.

I would like to thank you for having selected me as one that could give you help.

In July, 1952, we arrived in the United States. We spent our first year at K–. I was twelve years of age and because of my language difficulty, I was put in the third grade. It was very hard for me and I had to try hard. Fortunately, my teacher was nice enough to stay after school and help me. Some girls used to come over to my house and help me with my English with the condition that I had to do their arithmetic problems. Within three months I was able to understand and write almost everything. Two months later I was promoted to the fourth grade. Being the oldest one in the class, I still felt strange. I remember one time we had a Christmas party and I had to teach the girls how to dance because I was too big to dance with anybody.

In March, 1952, a very good job was offered to my father at H–. We came, and I continued my year in a Catholic school. I was the only Mexican so I had to learn how to speak English. Again, everyone was very nice. The nuns used to help me out a lot, and I helped them with their Spanish.

I remember that the priest used to have a Spanish dictionary in his hand before he would confess me.

The spring term was over. The only trouble that I had was with my English. I was afraid to speak it. My tongue did not want to move. People said I had a cute accent, but I wondered if they were only making fun.

When September came, I took a big chance. Instead of going into the fifth grade, I enrolled in a junior high school near my house. The principal was Mr. W–. I didn't tell him that I didn't know how to speak English well, nor that I had gone to St. T–. I just showed him my report card from Mexico and that was all. That year was one of the happiest ones of my life. At first I felt funny because I wasn't used to seeing so many boys, but I liked it. I remember an American boy named Marvin asked me for a date, but Daddy told him I was too young and he was too old for me.

During that time Mother and Dad decided that our house was too small. We moved into a neighborhood completely unknown to us. We were surrounded by Latin Americans, and we liked it since we hadn't seen very many of them. I had to go to another junior high school which was much different from W–. I noticed that some girls looked at me with malice and some told me to go back to Mexico. It surprised me that people of my own race would do that, but, of course, I did nothing about it. Daddy said that we would find people like that everywhere. Getting into clubs and activities helped me to forget.

I finished junior high and I started my most interesting years of senior high school. When I saw that book of biology and that thick algebra one, I got scared, but I got used to them and learned to like them. My teachers have always been very nice to me. I asked for advice and they gave it to me with pleasure. Thanks to God, no American has ever told me anything that would embarrass me or would make me hate him. On the contrary I loved them because they let me be in their country. In my opinion, when one is left out, it is because he wants to be left out. If he doesn't make friends, nobody is going to come and make them for him.

My main trouble is my accent. I really wish I didn't have it. Some words I just can't pronounce.

My ambition is to continue with my studies and later on get married and be the mother of many, many children.

Attitudes toward Spanish-Speaking People

The advantage of going to school with English-speaking children is emphasized by a senior high school boy who learned English before he entered the first grade. He points out the effect of lack of contact with English-speaking people, and he thinks that unfavorable attitudes toward Spanish-speaking students may develop in the upper grammar grades.

I have been very fortunate. I was taught to speak English before I went to school. Therefore I was one step ahead of the other Mexican children. My first two years were spent in a Mexican school of two rooms for four grades. Through the work of my father and some of the other parents, I was able to go to school with [English-speaking children]. Since then no major problem has arisen in my quest for an education.

My parents [have] concentrated on first our religion, and then our education. They have also been willing to sacrifice a lot, not only for me but also for my brothers and sisters, to see that we have the opportunity to get a good education and make the most of it. Unfortunately, not all the kids have had the understanding parents that I have had; so they have not made good their opportunities.

Most of the kids that live in town usually know a good quantity of English words by the time they go to school. This is not the case with the farm kids who do not come in contact with people who speak English very often. Therefore, they are usually behind the advancement of the other kids. This not only hurts the children scholastically but also mentally. It makes them feel out of place if they fail a few years.

Another factor that hinders some of the kids is the change in attitude that some of the [English-speaking] kids have toward them in the later years of grammar school. This change in attitude just helps the kids make up their minds in quitting school. It is an increasing problem because out of my class only three Mexicans will graduate this year. We had at least 15 in the eighth grade.

What the parents have failed to provide for these kids—a good home, incentive—the teachers have to try to make up. They should try to help them and give them sound counseling.

A senior high school girl, who herself could speak, read, and write English when she entered the first grade, adds her observations concerning those who have no practice in speaking English except at school. She thinks that lack of practice creates a feeling of insecurity, which in turn discourages practice even in the classroom. The result is retention of pupils in the lower grades and dropping out of school.

I was born in very humble surroundings in E– on July 5, 1941. My mother was also born here; my father is from California. I am the youngest and only girl, but I have two older brothers. The first seven years of my life were spent in a semi-rural part of town. I started school when I was six, but by that time I could speak, read, and write English. I was lucky to have seven members of my family who knew English well enough to instruct me. I have never had any problems in school concerning English. As a matter of fact, English has always been a favorite subject with me. In both Spanish and English I have achieved above-average grades.

My plans for the future are to work for about two years after graduation and then attend a business college. After completing a secretarial course I hope to obtain a good secretarial position, preferably in an office where my bilingual ability will be of special use.

In my opinion, a big problem the Spanish-speaking students have is that a majority have never heard, read, spoken, or written English until they go to school. Also, in many cases, they practice speaking English only at school, for at home no one knows the language. The lack of practice makes the students feel insecure; many times this insecurity holds them back from using English even in the classroom unless it is a dire necessity to do so. They find themselves in a terrible situation. After some years they find themselves still in the lower grades, but very much overgrown; so they quit school. When grown, they marry, have children, and then these children face the same problem their parents faced—that of not knowing any English at all.

Need of Understanding

Mutual understanding is emphasized by the next senior. She places importance upon the kind of teaching a child receives in the early grades.

One day the teacher in my first-grade class saw what I was trying to do, and she agreed to help me in my effort. She would take special pains to help me say words and express myself in English correctly so that in a very short time, I had begun to understand just what I was up against. Events did not continue to run so smoothly, however, for in the second grade I was in the class under a teacher with an entirely different attitude toward Latins. She just simply did not believe that I, or any other Latin, would ever amount to anything, and since my first-grade teacher had moved to another town, I was at a loss as to what to do. Fortunately, my older sister who was in high school by this time, agreed to help me as much as she could. It was quite a struggle in my second-grade class because of the indifferent attitude my teacher took toward my learning the language, but once I learned the basic fundamentals, it was much easier from then on.

From my second-grade teacher's attitude, along with many other similar experiences, I believe that I could stress certain points in what other people should or should not stress in dealing with students of Latin descent. They would be: (a) Do not emphasize the language barrier to the extent of embarrassment. That is, as I often noticed, the Anglo students in my class would laugh or snicker whenever the teacher called on a Latin to answer a question. If the student could not, they would say "Oh well, you can't expect much from a Mexican!" (b) This brings us to our second point— just because a Mexican student cannot express himself in English properly does not necessarily mean that he is stupid. (c) A third project would be for the schools to show the Latins how to speak both languages, for in the process of learning correctly the English language, a Latin-American will tend to become neglectful of his own Spanish.

In the following quotation a senior boy in a high school enrolling both Spanish-speaking and English-speaking students discusses the language barrier and the isolation of different groups. His comments on the nursery school suggest the importance which he places upon early contacts with English.

Although both of my parents could speak English well, Spanish was predominantly spoken at home during my preschool days. My mother was born in H– and my father, in a small town in Mexico. At the age of four my mother began taking me to a Methodist community house nursery school. I went there for two years and did not attend the public school kindergarten. I believe that I profited more by going to the nursery school than by going to kindergarten because here I and the other Spanish-speaking boys and girls learned English at our own speed. Most children that go to kindergarten are usually expected to speak and understand the English language. By the time I was ready for the first grade I believe that I was at about the same level with the other students.

After graduation in June I hope to attend either the Rice Institute or Texas University and study some type of engineering.

I believe that the big problem in the education of Spanish-speaking boys and girls is the language barrier. Even though it did not prove difficult to me, either in school or elsewhere, I know of several cases in which it has proven to be a problem. Therefore, I believe some type of preparatory institution for prefirst graders would be helpful as it was to me. This, in addition to teaching the English language, might also be helpful in preventing failures in the early grades and also preventing the large percentage of drop-outs in the secondary schools among the Spanish-speaking boys and girls.

I believe another problem, which might possibly not be included in educational problems of Spanish-speaking people, is isolation both on the parts of Spanish-speaking people and non-Spanish-speaking people. Many times I become rather angered at the expression "Latin-Americans" in the way it is used. For when it is used by someone, he does not refer to those of Spanish, Portuguese, French, or Italian descent; no, he is talking

Reading group using chart and textbook—El Paso city schools.

Reading group working with initial sounds—El Paso city schools.

Library—Austin city schools.

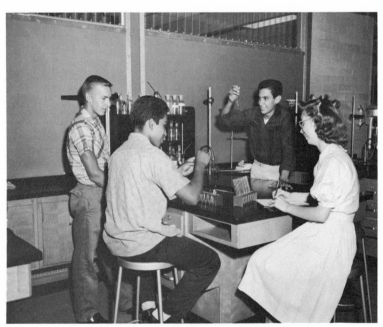

Laboratory—Austin city schools.

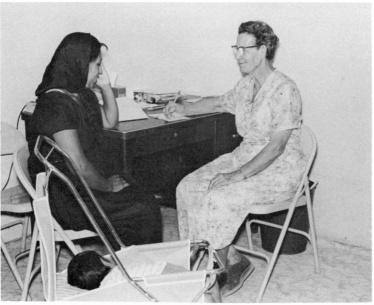

School and community cooperate—Tempe city schools.

Language-learning center—Los Angeles city schools.

Happy birthday—El Paso city schools.

A contrast in housing.

Halloween—
Alamosa city schools.

"Have we not all one father?"

Kindergarten—Denver city schools.

about one of the Mexican descent. In the newspaper a few weeks ago I read an article about the crime rate. The statistics were divided into three groups: those for Negroes, Anglo-Americans, and Latin-Americans. Why segregate the "Latin-Americans" from the rest of the white race? On the other hand, however, we are not totally without fault. We tend to set ourselves apart. For example, here at J– High, the Spanish-speaking boys and girls have set up their own Latin-American prom committee to plan their own senior prom. There is, of course, no discrimination in regard to the regular prom. As far as segregation goes, I have witnessed very little. I think the problems in general are not so difficult that they can't be solved with a little effort and work.

Good Relations a Joint Responsibility

In the preceding comments and in those to follow may be seen a feeling that creating good relations between Spanish-speaking and English-speaking people is a joint responsibility. Also in the comments of this boy, teachers will find support for providing reading material suited to the level of the pupil.

In our family there are nine in all, including my Dad and Mom. I have three sisters and three brothers. Before going into school I knew some English because I was the smallest kid in the family and my brothers and sisters being already in school spoke it at home. I remember when I first entered school the first thing the teacher taught me was how to spell my name. I also remember that I was having a hard time reading books until I was in the fourth grade. I guess that was my main defect, because I couldn't understand what I was reading. I didn't really think I was having trouble because the other Spanish-speaking students were in the same reading group I was in. After I moved out of one neighborhood into another, my fourth-grade teacher helped in reading books. She told me to read second-grade books and gradually work up. After that my grades started going up. I also found that I could get along with other students better.

When I got into junior high school I found that the Spanish-speaking students and the [English-speaking] students stuck to their own groups. I got a scholarship in the seventh grade and was trying to get another but was discouraged because other Spanish-speaking students were not trying. I just worked enough to pass. I guess I didn't like the idea of being a "square"; so I decided to just make passing grades like the rest of the kids. When my four-year plan came, I realized I soon would be out of school. I said to myself I'll just go to vocational school and learn a trade. After finishing one year in vocational school I decided to go back to high school and after that college. One thing I didn't like was when I was in the eleventh grade taking literature I remember a Spanish-speaking girl gave a report and when she finished the teacher said, "That's a good report considering your race." I didn't like this because this teacher underrated us and thought we were not as good as [an English-speaking] student.

I think the Spanish-speaking student should get down and go to work to help himself and his race to get along with the English-speaking student and make a world of equal rights.

The letter written by the next boy, a high school sophomore, is quoted at length to give his experience in different types of schools and his feelings toward different conditions. He notes a tendency for Spanish-speaking boys and girls to drop out of school.

I was born in a little town in south Texas. I lived there until I was six years old. I started school there. Then we moved to Washington state. I don't remember much about what they taught me. Then we moved here. I went to a Catholic school for a year and a half. I learned a lot there because they were very strict and hard.

From L– we moved to S–. I was in the third grade there. I was the only Spanish boy in the school because I was the only Spanish boy living in the district of that school. I think that was the year I liked and enjoyed school the most. I had a lot of friends and girl friends. I also made very good grades in school. I had a straight *A* report card. The education there wasn't as hard as the education in Catholic school. I guess the education in small towns is not as good as the education in cities. The only thing I didn't like about S– was the prejudice against the Spanish people. All the Spanish people were made to sit upstairs with the Negroes in the only theater in town.

From S– we moved back to L–. I went to a school named N– from the fourth to the sixth grade. My grades dropped a little there because it was much harder.

Then I went to N– Junior High from the seventh through the ninth grade. Education there was very good. The teachers were strict and the subjects were harder. But I managed to make the honor roll every now and then. But in junior high only a very, very few Spanish boys and girls made the honor roll. Many were failing. I guess that's why some of them quit school. Many Spanish boys and girls give up school when they go to junior high because the studies are harder and because others want to work and have money. And for other reasons.

Now I'm in T– High School. Here all the rest of the Spanish boys and girls and I get the best education offered in the whole state. But there are only a few of us who are in high school compared to when we all started junior high.

My plans for the future are to finish high school with the help of God, and to go to college. I hope very much that I do that because nowadays a person without an education is nothing. I realize the importance of school; that's why I haven't quit school no matter how hard it is.

The comments of the next boy should be read with care to see how his experiences have affected his attitudes and feelings. He seems to find it impossible to be fully accepted by both English-speaking and Spanish-speaking people.

While I attended elementary, there were not too many Anglos; so not many difficulties in race were present. After entering junior high there was little tension. But I could feel just a little dislike toward me because I spoke Spanish. No one actually said it but somehow I felt a little dislike. The way it is with Spanish-speaking students is that they feel that the Anglos hate them. When a Mexican mixes with Anglos naturally they are criticized by their own race; so they avoid the Anglos as much as they can. Personally, no one ever said anything about it, until I got to high school. They would call me "Mexican" in a way that did not sound so good and later came "wetback." It may have been a joke.

Concerning teachers, there are few who seem to dislike Mexicans and I have nothing to say about them. However, people that offer jobs will be silent just for a second or two when I say [my name]. It may be my imagination, I'm not sure.

As to some suggestions which I might have, there are few. One thing for sure is that the language which their parents speak is not right at all. This only shows that Spanish is not considered good enough to be spoken in an American school and yet they teach it in school. I think the textbooks describe Pancho Villa and other Spanish heroes as being the lowest class in the world. Maybe they were, but not according to what people say in Mexico. There could be better relations among the Anglos and Mexicans by allowing Mexicans to accept responsibilities, for I am sure that there are a few who would be qualified. How that can be established I don't know.

Another high school boy in another state gives his views on the treatment which Spanish-speaking people receive. Since he knew only English when he entered the first grade, language was not his problem.

Just because a person's skin is a little darker than another person's, we are referred to as Spanish or Spanish-Americans. In my opinion I believe that any person born in the U.S.A. is an American and should be treated as such.

I have always been treated just the same as the next person. As long as we try to get along with other people knowing that we are their equal, we will have a good understanding among all people.

Effects of Discrimination

The effect of discrimination is shown in the following comments of a senior high school boy. Especially remarkable is the change of the attitude of the family toward English, as is also the ability of the boy to rise above the hurts which he experienced.

In my opinion, the chief problem of the Spanish-speaking student is his unableness to speak the English language correctly or even to speak it at all.

When I first entered school in the first grade, I was not able to speak any English. Though I learned it quickly, it was a great hindrance to me until I learned how to speak it. I do not directly blame my parents for not teaching me. My father grew up in a small town where there were not too many Latin people. The town was populated mostly by Anglos. Being outnumbered, my father and the other Latin people got pushed around. Thus my father built a hate for Anglo people. When I was of school age, he didn't want me to learn English; in fact, he didn't want me to go to school because of his hatred for Anglos. Once I was in school my father's attitude changed. He realized the importance of my being able to express myself in English. Now one of Daddy's greatest desires is for me to go to college; and he is doing everything within his power to see that I do go to college.

We have been speaking English in our home ever since I was in about the ninth grade. My sister, who will enter junior high school in mid-term, can speak only English, although my parents are teaching her to speak Spanish now.

I had never experienced any discrimination until I was in the ninth grade. My best buddy (an Anglo) and I were going swimming. But when we tried to enter, he was allowed to go in, but I wasn't (this did not occur in school). Ever since that day I felt a little self-conscious in school or wherever there were Anglos, although I have gotten over it now; as I intend to fulfill my parents' desire to go to college. I plan to major in secondary education. There is hardly any trace of discrimination of Latins now. Therefore, I don't believe this is a problem to Latin students. But I do think that the students' grandparents and even some parents, who have experienced discrimination against them, influence the students.

A feeling of inferiority and a fear of discrimination are listed as problems by the next student. Note his closing comment expressing the opinion that this inquiry is not reaching the right students.

In my opinion, the main problem with Latin students is their attitude. Even if a student is bright, he'll feel inferior or he'll feel that he won't be given a chance. Since friends' opinions mean much to Latins, students only strive for average grades instead of trying to make superior grades for fear of being called a "brain" or a "square." One problem of Latins is that instead of trying to meet and beat their problems, such as speech handicaps, they avoid them by joining in a gang or crowd of Latins.

I look back with amazement at the progress I made in school. Before I started school, I lived in a farm where I seldom heard English spoken. When I started school, I knew only a few phrases in English. After a few weeks in school I started to catch on to the language. Since very few Latins attended that school I learned to get along with all the students instead of forming a group with other Latins. I don't believe I've had any special problems in school either with students or teachers. After I finish my postgraduate work in high school, I plan to attend the Coast Guard Academy to which I have already made an entrance application.

I don't believe that this survey will reach its intended point because the teachers usually select their better students to participate; therefore, the students that have had problems aren't reached.

A Frank Statement by a Mexican Student

The next comments provide a rare opportunity to see how a bright, cultured student with Mexican background feels toward the people of this country. She writes with delightful frankness:

The chief problems in the education of Spanish-speaking boys and girls are that they do not speak enough English and that they think in Spanish while trying to speak in English. They translate and the things said are not always the things meant or the correct way to say them. Pronunciation and vocabulary are a big problem to us.

I was born in Mexico and am a very good patriot. Whenever others try to make me speak English, I feel as if I am giving Spanish a second place or making it less, and I wouldn't do that. I don't get along too well with Americans because they are not Catholics and because of the way they think about religion. Also I think that most of them descend from the English, and I don't like the English because of the hatred they've always had towards the Spanish.

Ever since I was a little girl, I read stories and always I would read that the English were better than the Spanish or that the English had gotten the better of the Spanish or the Spanish would be portrayed as mean, ugly, cruel men while the English would be portrayed the opposite way, and *I* didn't like that! I know that when the English came, they killed most of the Indians, and the Spanish Christianized them and married them; so it was really the opposite.

In English literature the Spanish have always been given a second place and the Spaniard's good doings have not been recognized or mentioned.

I also don't get along with them because they always want us to speak English, but they never try to learn Spanish so that we can't tell each other what we really mean because *that* you can only tell in your native tongue.

The Latin American nations have never been given a thought by the U.S. or not as much as it should have been, *until recently*, and that is why I don't give Americans a thought either. These have been my problems. The good is that I'm a pretty good student, usually making *A*'s and a *B* or two.

I appreciate your doing this *very, very* much. Thank you.

Pride in her Mexican inheritance is shown also by the comments of a student from another city. In her autobiography she goes back to great-grandparents, Spanish and Mexican, in Chihuahua. She continues:

When I was five years old, I entered the kindergarten in Juarez. While there I participated in a program for the celebration of the 16th of September (Independence Day). I was in the group that danced the Mexican Jarabe. I was very proud to wear the traditional costume of the "china poblana." The dance was held in the Auditorio Municipal (the Juárez Coliseum).

The following year, I was going to enter the first grade in the same school, but I was not admitted because there was no more room. So, I entered a Catholic school in Juárez. We had to wear a navy blue jumper, white blouse, white bermuda socks, black shoes, and a beanie; for special occasions we wore a navy blue uniform decorated with white buttons on the front, white bermuda socks, black shoes, gloves, and a beret. We were taught to read, write, and sew. At the end of that school year, I had very good grades and could read and write Spanish.

The following summer I went with my parents to California. While we were there I had trouble understanding the people because most of them spoke English and I could not speak or understand it. When we came back to E–, my mother told me that I was to start school here. I was happy but scared. So in September, 1949, I started school at F–. I was seven, and most of my classmates were six and could understand and speak English; I didn't know any English at all. When I was learning to read I had trouble because I read the words the way they were spelled. The teacher would tell me that many words were not pronounced the way they were written. I think that my knowledge of the Spanish language helped me a lot, especially to tell the meaning of the word. I was given my first double promotion from kindergarten to first grade; the following years were easy; then from the third I was double promoted to fifth. My family moved to another house; so I transferred to A– school. I remained there until I graduated from the 6th grade on May 26, 1954. In September I entered the seventh grade at . . . Junior High; I have been here ever since and plan to graduate.

Both of my parents have always encouraged me to continue my education; therefore I have made it my goal to give this satisfaction to my parents. I believe that with God's help and my efforts I will accomplish it.

I visit my relatives in Chihuahua about once a year during the summer vacations. While there, we visit farms that are hidden by mountains, and the only way to reach them is by horse. Some Indians live there and they are always glad to welcome visitors. These people live the way their ancestors lived, with only slight changes. Chihuahua is a very beautiful and peaceful city; it is only 4 or 5 hours from Juárez.

Next are the comments of a high school senior who has overcome many difficulties. His explanations are impressive.

I was born in a Latin-American neighborhood. Consequently I spoke no English until the summer before I started school. That summer we moved into an Anglo neighborhood. There, with the help of Anglo children I learned a few necessary words. As I progressed in school, so did my ability to speak better English. A number of teachers were interested enough to further help me with outside work.

At the age of ten . . . my family moved into a poorer-than-average Latin neighborhood. I was at first resented and disliked. I found that I could win their favor if I behaved as bad as they did. This, of course, got me into trouble. After a number of brushes with the police, I changed acquaintances and habits.

I really enjoyed junior high. Once again I made a number of acquaintances among Anglos. Among my acquaintances was a pretty girl. I finally got enough courage to ask for a date. She was surprised and angered; with what seemed a terrible tone in her voice, she told me that she would not go out with a "greaser." About this time, I also noticed that my Anglo friends started drifting away. After a number of painful experiences, I gathered that my Anglo friends did not want much to do with me. An interesting observation I made at that time is that people coming from intelligent and educated families hold no specific dislike against Latins.

In senior high, the rift between Anglos and Latins is more noticeable.

There is little or none of Latin and Anglo close relationship. [Both] of them go their separate ways and even form two different social structures. I believe that this is largely due to the Latins. Latins are afraid of being hurt or embarrassed, because of what they are. To forget this hurt, they band together. This banding together hurts Latins more than exposure to the outside world. If Latins were to mix freely, they would soon be accepted. However, there is a stumbling block: the fact Latins cannot explain or communicate with others. Plainly speaking, most Latins cannot speak English. Better teaching may be an answer. A better environment may also be the answer. Latins should fight against complacency and turning away from challenges. Only by becoming aware of themselves as capable individuals can Latins become responsible leaders in our present society.

A Brief Summary

These are the problems of Spanish-speaking children and youth as reported by themselves. For the present the list will be allowed to stand as given. A few summary statements can be made: first, the reports show in a vivid and convincing manner that there are many problems in the education of Spanish-speaking children and that they are serious from the standpoint of education and public welfare; second, it is clear that the problems vary from child to child—in the matter of language, for example, some of the children do not even speak Spanish; third, many of the problems seem to cluster in three overlapping areas—language, economic status, and attitudes. Many of the children know little or no English when they start to school, and many suffer the privations of severely limited family income. In many cases the attitudes of English-speaking people or Spanish-speaking people or both make progress difficult.

A Study of the Plans of High School Students

Another study throws additional light on the problems of Spanish-speaking students. With the assistance of the counselors in a junior high school and a senior high school of a Texas city, a questionnaire on "Plans for School and for Work" was presented to pupils of grades 9 to 12. Usable replies were received from 559 boys and 489 girls, distributed as follows:

	Grade 9		Grades 10, 11, 12	
	Boys	Girls	Boys	Girls
English-speaking	40	38	397	324
Spanish-speaking	92	97	30	30

The students were asked two questions relative to their plans for vocation. In the first they were asked what they would *most like* to do as a lifework. In the second they were asked what they thought they would have a chance to do and would *really do* when they finished school. The girls were asked to consider work exclusive of homemaking in the first question, but no mention of it was made in the second.

There were distinct differences in the vocational plans of English-speaking and Spanish-speaking students. Sixty-eight per cent of the English-speaking boys and 47 per cent of the English-speaking girls listed professional and managerial occupations, in contrast with 44 per cent and 39 per cent of the Spanish-speaking group. Eight per cent of the English-speaking boys and 24 per cent of the Spanish-speaking boys listed skilled occupations. Forty-four per cent of the English-speaking girls and 47 per cent of the Spanish-speaking girls listed secretarial, clerical, and other service occupations.

The difference between their dreams and what they considered probable reality is reflected in the answers to the questions. The percentage of students listing professional and managerial occupations dropped from 68 per cent to 39 per cent in the English-speaking group of boys, and from 44 to 22 per cent in the Spanish-speaking group of boys. The corresponding decreases for girls were 47 to 29 per cent for the English-speaking group and from 39 to 16 per cent for the Spanish-speaking group.

The students were asked whether they would like to go to college after high school and were given three choices for the answer—"Yes," "No," "I am not sure." In the English-speaking group of boys the responses were 62 per cent yes, 14 per cent no, and 23 per cent not sure; in the English-speaking group of girls 53 per cent yes, 20 per cent no, and 26 per cent not sure. The percentages in the Spanish-speaking groups showed much less choice of college: boys, 34 per cent yes, 20 per cent no, and 46 per cent not sure; girls 31 per cent yes, 17 per cent no, and 51 per cent not sure.

The relatively unfavorable economic level of the students in general and especially of the Spanish-speaking students was reflected in answers to a question concerning the part of college expenses which their families *could* pay. Thirty-six per cent of English-speaking boys and 46 per cent of the English-speaking girls expressed the opinion that their families could bear all or nearly all of the expenses; the corresponding percentages of the Spanish-speaking students were 18 per cent and 20 per cent. Some left the question unanswered.

Two questions were asked to get some indication of parental attitude (as perceived by the students) toward college attendance. The
questions asked simply, "Do you think that your father [second question, "mother"] wants you to go to college?" The percentages answering with a definite yes were as follows:

	Father	Mother
English-speaking boys	82 %	87 %
English-speaking girls	63	71
Spanish-speaking boys	48	62
Spanish-speaking girls	43 %	54 %

The lower percentages in the *Father* column seem to result in part at
least in less knowledge of the father's attitude than of the mother's. If
the percentages may be taken at their face value, they seem to represent higher aspirations in the English-speaking group. Or perhaps
the Spanish-speaking parents view the possibilities more realistically.

A desire for more information "about schools, or colleges, or jobs,
or [my] own chances" was expressed by a large number of students,
thus giving support to the statement that counseling is a major need
of the modern school.

A question designed to reveal the students' perception of the difficulties ahead of them asked, "What do you think might keep you from
doing the work which you would *most like* to do?" Nine possible
answers and a blank space for a different answer were provided; the
student might mark as many as he chose. As far as could be judged
from the replies, the Spanish-speaking students were a much less confident group. Here is a tabulation of the replies in terms of the percentage giving each answer:

	English-Speaking Pupils	Spanish-Speaking Pupils
1) Nothing special; excellent chances	47 %	14 %
2) Not enough ability	11	27
3) Not enough money	12	32
4) Not good enough in my studies	25	43
5) Afraid I would fail	9	33
6) Too little help from my family	4	14
7) Feeling I might not have as good a chance as others	5	29
8) Sickness	1	6
9) Rather get a job	9	22
10) Some other reason	8 %	2 %

The feelings of both English-speaking and Spanish-speaking students regarding their future difficulties may be closer to reality than one would like to admit. Both economic level and school achievement vary over a wide range in both groups, but again the average finds the Spanish-speaking group at a disadvantage. In spite of the selection which has taken place through the dropping-out of less able students, the Spanish-speaking students in the senior high school (for which figures were available) made much lower average scores than did English-speaking students on tests of reading and mathematics.

The school, the home, and the community have a gigantic task to provide opportunities which will enable children to reach more nearly the capacities with which they are endowed.

11. The Problem of Language

Parents, teachers, and pupils in general agree that language is a major difficulty of Spanish-speaking children. Although a growing number of the children enter school with some knowledge of English and some indeed know English only, many start their schooling with little or no knowledge of English. In most cases even those who have some acquaintance with English use the language with much less facility than do English-speaking children. By and large, with many exceptions, the children use Spanish at home and in conversation with each other. By and large, again with many exceptions, they have at school little or no instruction in their native language until they have completed the elementary grades.

Differences in the ability to use English and differences in contacts with English out of school make the problem of teaching extremely difficult. To give children their best learning opportunity, materials and methods must be adapted to many levels of ability.

A Preview of Language Teaching

Language consists of symbols which represent objects, activities, or ideas. The deaf have a language for direct communication which consists entirely of making signs which typically have no reference to words. They have also a way of spelling words with the fingers, and many of them are taught to use speech and written language. In the sign language, however, the movement or position of the hands conveys directly an idea. There is nothing strange about this; indeed people with normal hearing use signs as language. The traffic policeman, for example, holds up his hand. This movement does not say or spell "Stop"; it just means "Stop." A red traffic light at a street intersection means the same thing.

The language (English or Spanish) which consists of words has two related series of symbols—the one made up of sounds, the other of odd-shaped, written forms which are to be looked at. The written forms (letters) are in some cases the remnants of pictures which once referred to objects directly, but now they refer to the sounds of the spoken word. Thus the letters *b o o k* refer directly to the sound which in turn means the object to which we refer. The letters *r u n* are symbols to stimulate the sound by which we refer to the act of running. (It is interesting to note that the blind use a pattern of raised dots to indicate the same sounds.) It is possible, of course, to relate the written symbol directly with the object rather than the sound of the word, and development in reading ability tends at least to suppress the use of sounds between the written symbol and the idea. In learning to read, however, the three—written symbol, sound symbol, and idea represented—are closely related.

From birth the child's experiences include objects and activities and sounds used by others to represent these objects and activities. We must never forget the necessity of experience, the necessity of contact with objects, activities, and relationships to which the sounds and later the written symbols are applied. It is possible to use sounds and to learn written words to represent these sounds without having the ghost of an idea of what they mean. Try yourself some time on a list of nonsense words, like *noq ird jes zam ven!* You could learn to read a whole book of these in a short time but they would still be meaningless. To a certain extent this is what sometimes happens in learning to read a foreign language (or even one's own language); one calls or thinks sounds, but that is about all.

In principle, learning to read is quite simple, and indeed in practice it need not be as difficult as some children find it to be. Here is an object, here is a sound which refers to the object, and here is a combination of letters which represent the sound. Knowing already the object and the sound which means the object, the purpose is to teach the child the combination of letters which indicate the sound. At one stage a child may know a word by its general form and certain identifying details without giving attention to the separate letters; but when he wishes to produce the written word, he must do so letter by letter. Again, when he wishes to find independently the sound of a word which he does not know, he needs to proceed by letters and combinations of letters. It is necessary at some time to know what a letter and a group of letters within a word "say."

A child needs to know the name of a letter in order to refer to it conveniently, just as he needs to know the names of persons. He needs to know the order in which letters occur in the alphabet so that he can use dictionaries and alphabetical lists. And he needs to know what letters and combinations of letters say. The name of a letter and what it says must be distinguished carefully. In fact, the same letter says different things in different languages, and often in the same language, certainly in English. *T* says one thing itself but with *h* it often says something different like "Tom" or "Thelma." *O* says one thing in "Tom" but another thing in "Tony."

Children are taught step by step with practice in language suited to their experience and interests. They are not given an analysis of language with all sounds and symbols before they start to read. First, a background of experience and a desire to read are developed. Parents can do much at this stage by reading to children what they are interested in hearing, and at times pointing out the words which say what is being read. In fact, parents can often teach their children to read in this informal way. There is a danger that the effort will be futile because of lack of maturity or interest on the part of the child, because of lack of skill on the part of the parent, or because of pressure which makes the experience an unpleasant one.

When a situation favorable to reading is developed, children are taught the written forms of words which they already know by sound. Very early also they are prepared to analyze some of the simple words into their component sounds and learn what the letters and combinations of letters say. It is interesting to sound the different letters and to note the position of the tongue and the lips and other parts of the voice apparatus. In sounding *n o*, for example, the nasal sound of *n* blends with the *o* coming from the throat with a characteristic mouth position. Incidentally, this kind of analysis may be helpful to pupils who have difficulty with certain unfamiliar sounds.

If Spanish is the home language of the child, or one of the home languages, the educated parent can teach his child to read Spanish if the child has no opportunity to learn it in school. An interest in reading can be developed gradually, and specific instruction started when the child is sufficiently mature. It will be helpful if he has very simple but interesting children's books in Spanish. The child is taught that most of the same letters are used in Spanish as in English but that sometimes they represent different sounds—that is, the letters speak both English and Spanish. Let us see what they say in Spanish; then we shall know two languages. Here is Tomás—the same boy is Tomás in Spanish and Thomas in English. It is probably best not to start formal instruction in reading in two languages at the same time. If the child knows both English and Spanish, the introduction to reading may be in either.

This discussion should not make the teaching of language or of a second language seem too easy. It requires effort and skill to deal effectively with twenty or thirty pupils of different background, to arrange a series of learning situations which lead progressively and systematically to higher levels, and to provide suitable materials. Cooperation of home and school can make the work easier and more productive.

How Language Is Learned

Learning a language is itself a matter of degree rather than an either-or situation. There is a great distance between the ability of a person who knows and can use only a few words in simple concrete situations and the ability of the scholar who knows thousands of words and can understand and use abstract and complex ideas expressed in language. It is easy to overlook this point and to discuss the situation as if one knows a language or does not. It can be said, and truthfully, that even high-level feebleminded persons are able to learn a language—in fact, they do learn to understand and speak a little language, and some of them learn to read a little. In contrast it is said that some persons, even high school graduates, cannot learn a foreign language. The truth is simply that they cannot learn at the speed, at the level, and under the circumstances in which they are being taught.

Learning a language has four interrelated but different phases: learning to understand spoken language, learning to use language in speech, learning to understand written language, and learning to produce written language. To a certain extent understanding spoken and written language precedes production of spoken and written language, and to a certain extent they go along together. A little understanding paves the way for production, and soon the two are going forward at the same time. In learning one's mother tongue the process is normally from speech to the written work, but speech and reading develop together, once the reading has begun.

It is possible for the learning of a second language to follow the pattern of learning the first language, as when a preschool Spanish-speaking child plays with English-speaking playmates and is addressed by his parents in English at least some of the time. If he has constant contact with and stimulus to use both languages, by and by he will do so. He hears, he understands, he imitates, and he communicates. This pattern, or some modification of it, is becoming more frequent in the Southwest as second-generation and third-generation Spanish-speaking parents use more English and move into closer contacts with English-speaking people. But it is still not the prevailing pattern in many communities. Even where there is some learning of English before school entrance, it is often relatively little. It has seemed to some a great accomplishment to know the meaning of four hundred or five hundred English words—and in fact it is—but we must remember that the native-language child has a vocabulary of two thousand to three thousand words, or even more, and is able to use with ease a large number of the patterns of expression of the language.

A comparison is given below of the scores of Spanish-speaking and English-speaking children in a test of their ability to understand spoken English. The pupils were in the first grade of a Texas school. The scores of the Spanish-speaking children revealed great differences within the group, but no Spanish-speaking child was quite up to the average of the English-speaking children.

Scores on Test of Oral English	Number of Children	
	English-Speaking	Spanish-Speaking
(Highest possible) 40	4	
35–39	35	
30–34	26	7
25–29	5	11
20–24	1	8
15–19		6
10–14		7
5– 9		2
0– 4		6
Total	71	47

Only two out of five Spanish-speaking children had scores above the score of the lone English-speaking child who was at the bottom of his group. Doubtless there are other schools in which the comparison would be much more favorable to the Spanish-speaking child, but the showing here was not at all unusual. Does anyone suppose that in such a situation, instruction which is well adapted to the needs of one child will be equally appropriate for another?

Estimating Language Ability

Without careful testing it is easy to overestimate language ability. A child seems to engage in ordinary conversations with ease; so the observer infers that he knows the language well. A child reads words from his reader, and that is taken as sufficient evidence of his understanding. Both may be far from the truth. It is a safe generalization to say that most Spanish-speaking children are handicapped in their understanding and use of English from elementary school through high school.

The language weakness of Spanish-speaking children in the primary grades is sometimes obscured by their apparent success in reading. In these grades the children may be working with a carefully controlled and limited vocabulary, and even their mastery of this may be less than appears. W. H. Sinninger, of New Mexico Highlands University, long a student of the education of Spanish-speaking children, presents a picture of progressive deficiency in a personal letter:

In the elementary schools the graph of achievement is similar to what it was twenty years ago. The pupils in the primary grades are up to national norms in achievement, or near them. They start dropping below norms in the fourth grade and lose ground in each of the succeeding grades. This results, we think, from inadequate meanings and vocabularies. The work in the primary grades is rather mechanical and concerned with developing a sight vocabulary and word recognition skills. It does not call for the word power demanded in the higher grades.

In January, 1960, Mrs. Afton Dill Nance, consultant in elementary education, California State Department of Education, conducted a study in thirteen school districts. Her inquiry was directed toward answering the question, "How do promotion practices affect children of Spanish-speaking background?" The reports covered thirty-one schools, 101½ classes, and 2,831 children in grade 1. In nine schools nearly all the children were of Spanish-speaking background, in fifteen schools about half were of this background, and in seven schools only a few were. It is significant that in all the schools except one most of the children had been enrolled in kindergarten the previous year. In four of the thirty schools about half entered the kindergarten with little or no English, and in twenty-six schools only a few had any background in English.

In twenty-seven of the thirty-one schools, 246 children (189 of Spanish-speaking background) were asked to repeat the first grade. To the question whether inability to speak English was one of the major reasons for the repetition of grade 1, the answer was yes in eleven schools and no in thirteen schools. (No answer was given by seven schools.) Of the twenty-four schools replying to the question whether inability to learn to read was one of the major reasons for repetition, the answer was yes in twenty-two schools and no in two. To the questions "Of the children of Spanish-speaking background who were retained in Grade 1, how many spoke Spanish at home" and "How many spoke English at home?" the answers were 159 and 112, respectively. When these numbers are related to the total number (189) in the group, it appears that 77 children (41 per cent of the group) spoke only Spanish in the home, 30 children (16 per cent of the group) spoke only English in the home, and 82 (43 per cent of the group) spoke both Spanish and English in the home.

No data in our possession illustrate more clearly a transition stage in the education of Spanish-speaking children. There are still many children in California who enter school with little or no knowledge of English, but in the districts surveyed they are in the minority. A letter from an assistant superintendent in response to the inquiry describes an interesting local transition. Until 1954 the district had a policy of segregation for its Mexican-American population. In that year about half of the pupil population of around five hundred were Mexican-American, living in a special section of the community and attending a school in that section. Today there are approximately five thousand other pupils in the district, the schools are not segregated, many Mexican-American families are moving into new subdivisions, there is very little first-grade retention, and no retention attributed to the lack of an English language background.

A final question on the questionnaire asked the extent to which an imperfect command of English appears to be a handicap to achievement in the later grades. Although the opinions of those who answered this question were not unanimous, most of the respondents expressed the opinion that lack of command of English is a handicap to achievement in the later grades. Some took occasion to list other contributing factors such as immaturity, lack of self-confidence, lack of a real drive to learn, poor nutrition, poor home conditions, lack of ability, emotional problems, irregular attendance, lack of experiential background, and a difference in cultural patterns. One person thought that "imperfect command of English has probably been overstressed as a factor in school failure," and that the "almost complete absence of academic achievement as a cultural value" was probably the primary causal factor. At least two were quite definite in their opinion that imperfect command of English was not a factor, and one of these thought that with the proper educational opportunity "children at an early age can learn, absorb, and master not only one language but three or four."

In one reply the opinion was expressed that an imperfect command of English results in a feeling of insecurity which affects achievement in all areas of the curriculum. One found that many of the children do not have "an adequate language in either English or Spanish." Some seemed to think that the handicap continues through the grades, but two expressed an opinion that language was less of a handicap in the upper grades. One of these pointed out that children who attend a school where most of the children speak English seem to suffer less in later grades. One expressed concern over middle-grade failures of children who are taught formal reading without sufficient attention to meanings. They may be unable to keep up because of a lack of comprehension of the words which they "read."

The report of the district which had no kindergarten bore witness to the value of a preparatory year preceding the first grade. "Much of the first-grade curriculum is devoted to teaching the speaking of English [to the children who enter without a knowledge of English], and naturally the teacher does not cover as much of the first-grade curriculum as in other schools."

A Dual Handicap

As suggested earlier, most Spanish-speaking children of the Southwest know neither English nor Spanish well. Generally speaking, their home language is a poor grade of Spanish. Even the fund of ideas which words express is limited. In their homes they lack the opportunity and stimulus to develop the concepts which other children normally develop. In school the growth of ability in their mother tongue is arrested by lack of instruction in the written forms of the language, and the development of English is retarded by the lack of sufficient contact with English.

Learning the vocabulary of a second language is not necessarily an addition of new concepts. The fundamental concepts of a language are the result of experience. Language then helps to deal with the concepts and to extend experience. A child's competence in language cannot be found by adding the ideas represented by the words which he knows in his mother tongue to those which are represented in a second language. Much of a new language duplicates concepts which a child already has in his first language. In the early stages of learning, time must be taken to attach new labels to old concepts and to develop new ways of expressing old ideas. From the beginning, however, the child in school has new experiences to which he attaches language symbols in his first language, in his second language, or in both. Often a situation develops in which some concepts are symbolized in one language and some in the other. A college student whose home language was Spanish once explained that she could not discuss science with her Spanish-speaking father because she had learned it in English!

Teaching a Second Language

The problem of teaching English as a second language to large numbers of Spanish-speaking children will persist in the Southwest for as long a time as can be foreseen. Geographical position, migration across the border, and the tenacity with which people hold to their mother tongue assure continuation of the problem. Because the teaching of English as a second language is difficult, and because ability in English is so important for the welfare both of the individual and of the community, language must be given high priority in the education of Spanish-speaking children.

In a thoughtful approach to the problem of teaching English to Spanish-speaking children, a question of basic policy must be raised at once. To serve the best interests of the child and the community, what part should Spanish have in the school program? Ability in the Spanish language may be in itself a significant objective of education. There is no doubt that the ability to use Spanish effectively can be a great asset to an individual and to the community. As the world grows smaller, the ability to communicate in a language which is used by millions of other people becomes a matter of increasing practical importance from the standpoint of international understanding and cooperation. Too, competence in more than one language widens the horizon of an individual and makes a significant contribution to his intellectual life. It provides a source of deep personal satisfaction as well. From this point of view, the ability in Spanish which a child develops in his home is an asset to be cultivated rather than carelessly cast aside. The chief practical hope for conserving and developing this asset is found in the school.

The fact that Spanish is a desirable objective of education does not dispose of the matter. At every level of instruction there is keen competition for a place in the curriculum, and there is not enough time for everything which might profitably be taught. An intelligent decision concerning the place of Spanish must be based upon a consideration of relative values. Including one area of subject matter may automatically exclude or limit another.

The case for or against Spanish does not rest solely on its value as an objective of education. Its possible use as a tool of instruction should be considered also, and the question should be asked whether part of the instruction of Spanish-speaking children should be given in their home language. At present in the Southwest, it is the policy of the public schools to use English as the language of instruction throughout the school grades. Spanish is sometimes used in speaking with children who know little or no English at school entrance and sometimes later to help in understanding English. It is the general practice, however, to minimize its use and to use English almost exclusively. In fact, many teachers have little or no knowledge of Spanish. In some schools Spanish is taught as a separate subject in the elementary grades, and of course later in the high school.

From time to time theorists have suggested the possibility of starting the schooling of Spanish-speaking children in Spanish, with English as the second language. This policy is followed in Puerto Rico, for example. In schools conducted on this policy the child becomes accustomed to the school routine, learns how to behave in a group, and learns to read in Spanish while he is learning an English oral vocabulary and simple English speech. Theoretically this suggestion has much to commend it. The transition from home to school and the process of learning to read are difficult enough under the most favorable circumstances. It is more difficult if the child is deprived of communication in his mother tongue and is plunged into a second-language environment immediately on school entrance. There is no doubt that the frustration and feeling of insecurity which a child experiences when confronted with such difficulties can be serious from the standpoint of individual development and school progress.

Initiating a child into the school routine in his native language, it is pointed out, enables him to meet the difficulties of the first year under the most favorable conditions. If this policy were adopted, most of the Spanish-speaking children at the end of the first year would be reading Spanish. A long step toward conserving this important language resource would be taken, and an avenue for extending his concepts through reading in a language with which the child is already familiar would be opened. It is theorized that at the end of a year or so he would have acquired enough knowledge of spoken English to make possible a fairly easy transfer of his reading habits to English, and at the end of the third grade he would have a reading knowledge of two languages rather than one.

The picture is not as rosy as it looks at first glance. Puerto Rican educators have not found it easy to teach English as a second language. Nor would it be easy in the United States. The Puerto Rican parallel breaks down at a critical point. There it is expected that English will continue to be a second language. There Spanish is the language of instruction in all grades of the schools and is the primary language of everyday life. The great handicap of children who are learning English in Puerto Rico is the lack of sufficient contact with English and the lack of practical motivation for learning it. In the United States' Southwest, on the other hand, English is the language of the majority of the people except in certain limited areas, and English is the language of instruction in all grades of the schools. If Spanish-speaking children are to learn English for effective use, they must have many contacts with it. In a policy of teaching Spanish first barriers might be placed to their learning of English by helping to preserve their Spanish-speaking background and by lessening both the motive and the opportunity for out-of-school use of English. It is possible also that less English would be learned in school if the time were divided between English and Spanish and if the children could meet their major needs in their mother tongue. According to the testimony of students in an earlier chapter, the learning of English is accelerated by placing a child in a situation where English must be used. It could be objected also that one group in Spanish and another in English would make it difficult to combine the two in the same working group and thus would tend to continue a social division which should be overcome as soon as possible.

The more generally applicable solution of the problem seems to lie in a very different direction—the teaching of English to Spanish-speaking children *before* they reach the age when reading is normally taught. This proposal puts a burden squarely on the shoulders of parents who know English. They can help their children a great deal by teaching them English and by helping them to have contacts with other English-speaking persons. The responsibility of the public is to supplement the efforts of the parents by providing formal school opportunities before the age of six, the customary age of school entrance. Preschool "education" could be organized to give such language and other experiences as would erase some of the handicap with which foreign-language children otherwise start their work in an English-speaking school.

Teaching English to Five-Year-Olds

A reasonable immediate goal is to make formal schooling available to all children of five years of age. What shall this year be called? "Kindergarten" is a possibility, but this name seems to set it apart from the schooling which is to follow. Unfortunately, we have committed ourselves to a numbering of school levels which starts with grade 1 for the six-year-old and the beginning of reading. It would be hard to start lower down and get accustomed to a new numbering. Perhaps the new year could be called the prefirst grade. In any case, it should have very definite educational objectives coordinated closely with the level to follow. Certainly, it should not be primarily an independent development or a place where children simply play and rest while their parents work. The idea that school properly begins at six years of age is an outmoded concept, and the whole primary division should be reconstructed to include children of ages five to eight instead of six to eight.

In California the provision of public schooling for five-year-olds is fairly common. Denver, Colorado, is an illustration of cities with well developed programs for five-year-olds. Texas has taken a long step forward in providing state aid for summer schools for non-English-speaking children who will be of school age the following September, but this is only a step toward the desired goal.

Before state aid became available, summer instruction for Spanish-speaking children was provided in a number of Texas communities, through the initiative of local school systems and to some extent through private support. With the assistance of the League of United Latin American Citizens, of which he was president, Felix Tijerina led a movement to provide privately financed summer schools for Spanish-speaking children who would enter the first grade in the following September. A modest goal of teaching four hundred English words was set. A few of these schools were established, providing a demonstration of the plan. In this effort Tijerina drew freely on his own resources. Also, as a member of a state committee considering educational legislation, he was a leader in the effort to get state sanction and public support for summer schools for preschool non-English-speaking children.

A decision to place the emphasis in the school upon English does not imply a lack of appreciation of Spanish, or a lack of concern that the transition to English be made with as little emotional shock as possible. Children may be led to have a high regard for both Spanish and English, and yet to give major effort to developing ability in the new language. Certainly, there is no place for a policy which makes a child ashamed of his mother tongue.

A Suggested Language Program

Although more research is needed for a better understanding of the learning problems of children whose home language is Spanish, enough is known to point the way toward fruitful experimentation. The following outline presents a program in which ability in both English and Spanish can be developed in accordance with the principles previously discussed.

(1) Provide a full year of education for children five years of age, with a gradual transition from speaking Spanish to speaking English and an emphasis on preparation for reading English.

This prefirst grade experience may be expected to prepare the children for more nearly normal progress with other children and thus diminish the retardation which in later years is a major cause of dropping out of school.

(2) Begin instruction in reading English when the children have reached an adequate stage of readiness.

(3) Begin instruction in reading Spanish when the children have mastered the basic techniques of reading English, and give instruction in Spanish as a language through the elementary grades to all who qualify.

The "mastery" of basic reading techniques may be tentatively defined as the average-and-above level of achievement reached by children in general at the end of grade 3. If English-speaking children are enrolled in the same school, they may be given instruction in oral Spanish beginning in grade 1, in preparation for beginning to read

Spanish when their achievement in English has reached the same level.

(4) Encourage the more able pupils to continue the study of Spanish beyond the elementary level.

The children who demonstrate interest and ability in language are the ones to whom we can look with greatest confidence to conserve and develop the individual and community assets of knowing Spanish as the first language.

Increasing Contacts with Standard English

Although this is not the place to discuss detailed techniques of teaching Spanish-speaking children in the schools, some facts and principles the public and teachers alike should understand. For example, the urgent need of increased contacts with satisfactory examples of spoken and written English both outside the school and in the school itself is a matter of common concern. These contacts are of supreme importance in the preschool years and in the elementary grades while the child's language habits are being formed largely by imitation. If the child's chief contact with English is limited to the time which he has in a class recitation or which he has individually with a teacher of twenty to fifty pupils, the outlook is discouraging for a mastery of standard pronunciation, speech rhythm, accent, vocabulary, and usage. The record of accomplishment and the testimony of the students themselves support this statement.

The effort to increase the contacts with standard English should be a very practical one adapted to the conditions under which children must live, but it should be imaginative. The parents of Spanish-speaking children must make opportunities and take advantage of those that exist. To leave all to the school is to invite inferior and discouraging achievement. Sentimental attachment to the mother tongue and conformity with the language pattern of the group may be satisfying to a parent, but it will not prepare his child to live and compete in an English-speaking environment.

The public—both English-speaking and Spanish-speaking—can help by supporting the efforts of the schools and of outside agencies to increase favorable language opportunities. Television is already a powerful educational instrument in teaching language, and it can be made a much more effective instrument. Special television stations can be established to devote themselves entirely to programs in the public interest. It is not too much, however, to ask of commercial stations a little time for carefully prepared educational programs at an hour favorable to children. Regarding television programs, Ralph Long, a student of English as a second language, has offered a suggestion which has unlimited possibilities: that language programs be prepared with children (nonprofessional actors) as participants. Anyone who has witnessed the keen interest of children in the simple dramatizations of the primary grades must be impressed by the possibilities of arranging such presentations for a wider audience. The language would be simple, for it would be children's language, and the listening child would tend to identify himself with the children in the performance.

Within the school, modern technical advances make it possible to add greatly to the language environment. If a schoolroom is properly equipped with a laboratory of projection apparatus, sound equipment, and listening devices, children can look and listen during periods when the teacher is busy with another class. Horse-and-buggy equipment of schools is not satisfactory in a jet-airplane age! Fantastic equipment or equipment clearly beyond a school's means is not urged, but efforts in the conservation and development of human resources should be modernized. Naturally, it will require a little larger slice of the tax dollar.

Drill with Understanding

The matter of drill is another common concern of public and professional staffs. The first principle here is that language must be based upon experience and must be motivated by a desire to communicate— to know what someone else is saying or has written and in turn to say something one's self. Pupils must want to talk and to write, and they must actually talk and write something which they wish to say. Teaching, at home or elsewhere, which is too far from the child's world or which contains too much criticism of the child's efforts can only result in a relatively barren drill. Why should a child try to think of something to say just to illustrate how something *can* be said? Language situations must produce the desire to communicate.

On the other hand, there is no royal road to learning a language, for incidental listening and imitation are not enough. There must be drill, and drill often requires effort. A person does not get ahead by dreaming and wishful thinking. Hard work is necessary, and children should learn to give it and expect to give it. The idea of calling everything a game, even in the kindergarten, is absurd; it does not prepare for life in a real world.

Four important points need to be made with regard to drill. The first is that drill should be carefully planned to give correct practice. A child learns what he practices, whether right or wrong. The second point is that the drill should be organized in steps adapted to the child's ability and previous learning. Haphazard drill may be a kind of merry-go-round, going on and on but not ahead. The third point is that drill should be conducted with a maximum of effort and attention. Motivation is important, and the time given to drill in one period should not be too long. A spread of practice over periods in which maximum effort is given will be better than a single long period of gradually decreasing interest and effort. Naturally, the periods should not be too short, for it often takes a little time just to "warm up." The use of self-teaching devices increases the possibilities of distributed and effective drill. The fourth point is that the child should know when he has made a correct response in a learning situation. If a learning situation requires repeated trials to make a correct response (as in learning to speak another language), the knowledge that a response is correct reinforces the tendency to make it again.

Techniques of Teaching

For more than thirty years educators have given serious attention to teaching English to Spanish-speaking children, and many helps are available, especially for teachers in the primary grades. Both individual school systems and state departments of education have prepared outlines and other forms of assistance. The late L. S. Tireman published a systematic treatment, entitled *Teaching Spanish-Speaking Children*, covering many topics and including an extensive discussion of the teaching of language.

Reading different accounts and visiting different schools, one is impressed by the variety of emphases in point of view and method. The fact is that children can learn from quite different learning situations. A linguist once remarked regarding a teaching situation in another geographical area, "The teachers were doing everything wrong, but the pupils were learning!" Although a careful evaluation would find that some methods are better than others, there is a great deal of room for variation in effective teaching.

In 1938 the Office of Education published a bulletin by J. L. Meriam with the provocative title *Learning English Incidentally*. This was an account of an experiment in which the emphasis was upon experience rather than language. The author pointed out the difference in these words:

... the activity program of La Jolla School is not used, as in most schools, to *motivate* the learning of English. Whatever of English is acquired by these bilingual children is strictly incidental to the accomplishment of a larger objective—the improvement of the normal activities of children.

He advocated the use of English in its various forms as one of many tools for reaching greater efficiency in normal life. "English at its very best is of value as it functions."

Although most students of the problem would regard Meriam's position as extreme, his insistence on the close connection of experience and language is quite sound. He does not at all preclude attention to other aspects of the situation, such as careful choice of the words to be taught and attention to the language as well as to the situation in which it is needed.

Robert Lado's discussion of the similarities and differences between English and Spanish (in his *Linguistics across Cultures*) emphasizes linguistic considerations in teaching a second language. As he points out, the languages are alike at some points and are different at others. The points of difference are the places of greatest difficulty in learning. There are differences in the speech sounds, in the sequence of sounds, in stress and rhythm, in word form and meaning, in intonation, and in grammatical structure. The teacher of Spanish-speaking children should know the points at which the greatest difficulties occur. In general, methodology is far behind in its adaptation to linguistic factors.

The listing of a few differences in the Spanish and English languages will illustrate the difficulties in learning either of the two as a second language. In word order, the adjective more often precedes the English noun but follows the Spanish noun. Thus "large river" is *río grande* (river large). In English, adjectives and the articles "a" and "the" are unchanged by the gender of the noun; in Spanish the endings of the articles and of many adjectives change with the gender of the noun, and many nouns which are neuter in English are either masculine or feminine in Spanish.

Except for emphasis, Spanish commonly omits the pronoun as the subject of a sentence, the subject being understood from the forms of the verb and the context. Thus "I tell a story" and "he tells a story" can be simply *digo un cuento* and *dice un cuento*. In English the pronoun "you" serves for both singular and plural, but in Spanish there is more than one word that means "you." *Usted* is used for singular and *ustedes* for plural; also, in more intimate relations *tú* (accented) is used rather than *usted*. To complicate matters further, *tu* (unaccented) is used for the possessive singular "your," and *tus* for the possessive plural; in English, on the other hand, "your" is either singular or plural.

Systematic differences in spelling may present some difficulty. Thus, "-tion" in English is *-ción* in Spanish; "nation" is *nación*.

Differences in the sound values of letters and syllables frequently lead to errors in pronunciation. The Spanish sound represented by *i* is close to that represented by *ee* in English. For that reason Spanish-speaking children will tend to say "leetle" for "little." The sound of *th* is not common in the Spanish of the Southwest. Children may need help in placing the tongue to get the differences between *t* and *th*, and between *d* and *th*.

Differences in rhythm and intonation in connected speech add to the difficulties of pronunciation and of understanding. Lado calls the rhythm of Spanish a "syllable-timed rhythm," in which each syllable tends to take the same time. In English on the other hand, the timing is more by phrases than by syllables. In both languages some syllables are stressed more than others, and differences in pitch are used in somewhat different ways.

In the elementary grades while speech habits are still flexible, it is rather easy to help a child produce a speech sound almost correctly by imitation, guided if necessary by suggestions on how to make a given sound. The difficulty is one of providing sufficient practice with that sound. Once the child leaves the teacher, he may practice a very different sound—and what he practices he learns. At this point recordings of correct sounds which may be used for practice away from the teacher can be very helpful. The purpose is to give the pupil almost constant contact with satisfactory models. The same principle holds when the child has learned to read. He must be encouraged to read a great deal. Whether he listens or reads, it must be with understanding.

Teachers sometimes become accustomed to nonstandard pronunciations, as do children, and do not hear them as errors. It is possible also to be too sensitive to errors and to be so critical that children are uncomfortable and avoid English as much as possible.

If children advance to the junior high school with glaring errors in speech, the correction of these errors is difficult. During these years, however, and even later much can be accomplished through special classes or individual help supplemented by increased contact with standard English. At this stage a special speech teacher who understands the difficulties of Spanish-speaking children can be of great value.

Other Problems

Two of the greatest difficulties in the teaching of English in the primary grades are (1) developing a program which leads systematically and at the right speed toward definite goals, and (2) giving sufficient content to the teaching. However interesting and valuable exercises may be in themselves, they should fit together in a sequence which leads toward some end. There was once a phrase "busy work" which still all too aptly describes many classroom activities. Giving content to language is difficult when the vocabulary is small. Take three hundred to five hundred words some time and try conducting an exhilarating conversation using only them!

In the higher grades it is sometimes difficult to find reading material of content appropriate to the maturity of the children and at the same time simple enough in language to allow the children to read without experiencing difficulty so great that they will give up the struggle. This, of course, is also true of English-speaking children, but the problem is especially acute with children who are learning English as a second language. There is another possible approach to the solution of the problem of difficult reading material. To a certain extent, instead of avoiding difficult selections or rewriting them to present the content in easier language, systematic help could be provided at the points where the difficulties are likely to be greatest. Difficult words and unfamiliar expressions can be explained in preparation for the reading, thus increasing the child's ability to deal with the material as written.

Sometimes Spanish can be used effectively in teaching English, particularly if it is hard to explain a word in simpler English or to develop its meaning through experience. For example, such a word as "however" may be explained quite simply by giving its Spanish equivalent. On the other hand, the use of Spanish can easily be overdone. Giving equivalent words in a language which a child already knows tends to make him translate rather than use the new language in his thought processes. Even Spanish-English dictionaries encourage translation. Thinking in English is stimulated by using as far as possible a dictionary in which the meanings of English words are expressed by pictures or by other English words already in the child's vocabulary.

Craftsmanship in Teaching

There is a certain craftsmanship in the work of the good teacher, a combination of skills which to some extent is individual. At the primary level, for example, a teacher who is musical and creative may make music of primary importance in learning language. Nearly any situation can have an appropriate song, sometimes composed for the occasion, to reinforce the learning. Similarly, a teacher talented in art may make the use of charts and illustrations especially effective. Another with a good literary background and the ability to tell a story may give the children an unusually rich experience in literature. A teacher with dramatic training may emphasize the role of make-believe and make common situations intensely interesting. Another with a scientific background may open a new world by helping the children to see the things around them through the eyes of science.

12. Children of Low Economic Level

The learning of a second language and the use of that language, while still imperfectly learned, as a tool for other learning place a heavy handicap on many Spanish-speaking children. Often added to this burden is the handicap of poverty. As pointed out, the average economic level of the Spanish-speaking people of the Southwest is much lower than that of the population as a whole. Fortunately, the level is rising, but there are still thousands of children who come from homes of poverty. Children in this large group have special educational needs because of the deficiencies of their homes.

Material Needs

The first problem in the education of children of low economic level is to get them enrolled in school and to see that they are in regular attendance. Related to this requirement is the problem of caring for physical needs and supplying educational materials which the home is unable to provide. To be ready for school, children must be clothed and fed, clean, and free from infectious disease. To do their school work they must have books, pencils, and other supplies.

If a community is well organized for child and family service, much of the actual load of helping children and families can be carried by outside agencies, acting both independently and on the recommendation of the school. Thus, instead of giving a child a pair of shoes at the school, the principal may send a recommendation to a family-service organization. In like manner the school nurse may recommend the help of a community clinic or of a club which has committed itself to the kind of assistance which the child needs—for example, the treatment of an infection or the provision of glasses. When there is less division of labor among community organizations, the school itself often finds it necessary to give the help directly, with the support of public funds or of community groups such as the PTA or a luncheon club. There is a feeling among some principals, however, that the aid given directly by the school itself should be reduced to a minimum, that the activities of the school should be limited as far as possible to strictly educational work.

Giving help in such a way that the assistance will be constructive rather than damaging to the personality of the person who is being helped is often a delicate and difficult matter. Handing out money or goods can be done in a way that is cruel and destructive of self-respect. It can promote continued dependency. In giving help the school is dealing not simply with hungry and ill-clothed children but also with personalities who are influenced by the manner as well as the substance of what is done. Giving clothing of style and quality different from that worn by other children may protect a child from cold, but it invites a feeling of inferiority and a withdrawal from normal social contacts. Continued giving without permitting the child to do something in return invites continued dependency. Giving help of any kind in a way that brings the child to the attention of his fellows as an inferior person undermines his position and challenges his self-respect.

In the whole field of dealing with dependency there is much to learn, or perhaps enough is known but not applied. Dependency tends to breed dependency. Adults to whom unusual help is given over a long period tend to believe, if they think at all, that the world owes them something. More likely, they simply accept the situation and go along with it as the natural thing to do. At the lowest level an ignorant, poverty-stricken woman who has had no chance to develop better ideals may fall easily into a pattern of accepting aid for dependent children and adding to the flock with the assistance of one man after another. A child from such a background, when other children are telling what they plan to do when they grow up, could find it reasonable to say for himself, "Nothing. We get a check." Similarly a mother, accustomed to being given help, might write to the school principal that her child will come to school if the principal will send some shoes.

In part, these people become victims of the community's efforts to help them. In order to awaken the more favored people of society to the needs of the less fortunate, those who want to help talk about forgotten people, needy people, underprivileged people. But the

people who are being talked about often hear what is said and find
it easy to wait for others to help them instead of helping themselves.
No one with a spark of human sympathy wants to deny relief to the
needy. In fact, in the abundance of the United States economy, giving
relief is fairly easy. The difficult part is to educate the people who are
receiving help to the point where help will not be needed, or to where,
with the help, the families receiving it can rise through their own
efforts to a higher standard of living.

The School Program

The special needs of children from homes at the lowest economic
level call for appropriate adjustments in the program of the school
which they attend. Some families have to be taught to deal effectively
with skin and hair infections and to keep their children clean. In a
school enrolling these children, facilities for shower baths and a program for using them are very helpful, for in many homes there are
only the most primitive opportunities for keeping clean. It is not easy
to bathe when eight or ten have to use the same washbowl and perhaps
to carry the water in and out of the house. Bathing is obviously a matter of concern to the teacher and to other pupils as well as to the child
himself.

Assuming that the children have been clothed, fed, and washed,
what then? Then one is ready to think of reading, writing, arithmetic,
and other areas of learning, and the teacher will find that significant
adjustments must be made to compensate for the cultural lacks which
accompany long-continued poverty. She has to remember that these
children do not have many of the experiences and educational opportunities outside of school which other children have.

Adjustment to the cultural lacks of Spanish-speaking children of
low-economic level requires that the school supplement the experiences provided by the home and to some extent correct the trends
established by a poor environment. One of the knottiest problems is
to provide experiences from which the concepts already acquired by
other children outside of school can be developed. Excursions, laboratory work, and activities in the schoolroom and on the playground
are fruitful sources. Direct experience can be supplemented by pictures, drawings, and simple explanations with the assistance of filmstrips, still and motion pictures, and television. Experience programs
are time-consuming and must be prepared with great care if they
make their full contribution. Although full advantage should be taken

of chance opportunities—for example, when something unusual but full of meaning for the children is brought to school—the schedule of experiences to be offered should be planned with as much thought as other parts of the school program. Parents and parent organizations can help by deliberately seeking new and meaningful activities for their children.

The general principle, applicable in all education, is that education must begin at the point reached by the learner and go on from there. No life is so poverty-stricken that there is nothing to develop. The teacher's difficulty is in finding where the child is in his development and then finding ways of leading him forward step by step as rapidly as he can go. Again the problem of individual differences occurs, for Spanish-speaking children are very different among themselves in all measurable traits. In group work there must be some compromise of different needs, but the goal is clear: learning opportunities adapted to each child. Among children from the poorest homes are children of very different capacities. At all economic levels there are retarded, average, and gifted children.

If there is to be an adequate filling in of the gaps in the experience of culture-deprived children, there must inevitably be a long school day. Then lengthening the school day becomes itself a problem requiring careful planning to avoid fatigue and boredom and to keep the level of learning high. With appropriate rest and recreational periods the whole day may be geared to learning. In the longer day, time for reading and study should be supplemented, not replaced, by various group activities. As rapidly as possible children should be taught how to go forward on their own, and conditions should be arranged so that they can do so effectively.

The Community School

Sometimes the school can be a regenerating influence for a whole community, particularly where other agencies of community welfare are lacking or are poorly developed. Such a school has been aptly called a community school. One of the most inspiring and helpful descriptions of a school of this kind is that published by Tireman and Watson in 1948, *A Community School in a Spanish-Speaking Village*. The authors tell of an interesting five-year experiment in a school in which the curriculum was built around the needs of the community.

A nine-grade consolidated rural school in the Sandia mountains of New Mexico near Albuquerque, visited a few years ago, provides another interesting illustration of a community school. The principal explained the history and program of the school in detail. It had been established in 1948, when seven struggling districts were brought together into one. There were now ten districts in the consolidation. Before the union the people of each little village had lived separately, and, as might be expected from their isolation, the people of one village were not very friendly toward those of another. The children who came to the new school reflected these unfriendly attitudes. The outcome of the consolidation was not at all certain. Perhaps the people would accept the school; perhaps they would not. To add to the uncertainty, an accident to the building forced the closing of the school early in the year. This circumstance might have discouraged a less devoted group of teachers, but while repairs were being made the teachers visited systematically in the homes of the community. These visits made the difference between success and failure. The school became and was at the time of the visit a center not only of learning but also of leadership and service in the community, a center to which the people turned with confidence and which they helped to maintain. In the years since the founding of the school, the economic level of the people and their standard of living have risen perceptibly, and in this improvement the school has had a significant part.

The principal reviewed this bit of history and explained the present organization and program of the school. She told how some of the needs had been met with meager facilities—for example, that the lunch program had been started with the furnace room as a kitchen and with utensils which the children brought from home. It was clear that the principal had brought great intelligence and skill to a difficult task. The motivation which had sustained her effort seemed to be expressed in a final, almost casual remark. She spoke with pride of the children, and with sympathy and understanding of their problems. Then in a kind of concluding statement she said simply, "These are my children."

Without being a community school in the complete sense of those used as illustrations, a school may be a center for significant community activities. Outside of school hours its auditorium and perhaps other rooms can be used by adults for public meetings, and its playground by children and others for recreation, provided adequate supervision is available. In a city a public recreation department may take charge of playground activities when school is not in session. Adult-education classes may be conducted in the evening. A school

library may be extended to serve as a community library when a
public library is lacking. The school itself may sponsor community
activities and provide counsel for members of the adult community
on individual problems.

The Problem of Separate Schools

If this book had been written several years ago, much greater attention would have been given to the problem of separate schools. In
some communities of the Southwest it was common practice to provide separate schools for Spanish-speaking children. This custom
was partly the result of the concentration of Spanish-speaking
people of low economic status in a particular section of the community, partly a reaction of persons of higher cultural levels
against the hygienic conditions found among children from the lowest
levels, partly the result of a lack of understanding and prejudice on
the part of the ruling majority in the community, and to some extent
the result of an idea that separation was a better educational policy.

The status of the segregation of Spanish-speaking children in Texas
some thirty years ago is discussed in the author's *Education of Mexican and Spanish-Speaking Children in Texas* (1930). At that time
many schools were struggling with unsatisfactory hygienic conditions
among children from the lowest economic levels, and in many communities there was strong opposition to admitting Spanish-speaking
children to schools for other children. There was a tendency to ignore
differences among children of Spanish name and to treat them all
alike. An account was given of a child "of unknown origin" who was
adopted in infancy by a Spanish-speaking family. The school district
in which the child lived maintained two schools, one for "children of
Mexican nationality" located in a ward "composed entirely of Mexican citizens," and the other for "white children of all other national-
ities." The child lived outside of the part of town in which the "Mexican" school was located, and the foster parents as..ed that she be
admitted to the other school. "The board of trustees assigned the
child . . . to the Mexican school and gave as a reason for said assign-
ment that the Mexican children were irregular in attendance and did
not advance as rapidly as American children and should have special
attention by the teacher which could not be given if they were inter-
mingled in the American school. The board of trustees disclaimed any
intention to segregate the Mexican children on racial grounds."

On appeal the question came before the state superintendent of public instruction and later the State Board of Education. Both upheld the right of the child to attend the school for non-Mexican children, although the state superintendent agreed with the notion that "it is probably to the best interests of such non-English-speaking children that they be placed in one room or in one school in order that the character of instruction given will be different from that given to English-speaking children." Such a conclusion is now generally recognized to need revision. The principle of individual differences, however, was soundly upheld. The child was found to speak English fluently and to be able to translate from Spanish to English and English to Spanish.

In 1951 George I. Sánchez, who has been both a student of the education of Spanish-speaking children and a leader in the struggle for their legal rights, published a pamphlet, *Concerning Segregation of Spanish-Speaking Pupils in the Public Schools.* Sánchez quotes decisions of courts—(1) the United States District Court of the Southern District of California, Central Division, in 1946, (2) the Ninth United States Circuit Court of Appeals, in 1947, (3) the United States District Court, District of Arizona, in 1950, and (4) the United States District Court, Western District of Texas, Austin Division, in 1948—which hold in effect that the segregation of children in separate schools and classes on the basis of Mexican descent is illegal. The Texas decision provided that the schools might maintain

separate classes, on the same campus in the first grade only and solely for instructional purposes, for pupils in their initial scholastic year who, at the beginning of their initial scholastic year in the first grade, clearly demonstrate, as a result of scientific and standardized tests, equally given and applied to all pupils, that they do not possess a sufficient familiarity with the English language to understand substantially classroom instruction in first-grade subject matter.

The opinion of many educators who are familiar with the problems of Spanish-speaking children is well summarized by L. S. Tireman in this quotation from Sánchez's volume (pp. 56–57):

It is my opinion, based on twenty years of study, that native Spanish-speaking children should not be automatically segregated in separate school buildings from the native English-speaking children. Such an artificial separation intensifies anti-social feelings in both groups. The Spanish-speaking children become timid and sullen. The English develop false attitudes of superiority. Neither group learns to appreciate the good qualities inherent in the other group. The great democratic tradition of respect for others and the splendid American trait of working co-operatively with others are given no chance to be practiced.

Our experience in New Mexico shows clearly that native Spanish-speaking and native English-speaking children will play and work together in harmony if the public school system be developed with that in mind. Both groups should be mixed up together and treated alike. By so doing, we develop Americans.

Grouping for Instruction

There are still a great many schools whose enrollment is largely or wholly of Spanish-speaking children. These schools are usually located in districts having a heavy concentration of Spanish-speaking people. If the buildings are fairly adequate, there is a tendency to maintain schools once established even though a different location would bring Spanish-speaking and English-speaking children together and serve the community better. In some communities the concentration of Spanish-speaking people in certain sections is so great and the number so large that schools enrolling Spanish-speaking children almost exclusively are likely to continue for an indefinite future. There is no doubt, however, that a professional and nonprejudiced approach to the problems of housing will change the location and enrollment of schools in many communities.

The grouping of children for instruction is a professional problem, and one which is extremely difficult. It is difficult because of the conflict between measures which are appropriate to preparation for co-operative living and measures which are appropriate to provision for individual differences. The first requires that children live and work together. The second requires a degree of separate grouping to meet widely divergent needs. Inevitably the practical situation requires a degree of compromise in which the needs of no group are fully met. The problem is to find the solution which is fairest and best to all children. Neither the theory that retarded children may be neglected because they will not accomplish much in any case, nor the theory that because of their handicaps they must have much more consideration than others can be accepted. The welfare of the community and the welfare of the individual both demand that the gifted child and the child who has already achieved a great deal have the opportunity to go forward to their maximum potential.

The conflict between the kinds of educational opportunity best adapted to children of different needs is illustrated in the language situation previously discussed. The Spanish-speaking child desperately needs contact with other children who have a better command of English. At the same time the English-speaking child needs contact with children who already have a command of English and with whom the language work of the school can be on a level appropriate to his advancement. Again, the child whose home life has brought superior opportunities needs educational experiences at a different level from those appropriate to culture-deprived children of similar age.

Early Educational Opportunities

The need of *early* educational opportunities should again be apparent. Although no outside help can completely overcome the disadvantages of children in culture-deprived homes, much can be done to diminish their handicaps. But to be most effective this help must begin at the earliest possible age. The minimum essential for the immediate future is clearly a prefirst grade for all five-year-olds. But a beginning of education in nursery schools would be much better—nursery schools, that is, which are more than baby-sitting institutions for children of working mothers. Much less remedial work at a later age will be required if children can be given an opportunity to develop normally.

13. Education of the Migrant Child

The education of the child of low economic level who moves with his family from community to community during the school year presents special problems. He is usually the child of an agricultural laborer who moves from a home base as needs for additional labor develop in different sections of the country and then moves back again at the close of the cycle. Some migrants indeed find permanent places in the communities to which they come as migratory laborers, but most of them return to a home base.

The migrant laborers of interest here are residents of this country. This group does not include the large number of laborers who live in the Republic of Mexico and who come, under contract or illegally, to help with the crops and then return to Mexico. Most of the laborers from Mexico are adults and for that reason are not themselves serious school problems.

Studies of Migratory Labor

Many persons have studied the problems of migrating workers. More than thirty years ago the National Child Labor Committee issued a pamphlet, *Migrating Child Workers*, by George B. Mangold and Lillian B. Hill. In this pamphlet Mangold dates the probable first study of the migratory child worker as 1907, a study made by the Consumer's League of New York City. Mangold cited two reasons for migratory child labor: (1) seasonal occupations, chief among which he named "fruit and berry picking, cotton picking, truck gardening, work in beet fields and tobacco fields, picking hops, and harvesting peas and beans"; (2) facilities for locomotion by automobile, with a development of "taste for travel." He reported that much migratory labor was of Mexican origin. Discussing conditions in California at that time (1929) he said: "Fruit growers desire the Mexican partly because the labor is cheap; partly because they feel but little moral obligation for his welfare and that of his family."

Miss Hill, then chief of the Bureau of Attendance and Migratory Schools, California State Department of Education, referred to an act (1927) which was passed to protect the educational rights of migratory children. This act provided for maintaining schools for the children of migratory laborers engaged in seasonal industries in the rural districts of the state. On the dark side of the picture she reported seeing classes of 125 migratory children with only one teacher in charge. On the brighter side, she reported a migratory school in which there were splendid teachers, good equipment, provisions for pupils to progress at their own rates, and happy children.

A mimeographed report by Miss Hill in 1930 stated that according to the school census obtained in 1927 there were in California 36,891 children "who declared that they were migratory and definitely stated that they and their parents had no permanent place of residence." She reported also that, according to the same census, there were 102,405 Mexican children in the state.

In the thirty-odd years since the publication of these early studies much has happened to improve the status of the migratory child and his family, but he is still a serious problem. A pamphlet issued by the U.S. Department of Labor, Bureau of Labor Standards, September 1956, summarizes the *Status of Agricultural Workers Under State and Federal Laws.* According to this pamphlet, in general the legal protection of agricultural workers lags behind the protection provided by law for workers in trade and industry.

Here are some of the statements:

(1) "Only five States, two Territories, and the District of Columbia now expressly provide a minimum age for work of children in agriculture outside school hours."

(2) "For agricultural work during school hours a minimum age expressly applies in 12 States, two Territories, and the District of Columbia."

(3) "Compulsory school attendance laws supplement the standards set under the child-labor laws by requiring boys and girls to attend school to a certain age. . . . In many States, however, these laws permit children [of certain ages] to be excused from school to work in agriculture. The situation as it relates to migra-

tory children is even more serious, since the school laws often do not apply to them."

(4) "Two Federal laws affect the employment of children in agriculture. The Fair Labor Standards Act establishes a 16-year minimum age for agricultural employment during school hours. Under the Sugar Act, if the producers are to obtain maximum benefits they may not employ children under 14, or permit those of 14 and 15 to work more than 8 hours a day, in the cultivation or harvesting of sugar beets or sugarcane."

(5) In a few states the minimum-wage laws are "broad enough to cover agriculture. . . . The wage and hour provisions of the Federal Fair Labor Standards Act do not cover agriculture."

(6) "Approximately half the States . . . have laws or regulations that apply to all labor camps or to migrant camps specifically."

(7) "A few States . . . have laws or regulations setting safety standards for vehicles used in the transportation of farm workers. In addition, a Federal law now provides for the regulation of the interstate transportation of migrants."

The first progress report of the President's Committee on Migratory Labor was published in 1956 by the U.S. Department of Labor. This committee was appointed "to assume national leadership in improving the social and economic welfare of our domestic migratory farm workers." The report estimated the domestic migrant work force, including dependents, as about three-quarters of a million people. It noted that

This work is highly seasonal and in many areas is frequently of short duration. Annual earnings from this type of employment are generally low, traveling and housing conditions are often below minimum standards, and, as a result of migration, the educational opportunities for migrant children are reduced.

The report suggests standards for regulating agricultural labor camps and for the transportation of agricultural workers by motor vehicle.

There is reason to believe that the need for migratory farm work will continue for many years. In 1956 O. J. Scoville of the U.S. Department of Agriculture presented a *Summary of Prospects for Reducing the Need for Migratory Farm Work* (pamphlet of the Department). It was his view that, ignoring effects of improved mechanization, "there would be a moderate increase in demand for migrants in cotton and potatoes and a more substantial increase in demand for migrants for work in truck crops and fruits." He recognized that there is substantial progress in mechanizing jobs but expressed the belief that heavy demands for migrant labor will continue for many years. Indeed, he pointed out that partial mechanization of work may displace resident workers and increase the demand for seasonal workers in the tasks which are not mechanized.

Dr. Daniel G. Aldrich, Jr., Dean of Agriculture, University of California, expressed similar views in the Report of the California Third Annual Conference (1961) on Children Who Follow the Crops. He pointed out the need of the migrant for more education:

Many of the undereducated and unskilled, instead of finding a haven in farm labor, could be forced out of agriculture by today's and tomorrow's farm machines. Unless these people get more education or training, they may have difficulty finding employment in either mechanized agriculture or the general labor market. . . . For the children of our migratory families, sometimes five years behind others of their ages, who is to say that enough farm jobs, or any jobs, at the grade-three educational level will still be available when they grow up into an advancing world?

The main streams of the northward movement of domestic agricultural workers are shown in Figure 6, a map reproduced from U.S. Public Health Service Publication No. 540. The migration of Texas farm workers in May and October, 1955, is shown in Figures 7 and 8, reproduced from maps of the Texas Employment Commission. In interstate migration the workers usually travel in crews under crew leaders. The Texas Employment Commission reporting "Migration 1961" estimated the total migration from Texas in that year as being 90,000 people. Records in the office of the Commission included 5,290 groups of workers, a total of 81,641 persons of whom 27,277 (approximately one-third) were children under sixteen years of age. It can be estimated that in 1961 migration interfered with the schooling of some 15,000 children of Texas migrant workers—enough families for a city of ninety thousand and enough children for five hundred classrooms!

Problems of Education

From the facts presented in the preceding paragraphs it is clear that the education of the children of migratory laborers is a problem of great magnitude and that it is a problem in many different states.

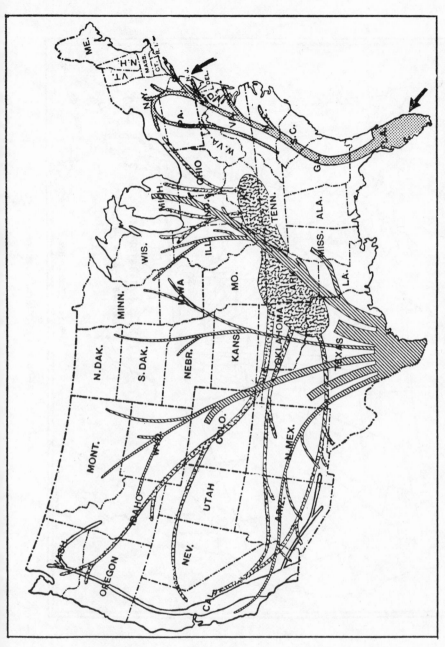

Fig. 6—Travel patterns of seasonal migratory agricultural laborers throughout the United States.

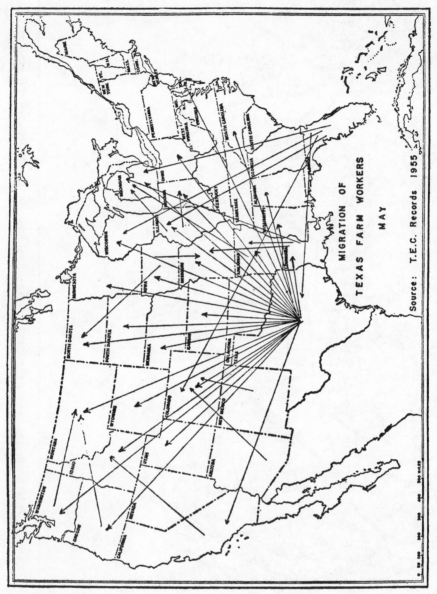

Fig. 7—Migration of Texas farm workers—May.

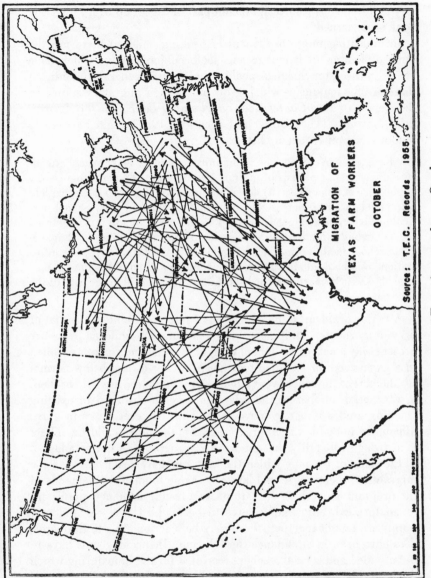

Fig. 8—Migration of Texas farm workers—October.

Since a large proportion of the migrants are Spanish-speaking, migratory children constitute a significant part of the group with which this book is concerned.

In educating migratory Spanish-speaking children there are the same difficulties of language and socioeconomic status which have been discussed for Spanish-speaking children in general. In addition there are the handicaps which grow out of their migratory status. In the *Report of Two Conferences on Planning Education for Agricultural Migrants* (U.S. Office of Education, 1957) eight barriers to school accomplishment are listed:

(1) Frequent moves from one community to another make school attendance difficult; (2) parents of migrant children often do not recognize the importance of schooling; (3) school organization is not flexible enough to accommodate large increases of non-resident children; (4) school curriculum experiences are not adapted to the needs of migrant children; (5) community indifference or rejection of migrant families; (6) inadequate school facilities and lack of funds; (7) inadequate advance information by school administrators about number of children and time of arrival; and (8) meager records of the previous school experience of the children.

A major problem in the education of migratory children is that of providing rooms, equipment, and teachers for children who are present only a part of the school year. If the number of pupils enrolled in a given room or assigned to a given teacher is kept below normal for the part of the school year when migrant children are not enrolled, a substantial number of the migrants may be absorbed in existing teaching units without overcrowding. This, however, leads to grave difficulties both for the migrants and for the other children. There is a strong probability that the work in progress will not be adapted to the stage of learning which the migrants have reached. Often the migrants who enter a school late are unable to meet the demands of the program which is in operation. As a result, if the new pupils are to go forward, adjustments have to be made. If the old and new pupils are taught together, there may be a serious loss to the pupils who have been in attendance the full time. If special rooms have to be provided and special teachers recruited for the time during which the migrants are enrolled, special problems of finance and personnel arise. One school system in a Texas community which is the home base of a large number of migratory workers reported an enrollment of about 2,100 in the fall and about 3,000 in February.

A second problem, more acute in the communities to which the children migrate, is the problem of attendance, getting the children in school for the time during which they are in the community. If they are old enough to work, they are likely to be employed to supplement the family income. Children who are not working sometimes stay out of school to look after other children or simply stay in the labor camp in idleness. Even under favorable circumstances the adjustment of a family and the children to constantly changing communities is a difficult problem. It is easy to remain isolated in the working group.

Probably the most difficult problem in the education of migrant children is that of providing a school program which is adapted to their needs. Even if it could be assured that migrant children would be in school somewhere during the entire school year, the lack of continuity in their learning could be almost disastrous. Differences in programs, lack of knowledge of what the child has accomplished elsewhere, lack of acquaintance with the child himself, and the tremendous range of individual differences among the children make it almost impossible to shape one short division of the child's schooling so that it will fit neatly with the others. It is easy in such a situation to mark time or to arrange work in segments which contribute little to movement toward a well-conceived goal.

During the school year 1963–1964 a number of school systems in the Lower Rio Grande Valley, with the cooperation of the Texas Education Agency, experimented with a shorter school year and a more intensive educational program for children of migrant laborers whose home base was in their districts.

The Fresno Project

Many educators have given serious attention to the educational needs of migratory children. One of the best of the local efforts is illustrated by the ninety-five-page book, *Teaching Children Who Move with the Crops,* a report and recommendations of the Fresno (California) County Project, the Educational Program for Migrant Children (published by Walter G. Martin, Fresno County Superintendent of Schools, in 1955). The project out of which this publication grew was a "two-year program of practical experimentation," in which school and community workers of nineteen school districts participated. It was directed by Helen Cowan Wood and assisted by grants from the Rosenberg Foundation.

The first two paragraphs of the first chapter of the book set the tone
for the whole discussion:

School is the measure of opportunity for thousands of children who
move with the crops across our farm country. To the child, a good school
in the new neighborhood means friends and belonging, interesting things
to do, growing ability and self-confidence. To his parents and to the
community, a good school means a healthy, happy child; a good citizen;
and hope for the future. For many children there will be no opportunity
except that offered by the public school.

When the classroom door opens to admit a new child in the middle of
the school year and in the middle of the lesson, this is what the teacher
must understand: Unless this child finds opportunity here, he will find it
nowhere. His education is the sum total of temporary school stops in classrooms like this, always at the busy time of the year. It can be no better
than what I offer him now, for whatever time he is here.

Teachers are advised in the report to visit the homes of at least a
few pupils for a better understanding of the children. At the same
time they are reminded that generalizations about groups, which have
value for "over-all planning of the school program" can not be applied
to individual children. "One of the dangers everyone has to guard
against in becoming acquainted with any new group is the human
tendency to make sweeping generalizations based on experience with
only a few members of the group."

The home of the migrant child as long as his family follows the
crops is a "temporary shelter," the report points out. "Usually it is
one room in a tent or a cabin, for all family activities." The children
live under conditions very different from those which are reflected in
stories, poems, pictures, and ordinary courses of study. Among the
simple and obvious points to consider are differences "in meal planning, cooking, and serving; in bathing and laundry; in care of the
sick; in bringing up babies and small children; in the availability of
books, magazines, and music; in types of recreation; in opportunities
for home work; in hours of sleep and quality of rest."

According to the report:

Family relations are often warm and close. . . . Many families are
large. . . . Boys and girls take a large share of the family responsibility,
especially in taking care of younger children; they become wage earners
as soon as they can; they grow up young. A great deal of permissiveness is
typical in the way small children are brought up. . . . At the same time the
authority of the parents is stronger and more unquestioned. . . . Anxiety

and emotional tension seem to be less. . . . The Spanish-speaking child has the difficult task of growing up in two languages and in home-school cultures which contrast even more greatly than for his Anglo or Negro neighbor.

The difficult conditions under which the children live, their frequent moving, and their poverty contribute to limiting their school attendance, but the authors agree with the earlier discussion in this book in saying that the knottiest problem of all is that of "providing a school program which has meaning and importance for these children, which helps each child to learn at his own level and his own pace, which takes into account the special needs of children who move, and does all these things without limiting opportunity for the children who stay." It is pointed out that "migrant children do not fit the traditional school pattern at all." The suggested solution, however, is not special schools for migrant children. It is rather the making of a school program which will fit the needs of both migrant and non-migrant children—"a flexible program, focused on individuals." Most of the book is devoted to outlining in some detail a program "built to the special requirements of a school which serves the needs of children who move."

Dealing with the problems of continuity as the children move from school to school the report describes a "transfer packet" which goes with the pupil when he moves. Additional information from school records is sent on request. But "the best guarantee for continuity is a goal-centered child who wants an education." Boys and girls should have guidance in broadening their own ideas of education, in understanding themselves, in believing in their potentialities, and in setting goals for themselves.

The Colorado Research

The Colorado State Department of Education has completed a significant Migrant Education Research Project under the direction of Alfred M. Potts, with the assistance of a grant from the U.S. Office of Education. A summary report of the project was issued by the Department in 1961 under the title *Providing Education for Migrant Children*. The report carries twenty-three specific recommendations, some of which refer directly to the Colorado situation. Others are more general in their application.

Since 1955, the report points out, summer schools for migratory children have been operated in Colorado, and a program of state support has been developed. The report recognizes, however, that the chief means for the education of these children as of other children is the regular school session.

The chief concentration of effort in a migrant education program should be centered on getting the children into the regular terms of schools, wherever they go for whatever period of time they are in each school district.

Workshops at Adams State College (Alamosa) were jointly sponsored by the College and the Migrant Research Project for the "education of teachers for work with migrant and bilingual children" and to develop materials for classroom use. The 1959 workshop under the direction of Neil W. Sherman, general curriculum consultant, Phoenix Elementary Schools, resulted in a State Department publication, *Learning on the Move: A Guide for Migrant Education.* The purpose of the workshop was to develop "the philosophies best suited to education of the children of migratory workers," and to transform these philosophies "into suitable examples of curriculum materials." As in the Fresno report, it is claimed that "the kind of a program which meets the special needs of migrant children is a better program for all children." The 220-page book includes a discussion of the needs of the children of migratory workers and offers concrete and definite suggestions for meeting these needs.

A 1962 Migrant Education Workshop, again jointly sponsored by Adams State College and the Colorado State Department of Education, produced a *Guide to Organization and Administration of Migrant Education Programs.* The *Guide* is broad in scope and "is intended to be useful to all who seek to improve educational experiences for the children of migratory workers."

A Wisconsin Study

In January, 1961, Professor Donald R. Thomas reported a study of children of migratory workers in Wisconsin. A total of 4,478 persons, "a large segment of the total migrant stream," were reported to the research project as expected members of agricultural migrant crews entering Wisconsin in 1960. Of these, approximately one-third (1,528) were children under sixteen years of age. Most of these migrants "originated or came directly from the State of Texas," and "the great majority are Spanish-speaking migrants born in the United States of Mexican ancestry."

One objective of the study was to find the extent to which "the arrival of specific children in specified places at specified times" and with "certain educational strengths and weaknesses" could be predicted. The research had the cooperation of the Texas Employment Commission, the Wisconsin State Employment Service, the Texas Education Agency and many local school systems, Wisconsin growers and canners, many crew leaders, and others.

Although the study included only a part of the estimated number of migrant children, the results were such as to lead to the estimate that with additional cooperation of employers approximately 55 per cent of the total migrant child population might be successfully predicted to arrive at a specific place at a specific time.

The problem of obtaining advanced information on the educational problems of specific migrant children must be considered unsolved, as only 21.5% of the total sample had partially or fully completed Educational Assessment forms returned for them.

The following generalizations are based on the sample for whom educational data were available: (1) 42.5 per cent of those who were given health ratings were rated as in "fair or poor health" as distinguished from good or excellent; (2) 84.1 per cent of those whose English was evaluated were said to speak "poor or fair English" rather than good or excellent; (3) 93.7 per cent of the sample population were from one to six years below the normal grade placement, 75.5 per cent from two to six years below; (4) test scores reported for a sample of the population revealed generally greater average scholastic retardation than average age-grade retardation. It was suggested "that experimental schools should plan for a population which is educationally retarded from one to four years, the range increasing with age."

Cooperation on Problems of the Migrant Child

The problem of educating the migrant child is part of a general problem situation which must be attacked cooperatively by persons representing many different interests and agencies. This point of view is vividly illustrated in a series of Annual Conferences on Families Who Follow the Crops, organized under the leadership of the Subcommittee on the Migrant Child of the California Governor's Advisory Committee on Children and Youth. The third such conference (1961) had 362 registered participants, including growers, farm workers, teachers, doctors, nurses, county supervisors, public or private agency workers, and others.

Our philosophy [says the letter of transmittal of the Report] has been to encourage self-reliance and to strengthen the family and those basic local services which should be within the reach of all of our citizens whoever they are—a goal we have not yet attained. Together with our dedicated group of co-sponsors [forty-nine persons of varied interests and affiliations] we hope to find the way to enable all families in our rural communities to prosper and raise their children to be strong, healthy, good citizens of America.

~.~.~.~.~.~.~.~.~.~.~.~.~.~.~.~.~.~

14. Personality and Social Adjustment

Educators are interested in the personality and social adjustment of children for two reasons. The first is that the learning of a child is profoundly influenced by the kind of person he is. A sick child, an undernourished child, a confused child, a worried child, a disinterested child, a child with inferior work habits, a child who is at odds with his group, or a child who is preoccupied with his own problems is handicapped in learning. The condition of the learner is a significant factor in determining the outcomes of teaching.

There is an even more compelling reason for interest in the child as a person. The traits which are valued because of their influence on learning are also *goals* of education. Knowledge and ability alone are not enough. In the product of the schools other traits are sought which contribute to the happiness and effectiveness of the individual and in turn to the welfare of the community. The goals for every child are the development of a healthy organism, efficient work habits, emotional balance, a feeling of security and confidence, constructive interests, a sustaining philosophy of life, and good will toward others.

The Psychology of Learning

The situations in which a child finds himself do not automatically produce corresponding learning. It is his response—thought, feeling, or action—which produces the learning. Always the parent, the teacher, and the counselor must consider what the child thinks, how he feels, and what he does in response to the conditions around him. This holds true for conditions which are not intended for teaching as well as for those which are arranged to stimulate learning. Home conditions, conversation, play, television, rewards, penalties—all must be judged on the basis of the responses which children make to them.

There are two variables in every learning situation: the child himself, and the conditions to which he is responding. Because of differences in children and differences in the same child at different times,
the same situation produces different responses and hence different
learning. Conditions which on the surface seem the same may have
important differences. It is the total situation which produces one response or another, and the addition or subtraction of an element may
produce a different response and different learning. Thus a tired child
responds to an irritating event with anger more readily than does a
rested child, and a child in a dangerous situation is more likely to be
afraid if an adult accompanying him exhibits fear. Poverty in a home
which is characterized by self-dependence and high ideals of conduct
presents a situation very different from that presented by poverty in
a home which is characterized by dependence and irresponsibility. A
broken home in which some substitute for the absent parent has been
found is very different from that in which there is nothing to compensate for the loss.

There are two avenues of approach to problems of personality and
behavior. The first is to create conditions as far as possible which lead
toward healthful attitudes, interests, and behavior, and to remove
conditions which present unusual and unnecessary difficulties. The
possible unfavorable results of undernutrition are avoided by feeding
a child, the hatred engendered through unfair treatment is avoided by
substituting fair treatment for injustice, and confusion resulting from
impossible tasks is avoided by giving tasks which can be accomplished. Home, community, and school share the responsibility of
making the world a better place in which to rear children, a world in
which the responses of children are more likely to lead to healthful
permanent habits of feeling and action.

But we cannot wait for a better world. Time goes on, and those who
are now children will soon be adults. Some things can be done to make
conditions better for those who are now growing up, but other conditions are beyond the possibility of immediate change. The handicap
of poverty cannot be removed from thousands of homes, the home
language cannot be changed overnight, or unfavorable community attitudes cannot be quickly reversed. These are conditions which for the
present must be met otherwise. The only alternative to creating more
favorable conditions is to help a child to meet effectively the difficulties which he cannot escape. By adding something to the total situation confronting a child, one may help him to make a healthful,

constructive response rather than leaving him to disintegration and defeat. By helping him to meet difficulties which are not beyond his strength he may be prepared for greater difficulties ahead.

Special Difficulties of Spanish-Speaking Children

To see some of the special difficulties of Spanish-speaking children in relation to personality and behavior, consider first the five-year-old or six-year-old who enters school from a home of low economic level with little or no knowledge of English. Even the poorest home has offered him some security. Usually because of his experiences in the family he will be quite dependent upon his mother and his older brothers and sisters. If he has had contacts with English-speaking people and places far from his home, it has been with the "protection" of older members of the family. The blackboards, seats, pencils, group routines, and often the sanitary arrangements of the school are new to him. Suddenly he is alone in this strange situation controlled by an adult with whom many times he cannot communicate. At best it is a confusing, fearful, insecure situation, and it can be even worse. The teacher's task is to give confidence, relieve fears, and help the child to find his way. The very atmosphere of the room, perhaps some use of the child's own language, and skill in dealing with young children can save the situation. Children are quick to respond to understanding and sympathy.

Persistent Conditions Affecting Personality and Conduct

It is not, however, the transition from home to school which offers the greatest hazards to the Spanish-speaking child. This is soon overcome, and in general both kindergarten and primary teachers show a great deal of skill in helping children to make this transition. The greater hazards are those presented by conditions which persist until they adversely affect personality and behavior. Hardship can be met and dismissed as part of life, or it can contribute to personality defects, inefficient efforts, and antisocial action. The concern of educators should be not so much with the pain suffered at the moment as with the long-range effects of a painful situation. To be afraid or to feel insecure at the moment is painful, but it is tragic when fear and feelings of insecurity become a permanent characteristic. Confusion is bad enough at a particular time leading to a single failure; it is infinitely worse when it becomes a habitual reaction to problems. Aggressive reaction in a single crisis may lead to quite painful consequences, but a whole life is lost when the aggressiveness becomes habitual and the behavior intensely antisocial.

To repeat a point made earlier, the Spanish-speaking child is often the victim of a conflict between the Spanish-speaking and English-speaking groups in the community, a conflict deeply rooted in the past. It is a conflict nourished also by cultural differences, by differences in economic level, by differences in place of residence within the community, and by acts which are regarded as unfriendly. Antagonisms, like traditions, tend to persist from generation to generation. They are learned in the home and reinforced by conditions outside the home. It is a two-way affair: the Spanish-speaking child brings from his home the attitudes of his subcommunity, and he comes face to face with the opposing attitudes which he finds in the larger community.

The minimum result is a divisive consciousness of "we" and "they" and of apparently conflicting interests. The parents of Spanish-speaking children think of themselves as different, and the children gradually come to share that opinion. They not only share that opinion, but they act the part as well. The opinion that they are different and the attitudes which go with it are reinforced then by the actions of the English-speaking group who regard themselves as different, and who also act the part. Patterns of behavior are developed which continue to place the groups in opposition to each other. Also developed are habits of working in and for their own subgroups rather than participating in common activities for the good of all.

A sharp division separating the Spanish-speaking group from the main current of community life tends to create in adolescent boys and girls a devastating emotional conflict between loyalty to their homes and a desire for at least a part of the kind of life which they see in the larger community. Rejected, partly indeed because of their own attitudes, by the English-speaking group and attempting to break away from their present environment, they find no place of security, and tend to give up the struggle or to strike out in unreasonable ways against the barriers which seem to hem them in. Basically in this behavior they are simply trying to satisfy their needs.

Since differences between groups tend to increase group consciousness, obviously one way to decrease the "we–they" awareness is to decrease the differences between the groups. Little can be done about some differences—at times, for example, a difference in skin color—

but many differences can be erased or at least minimized. A difference in language is one of these.

Isolation and Feelings of Inferiority

Wide differences in economic level tend not only to keep people apart but also to nourish feelings of inferiority in those of lowest income. Typically, with long-continued poverty families come to accept inferiority as a permanent state and to develop an attitude of dependency from which it is hard to escape. This the child shares. One of the greatest tasks of the school is to give the child of poverty a new outlook on life, to help him develop ambition and hope, and then to see that the hope thus kindled is not in vain. The need is especially great at the junior high school level as the age for leaving school approaches.

The attitude developed in the home is often strengthened by experiences at school. In so basic a matter as food and clothing, for example, the inferiority of the child is forced upon him as he is brought into contact with more favored children. Some of the children are very brave and try to keep a protective bold front. A Scout leader, for example, told of a boy who took only a carrot or two to camp, maintaining that he did not eat much anyhow. A teacher told of a boy who, not having the money for a special luncheon, came to school with his lunchbasket, apparently to eat his own lunch, but the basket was absolutely empty. Some retire and avoid contacts because they are unable to compete. Over and over illustrations can be found of high school students who avoid occasions where their shabby dress would place them at a disadvantage. One boy who had only one pair of shoes throughout his high school enrollment failed to attend a meeting to receive a scholarship award. These are not occasional hard-luck stories. They are real-life illustrations of an influence pushing many children toward feelings of inferiority and toward isolation.

When poverty is accompanied by language difficuⅼties, small success with school work, and rejection by others, the situation is very difficult indeed. There is little wonder that many Spanish-speaking youth develop a feeling of futility and want to give up the struggle. But the situation is not a hopeless one to be dismissed with the superficial explanation that these young people lack ambition. A more thorough analysis of conditions shows that much can be done to kindle hope and to raise substantially the level of achievement.

Every child needs to taste success and to enjoy prestige. Spanish-speaking children, as other children, have their confidence strengthened by real success and by being given the symbols and rewards that go with status. An attempt to impart this confidence does not mean the school should try to conceal differences among people. Different levels of attainment are normal parts of everyday life. It does mean setting goals that are reasonable for different individuals and marking the attainment of the goals with approval. It means there should be honors, medals, and recognition for achievement in different fields, and a cultivation of admiration rather than jealousy for those who succeed. A school in a depressed area in which children are weighted down by discouraged parents and teachers can be transformed by a change of attitude, policy, and method—a change that goes with the expectation of success and a belief in the possibilities of boys and girls. It has been done. A restless, discouraged, unruly mass of pupils can be transformed into a happy, confident, working group through a student council; a glee club, a band, and an orchestra, all with suitable uniforms; a neat and attractive building and grounds; a science fair; a challenging curriculum; a well-chosen library; well-equipped laboratories; recognition of work well done; a fundamental interest in children; note it well—hard but productive work; and a firm but kindly discipline.

Antisocial Behavior

Sometimes maladjustment shows itself in antisocial conduct. The young man or young woman rebels against authority or commits acts destructive of property or harmful to persons. The many accounts of delinquent behavior by persons of Spanish name are discouraging. As this is written, the local paper carries a report of the arrest of three persons of Spanish name for vandalism. Statistics add no comfort. The Annual Report of the Texas Youth Council for the year ended August 31, 1962, gives a sobering comparison of the number of children of different groups admitted to the training schools within the year. Of 2,283 children, 705 (30.9 per cent) were Spanish-speaking. This number is far out of proportion to the number of Spanish-speaking children in the total population. Information from other states also suggests that the proportion of Spanish-speaking youngsters who get into trouble with the law is generally greater than their proportion in the general population.

Some observers, in defense of the child who gets into trouble, point out that for the same offense the child of lower income levels is more likely than other children to be committed to a correctional institution. The suggestion is that perhaps the situation among Spanish-speaking children is not as bad as it looks. Even so, the statistics of actual commitments reveal a serious maladjustment and a heavy social burden.

There is need, of course, to distinguish between the real delinquent and the boy or girl who makes an occasional mistake. The public must not be too hurried in tagging a youngster with a delinquency label. A certain amount of misbehavior is to be expected, though not invited or approved, as an adolescent struggles toward adulthood. It is the task of everyone to prevent as far as possible even isolated outbreaks of misbehavior, which can be serious in themselves, and to foster development in the right direction.

The first step in dealing with misbehavior is to diagnose the difficulty, to understand as far as possible its cause, and to interpret its meaning in the development of the child. As in the emotions, misbehavior is the result of a total situation, and the chief causative factor may be difficult to find. Among the hazards which may be found in the history of the delinquent are these: retardation in school work, advanced age for grade level, lack of continuity in schooling, a conflict between the culture of the home and that of the community, discipline which is too lax or too severe, lack of suitable activities to occupy spare time, lack of security or affection, economic stress, residence in a "bad" neighborhood, low standards in the home, association with maladjusted persons, and rejection by others. Danger signals in the youngster himself are: inability to compete with others by normal means, attitudes of hate and hostility, a tendency toward bullying and destruction of property, isolation from normal contacts with others of his school group, undue responsiveness to suggestibility, opposition to authority, emotional outbursts, an underlying feeling of his own inferiority, an apparent lack of moral sensitivity, and a feeling that others are against him.

Children are helped in their behavior in precisely the same manner as they are helped in their emotional life. Unnecessary hazards should be removed as far as possible, and they should be helped to meet their difficulties more effectively. They will have a better chance if a better environment is provided; their physical needs are met; they are given security, acceptance, and affection; and tasks which are challenging but not overpowering are provided them.

Discipline, the training which is designed to develop orderly conduct, is one of the most difficult problems of the home, the school, and the community. Punishment undoubtedly has an important place in the control of behavior. One of the significant things that a child has to learn is that he may expect a penalty for misconduct. Acceptance of a person does not mean approval of what he does or protection from its consequences. But punishment can be and often is misused. Its probable effect on the person who is to receive it should always be kept in mind, for the goal is not to get even in some way but to influence the child toward right conduct. Punishment is only one aspect of discipline. Orderly conduct is developed, not simply or chiefly by punishment of misbehavior, but much more by a positive and orderly program in which the child participates.

Personal Responsibility

So far the discussion has been of the responsibility of the home, the community, and the school. But there is another side of the coin. As children move toward maturity they must also move toward adult responsibility. They must learn to help themselves. They must increasingly become partners in their own advancement. A careful reading of the statements contributed to this study by high school students reveals a most encouraging awareness of the need of an aggressive effort on the part of the Spanish-speaking students themselves. This is the more remarkable because as a group they are continually being reminded of their handicaps and encouraged to think of themselves as neglected if not actually mistreated. In many cases it is true that they have had unusual difficulties. The danger, however, lies not so much in the neglect or mistreatment itself, but in the sense of futility, the resentment, and the attitude of dependency or submission which easily develops. A chip-on-the-shoulder attitude is formed, so that the failures which come to everyone are shrugged off with the glib explanation that it wouldn't have happened if my name had been Jones. The damage which results is a damage to personality, and it makes the road ahead even harder. It is unfortunate to have a bad deal, if in fact it is true, but it is immeasurably worse to let that experience warp one's outlook on life. Getting ahead is a struggle, and a person with handicaps must accept the fact that circumstances have made it harder for him than for others whom he may know. That is the way of the world. Such a person cannot wisely waste time feeling sorry for himself or dissipate energy in futile anger and resentment.

The need to develop a sense of individual responsibility extends to all groups and to every level of education. One can be so intent on pointing out the responsibilities of the community at large, of parents, and of teachers that one weakens the sense of individual responsibility. As said in another connection, the persons under consideration hear this talk and are influenced by it. If the teacher is responsible for my learning, the child thinks, why should I worry? If the teacher can make the work interesting, well and good; I'll learn. If not, well it's his fault! This attitude can be seen as high as the level of the graduate school. If a child shows delinquent tendencies, a ready explanation is that something is wrong in his parents or in the community; he has been made that way, and so that is the way he must behave. As this is written the current issue of *Time* reports the case of a young man being chased by an officer who shouted, "You can't shoot me; I'm a teen-ager."

It is possible that the theorists who have been so bent on showing the responsibility of the community have overplayed their hand, and have forgotten that developing a sense of individual responsibility itself alters the factors which help to determine individual conduct. Perhaps they see the situation more realistically than appears, and have simply neglected one side of the story. In any case, in school and out, a little more of the spirit of the poem "Invictus" seems to be needed. Proclaiming one's self "master of my fate" and "captain of my soul" may be a little extreme; certainly, it will not change the hazards and conditions of life's voyage; but it may help to put one on the way to some worthwhile port.

Spanish-speaking boys and girls who think, perhaps rightly, that their difficulties are unusual may receive encouragement from the examples of persons within their group and outside who have found a realization of their dreams, often in spite of many barriers. Lino M. López has produced a remarkable booklet *(Colorado Latin American Personalities)* of biographies of "leaders of the Latin American community in Colorado." The seventy-six men and women included are only some of "the hundreds of examples of courage and progress among persons of Spanish heritage in this state." The positions held by the seventy-six include a great variety of jobs: legislator, attorney, minister, priest, union official, superintendent of schools, teacher in school and college, owner or operator of business firm, contractor, secretary, salesman, pharmacist, physician, dentist, laboratory technician, rancher, and others. One of the attorneys included in the booklet is quoted as giving this advice to "young Latin Americans today":

Work hard. Don't be discouraged by lack of money. Do not marry early. Be active in community work. Don't carry a chip on your shoulder about discrimination. Get an education. Vote and discharge all your other civic duties.

Another, a teacher, tells his students:

Get an education. In most instances it will mean a good deal of sacrifice, but in the long run it will pay greater dividends than any investment in time or money that an individual can make.

Another person said simply:

Never give up. If they can do it, so can you.

One of the women included in the study emphasized the importance of individual effort, saying:

I believe despite prejudice and ignorance, it is entirely up to the individual what he (or she) can become.

15. The School Staff

The quality of the educational opportunity provided for any children depends upon three interrelated factors. The first is the educational climate of the community and state, the will to educate and to provide the means for carrying forward a modern program of education. The second is organization and material equipment. Schools must be organized, housed, and provided with the equipment and supplies which are required for efficient teaching. The third—and if one of the three necessary factors can be emphasized above the others, the most important—is the professional staff. An able and inspired teacher can transform the most drab and uninteresting schoolroom into a learning laboratory in which children find security, happiness, and progress. But the drab and uninteresting schoolroom is likely to reflect both a poor educational climate in the community and a staff of poor quality. The principal who has no vision and the teacher who has neither interest nor preparation can do a miserable job even in the best of surroundings. But when the educational climate of the community is poor, when the material needs of modern education are not met, and when, in addition, the school staff is unqualified and uninspired, the situation is nearly hopeless.

One has only to visit schools to observe differences which stem from differences in the quality of administration and supervision. The responsibility begins with the community, first to give high priority to the education of all the children and then to see that the board of education is composed of capable, unselfish, and forward-looking citizens. It is then the duty of a board of education to employ the best chief administrative officer available, with his assistance to provide a professional staff of the highest quality, and then to demand and support a sound educational program. Strong community leadership may be required to see that the emphasis is not misplaced. It is easy to forget that education is now a serious professional job, requiring more time and effort than ever before. Some communities find it difficult to keep athletics, marching bands, entertainment, and the like in proper perspective. Some school staffs seem to be unaware of the vast amount to be learned to prepare for modern living and of the need to make the most of every hour and every day.

Personnel for Special Services

In the division of labor characteristic of modern schools there are four special staff members who should be available in every school system. The first is the school counselor or school psychologist, a professionally trained person to whom parents and children can go in confidence. He (or she) is not a disciplinarian. He supplements the work of the teacher in direct contact with pupils, and he provides the teacher with information which will be helpful in dealing with individuals. Problems of study programs, study skills, and vocational choice come to his attention. He assists boys and girls with personal problems, emotional difficulties, and social adjustment. It is not his business to hand out solutions to problems; it is to assist pupils to solve their own problems and to grow in self-direction.

A second specialized service is that of the visiting teacher, a social worker in the schools. To a certain extent the visiting teacher (usually a woman, but not necessarily so) is a counselor, but her main service is to provide an additional professional contact between the home and the school. She helps to interpret the school to the home and the home to the school. She is not an attendance officer, though obviously a better understanding between home and school promotes better understanding, better cooperation, and hence better attendance.

A third specialist on the modern school staff is the school nurse, who works in cooperation with the school physician as well as the teaching staff. It is her duty to help children keep strong and healthy, to help guard the school against infection, and to assist in dealing with unfavorable physical conditions, such as poor eyesight, defective hearing, undernourishment, and chronic heart difficulties.

A fourth special service is that of librarian. This specialist is not simply a custodian who issues and receives books from pupils and teachers. He (or she) is a specialist in children's literature and in library procedures. He helps teachers and pupils find materials suited to the interests and reading ability of the pupils who are to use them.

He helps make reading a successful, productive, and happy experience.

These are specialties which require preparation on the one hand and an opportunity to give the specialized service on the other. These points need to be emphasized because many people do not know, especially in relation to counselor and visiting teacher, that a high level of professional preparation is required, and because specialists are often unable to do their full jobs because of other work which is assigned to them. It is too easy, for example, to make a counselor merely by giving that label to a teacher, and to divert a visiting teacher from social work to attendance details.

The Teacher

The teacher is the chief working point of the whole educational machine in relation to the pupil. Others provide a background and assistance at various places, but the teacher carries the major responsibility for setting up the learning situation. Here is where weakness or strength has its most direct and most devastating or helpful influence on the pupil. It is a terrifying responsibility to determine, in the degree that a teacher does, the quality of the educational opportunity which a group of children has.

This is not the place to outline in detail the qualifications for teaching. As a matter of fact, very different people make excellent teachers. Except for some fatal weakness—character, for example—quite different personality patterns may be accepted as the basis for successful teaching. Exceptional strength in one direction may compensate for weakness in another. There are, however, three general areas in which the qualifications of teachers should be carefully considered.

The first is that of the teacher as a person. The teacher is himself a pattern which will be imitated and which will stimulate one kind of response or another. That is not the whole story. The kind of person a teacher is helps to determine the direction and intensity of his professional service. His ability, his interests, his ideals, and his patterns of action have an immediate influence upon his work.

Much is written about salaries as inducements for upgrading the teaching profession. There is no doubt that, by and large, poor financial status exerts a strong influence in the selective process and diverts many excellent prospects from teaching or takes them from the profession after a brief service. Better salaries will lessen adverse selections, but finance is only part of the teaching personnel situation.

Although ideally every man's occupation should be a "calling" in which a person tries to invest to the best advantage "that one talent which is death to hide," teaching is strongly influenced by the underlying motive of wanting to help people and to make the world a better place in which to live. Dollars can and should help teaching to compete with other professions, in which also one may give unselfish service, but there is need for a selection of persons who have the ideals and the zeal which are characteristic of great teachers.

The second area in which the qualification of teachers should be examined is sometimes called the subject-matter area. Obviously, teachers should themselves be well prepared in the knowledge and skills which they are to teach.

The third area is sometimes called, but somewhat incorrectly, professional preparation. This includes: (1) knowledge of the nature of children and society, of the educational system, and of techniques of teaching, and (2) skill in the process of teaching. Actually, professional preparation includes attention to the subject to be taught as well as to the person to be taught and the social structure in which the teaching is to be done.

There has been a great deal of confused thinking in relation to the "subject-matter" side and the "professional" side of a teacher's preparation. There is now such a large body of material in both areas that it is extremely difficult to strike a proper balance between the two in the time which can be devoted to teacher preparation. Whenever one college faculty has direction of one set of courses and a different faculty has direction of the other, coordination becomes a major problem. The result can easily be a power struggle which is difficult to resolve.

"Educationists" are frequently taunted by the fact (perfectly true) that many obviously excellent teachers have had few or no courses in education. It does not follow, however, that courses in education have no value or even little value. Nor is it true that teaching improves in proportion to the facts learned about education. Teaching is an art in which a considerable number of persons with favorable personal characteristics acquire skill without the benefit of formal courses in education. On the other hand, some who know a great deal about schools and teaching never master the art of teaching. It is not logical, however, to twist these facts into an argument for avoiding courses which deal specifically with professional problems. The pertinent question is the content of the courses, their relation to the teacher's job, and their place in the pattern which constitutes the total preparation of the teacher. A well designed internship in teaching helps to bridge the gap between knowledge (of both subject matter and child nature) and skill in teaching.

Special Qualifications for Teachers of Spanish-Speaking Children

What should be the special preparation for teaching Spanish-speaking children? In general outline the answer is obvious. First, these teachers should know the subject matter and should know ways of teaching the subject matter at points where it differs from the subject matter taught to other children. The chief points of difference are that English is taught to most of the children as a second language, and that a large number of Spanish-speaking children must be taught many things which at least a larger number of other children have learned outside of school. Second, these special teachers should know more about the Spanish-speaking child, his culture, and his problems, and more about the general problem of building a democratic society out of diverse populations. They should know more in these areas than they will likely know either from general education or from the usual professional courses. In other words, the teacher of Spanish-speaking children needs to know how to teach English as a second language, how to teach other materials to children who have a limited acquaintance with the language of instruction, how to teach children of below-average economic status and cultural level, and how to deal with problems of democratic living with different population groups. More than this, he needs to know how to recognize and deal with individual differences within the Spanish-speaking group itself, giving the intellectually able child and the less culturally handicapped child the opportunity from which each can profit most. No child should be neglected and no child should be held down by the weight of those who are less fortunate.

There is a question whether the special preparation for teaching Spanish-speaking children should be given in special courses. One runs headlong into the danger of trying to put too many courses into a preservice training program. The basic preparation for teaching is time-consuming. At present the prevailing tendency is against special courses for teachers of Spanish-speaking children, but the needs of these teachers are not necessarily forgotten. Certainly much can be included in regular courses and in practice teaching, provided the internship is with a group in which Spanish-speaking children are enrolled. Because of the mobility of teachers, in-service training—that is, training on the job—assumes special importance.

Replies to an inquiry made in this study indicated that only seven of sixty-six institutions currently offered special courses dealing with the education of the Spanish-speaking child. Three of the special courses were graduate courses. In one institution in New Mexico a course had been offered but had been abandoned because of dwindling enrollment. In another institution, a course was advertised but failed to attract enough students. Whether by special courses or otherwise, it is clear from visits to schools that the preparation of teachers is still a major problem. On the other hand, one finds a great deal of excellent teaching.

Should Spanish-speaking children be taught by members of the population group to which the children belong? Certainly the knowledge of Spanish which most members of the group possess can be an important asset if it is used skillfully, and membership in the group may increase one's sympathy for the children and one's understanding of their problems. But knowledge of the Spanish language, sympathy, and understanding are only part of the qualifications for effective teaching, and these characteristics may be found in persons who belong to a different population group. There is no sound basis for either special favor toward or discrimination against a teacher because he belongs to the Spanish-speaking or English-speaking group. If no Spanish-speaking teachers are employed in a community in which there are many Spanish-speaking pupils, there is cause for a strong suspicion that prejudice may have had an influence on teacher selection, but not necessarily so. Schools are not operated as welfare agencies to give employment in ratio to the size of subgroups, nor should membership in a particular subgroup rob one of equal chances on the basis of equal qualifications. Lack of mastery of English is likely to be the factor that will tip the scales against some applicants. Helen Hefferman, chief of the Bureau of Elementary Education in the California State Department of Education, notes in a personal letter that "hundreds of second and third generation Mexican-American young people" are teaching in the schools of that state and that "a creditable number have achieved positions in school administration and supervision as well as in the field of teacher education."

The Profession of Teaching

Teaching can be a drab and uninteresting occupation. Spending day after day alone with a group of children, struggling with the difficulties of those who learn slowly, trying to keep order among twenty or thirty wiggling children, grading papers, attending to school routines, making report cards, preparing lesson plans, going over the same material year after year—such a picture does not look very inviting. And if that is all which one can see in teaching, it is a job to be avoided.

On the other hand, teaching can be a profession full of interesting activities, and even routine work can be transformed by a realization of its significance. At whatever grade level the teacher operates he is passing on to a new generation the inheritance of the ages. He is helping individuals to find direction and to develop their capacities. He is increasing the value of human resources, the world's greatest asset. Teaching in communities in which both Spanish-speaking children and English-speaking children are enrolled is especially challenging because of the opportunity to deal constructively with problems of exceptional difficulty. It is reassuring and inspiring to visit schools where gifted and devoted teachers and other members of the professional staff are at work. It is doubly so if the community has provided the physical plant, the laboratories, the libraries, and the equipment of a modern school.

16. Cooperation in the Educative Process

The education of children is a community-wide project. In fact the responsibility goes far beyond the local community. The school is a special agency set up and maintained by the people, but it provides only a part of the learning opportunities of children. The community is itself an educational agency. It cannot be otherwise, for children learn from their total environment. The out-of-school environment can reinforce or weaken the work of the schools. It is not enough that a community support its schools; it should mobilize its resources to make the out-of-school environment one which will promote the highest and best development of its children.

The Home

Normally the home is the agency which gives children their early learning experiences. Here they learn the basic skills of everyday life, here they learn the use of language, here they form their early attitudes, and here they develop the emotional trends which help or hinder them in later years. If the home environment is culturally rich, their learning may be deep and extensive in language, literature, art, music, vocational skills, citizenship, religion, and other areas. On the other hand, if the home environment is culturally poor, their learning is correspondingly limited.

It would be difficult to overemphasize the importance of doing everything possible to make the home of every child a center which provides suitable educational opportunities in a secure and helpful environment, a center free from social and emotional disorders, a center stimulating the child toward high ideals. The tragedy of long-continued poverty and accompanying low cultural level is that the child from such an environment is deprived of a significant part of a normal educational opportunity.

Although a home is limited by economic conditions, it need not be entirely a victim of external circumstances. Within the conditions which circumstances force upon them, the parents can do much or little toward giving their children a suitable learning opportunity. In this they often need guidance in order to see the opportunities open to them. Relief is not enough; indeed, as previously stated, without guidance, relief tends to be self-perpetuating. Many parents who are handicapped by poverty need to be shown a better way of life than they have ever known, and they need to be shown what can be done within the means available to them.

Professional workers and organizations which support the home to make it a better place for children are by the nature of their work important contributors to education. The public-health nurse, the social worker, and the minister or priest who give support and guidance to the family are thereby doing an educational service. Similarly a labor union, a chamber of commerce, a community house, a social organization, a guidance clinic, a church, or other agency is contributing to education when it helps to raise the economic level of the family or to improve the insight, the habits, the emotions, and the interests of the parents. In short, whatever makes the home a better place for children helps with their education, and whatever weakens the home is an enemy to education.

Perhaps this is the place to point out that one of the greatest enemies of the home at all economic levels is alcoholism. All of the devastating effects of the misuse of alcohol alleged by the temperance advocates of another generation are still to be found. Alcoholism is a social and health problem for which the community has found no adequate solution. In the meantime, drink leaves a ghastly trail of ruined careers, broken homes, economic loss, disease, crime, poverty, death —and children who never have a fair chance. More time and energy are spent dealing with the ugly results than finding effective ways of prevention.

The magnitude of the problem is suggested by the following quotation from the *Journal of the American Medical Association* of February 16, 1957, (a guest editorial by Dr. Marvin A. Block, chairman of the Committee on Alcoholism):

Chronic alcoholism in the United States has reached the alarming degree where it directly affects about 20 million people, who are the families of alcoholic patients, estimated at almost 5 million. Indirectly, every man, woman, and child in the United States is affected sociologically, psychologically, and economically by this problem. For many years, the problem of coping with alcoholism was left for the most part to law enforcement, religion, and the social agencies of the country. Only comparatively recently has the public begun to accept it as a disease entity that requires medical attention. This offers to the medical profession a challenge it cannot ignore.

The *Spotlight on Alcoholism* (Winter, 1960) issued by the Texas Commission on Alcoholism quotes an estimate that the bill for alcoholism in the United States is a billion dollars a year "in time lost, accidents, reduced and spoiled work output, [and] welfare payments to the families of sick alcoholics." It points out that this direct cost does not include "crime attributable to alcoholism, human misery, broken homes, frustrated children, warped personalities, [and] dulled minds."

The Church

Have we not all one father? hath not one God created us? why do we deal treacherously every man against his brother . . . ?

—Malachi 2:10

Neither pray I for these alone, but for them also which shall believe on me through their word; that they all may be one . . .

—John 17:20–21

The teaching of the fatherhood of God seems to commit the church, not only to an interest in Spanish-speaking people on an equal basis with other people, but also to an interest in brotherly understanding and brotherly attitudes between members of different groups. In theory at least, it is only a short step then to the concept of a united community consisting of both English-speaking and Spanish-speaking people. The church now ministers to both groups, but its ministry is often given to each group in relative isolation from the other. Typically the Spanish-speaking people of a community are in one congregation and the English-speaking people in another, even when both are part of the same denomination.

The isolation of Spanish-speaking and English-speaking people in different congregations is partly a matter of geography and residence. The two groups often live in relative isolation. Related to this is economic status, which tends toward separate residence and separate congregations, not only for the two groups, but also for subgroups within each group. The factor of chief influence on isolation, however, is language. Expressing the influence of residence, a Protestant churchman wrote in a personal letter:

We have a policy in our Church where we begin no churches which are exclusively for one particular ethnic group or any other kind of group but are simply churches for the people, and if it happens to be in a predominantly Mexican-American area, the majority of the people undoubtedly will be of this background.

A Protestant bishop explains in a personal letter that the existence of separate churches for Spanish-speaking people is necessary to reach these people:

I know of no congregation of a Christian church that restricts membership to a certain racial group. . . . Any Latin-American is welcome to become a member of any Anglo Church [of the Bishop's denomination] . . . scores, if not hundreds of Latin-Americans are members of Anglo Churches [of his denomination] in Texas. . . . The vast majority of the Latin-Americans in this country are in language, culture and customs aliens, and unable and unwilling to attempt to become integrated into Anglo Churches. It is to reach these that the . . . Conference, of its own free will elects to be separated; they do not call themselves segregated; rather they proudly call themselves autonomous, and they are able in this fashion to establish contact with the vast throngs of Latins about them, who would never enter an Anglo church.

Another churchman points in a personal letter to programs for bringing Spanish-speaking and English-speaking people into the same congregation:

This is often done by means of Spanish-speaking activity being carried on simultaneously with English-speaking activity in the same church so that the members of the families of Spanish-speaking background may choose according to their own personal preference which language they will use.

The complexities produced by the language situation are illustrated by a statement of the same writer that

many of the Spanish-speaking churches are using English literature for all age groups except the very young and the very old . . . because of the fact that all of the young people, except a few who are more recently come from Mexico, have received their schooling in the United States and read English rather than Spanish.

The partial conflict between assimilation and service is well recognized by the same writer, who sees an advantage in a homogeneous group from the standpoint of service and points out that even with these groups there is some opportunity for assimilation:

. . . in some cases, we find that in order to obtain the spiritual results desired, it is preferable to deal with the people in a homogeneous group where you can communicate with them more acceptably in their own language rather than to have them in the English-speaking group where they would no doubt progress toward assimilation more rapidly, but on account of the difficulty of communication, might not be so well served spiritually. But, on the other hand, these Spanish-speaking congregations are an integral part of the general organization of [the church] life in the district or county associations, in the state organizations, and in the . . . Convention. Thus they participate in the life of the denomination with everyone else, and thereby have opportunity toward assimilation.

Another churchman lists in a personal letter different programs according to language facility, and finds that many parents are eager to retain the Spanish language for their children:

In our churches we have three separate types of programs that ultimately blend into one. The first type is for the group of Latin Americans who speak and understand Spanish. The second is for that bilingual group which speaks both Spanish and English but feels more at home speaking Spanish among Spanish-speaking people. The third group is for those who speak English and prefer it and are thoroughly assimilated into the social and sociological atmosphere of our Texas life. It is our hope and aim to bring all of these people to be thoroughly assimilated. Interestingly enough, there is more resistance on the part of the Spanish-speaking people to assimilation than there is on the part of the Anglo Americans with whom they associate. For example, among the parents, particularly those with limited training, there is an insistence that even the worship service and study in Sunday School be in Spanish, because they want their children to retain the mother tongue. Often it appears more important to the parents for their children to learn Spanish than it is for them to learn religious truths.

The Catholic Church, to which by far the greatest number of Spanish-speaking people belong, is also interested in bringing the groups together and is working toward that end. A churchman who is acquainted with the work of the Bishop's Committee for the Spanish-Speaking expresses in a personal letter a most hopeful point of view and emphasizes the role of education:

Segregation is still a very vicious element in our society. I do believe we can assimilate these people into our way of life without losing their identity altogether. This assimilation will come about quickest through education. An educated people never remain subservient to the desires of others. The Church is certainly interested in this but frequently through separate Churches for the Mexican people the contrary idea might be given. Here . . . [the Archbishop] has eliminated all national churches and the process of assimilation into parish life is progressing rather well although not as swiftly and perfectly as we would wish.

He quotes a memorandum on the progress achieved:

The assimilation of our Spanish-speaking people here has progressed remarkably in recent years so far as the educated Mexicans are concerned. Many of those who are uneducated are illiterate and their assimilation will not be easy . . .

The American Friends Service Committee, "a Quaker organization devoted to peace and good will among men," includes in its many activities a direct approach to the problem of better intergroup relations through bringing members of different groups together and increasing understanding and friendship in various ways.

The discussion of the work of the church in intergroup relations should not leave the impression that this is its chief contribution to education. The spiritual service of the church in giving a helpful philosophy of life, in providing an escape from the feeling of guilt, in helping people to adjust to the stern conditions of life and to have confidence in the future, in stimulating its members toward high ideals and vigorous support of the right, and in providing comfort as one approaches the "valley of the shadow of death"—this service is distinctly and directly educational. Many denominations also support schools, as well as community centers, clinics, and other welfare services.

A Catholic correspondent lists a number of agencies which show the interest of this church in its Spanish-speaking population:

Administrators in the Archdiocese of . . . take an active interest in the education of Spanish-speaking children. . . . Every parish is instructed to provide a school for the children of its boundaries. . . . Many archdiocesan agencies are devoted almost exclusively to the welfare of the Spanish-speaking, and the benefits of this devotion redound indirectly, and sometimes directly to education. These include: Bishop's Committee for the Spanish Speaking, Catholic Action, Catholic Boy and Girl Scouts, Catholic

Welfare Bureau, Catholic Youth Organization, Four Community Centers (some with clinics), Day Nurseries, Home for Working Girls, Confraternity of Christian Doctrine.

The interest of other churches in the welfare of the Spanish-speaking people is illustrated by the 1959 Conference on Latin-American Relations in the Southwestern United States conducted under the auspices of the Division of Racial Minorities of the National Council of the Episcopal Church. In this Conference, with the assistance of nationally known Spanish-speaking leaders and others, the members sought to define the problems of the Spanish-speaking people of the Southwest more clearly and to find ways of improving the work of the Episcopal Church with them. One of the Spanish-speaking participants, Ralph Estrada, supreme president of Alianza Hispano-Americano (a regional organization devoted to improving the status of Spanish-speaking people), expressed the belief that the two populations of the Southwest would become one:

The day will come, I believe, when the people of the Southwest will be one people and not two, a blending of two societies and two cultures, of which we can say only that the members thereof are Americans.

The church faces the task of continuing to interest and challenge the loyalties of the people whom it would serve. This may require special attention. At any rate, as quoted in *Time* (December 1, 1958, p. 38), Cardinal Cushing of Boston notes a lessening of interest in the church on the part of poor people:

When I was a boy living in a poor section, coming from hardworking people, it was unknown that the poor would not go to church. It was the last thing they would neglect. Now, with social security checks coming in, they are not interested in the church. They go from day to day knowing that tomorrow will take care of itself. Their former dependence on God, upon the personal charity of those representing religion, has been psychologically unsettled by the welfare state.

Other Agencies—the Denver Program

Denver, Colorado, is outstanding in its work with the problems presented by the presence of a large Spanish-speaking population. In the 1960 U.S. census the Spanish-surname population of the Denver "standard metropolitan statistical area" was 60,294 about 6-½ per cent of the total. Conditions which facilitate the progress which Denver is making in dealing with these problems include (1) its distance from the Mexican border and the resulting smaller migration into the city of persons directly from Mexico, and (2) the small proportion of the total population who are Spanish-speaking. One bit of evidence of the relation of the changing nature of the population to distance from the border is the fact that relatively few children enter the Denver schools without some knowledge of English. It is significant too that the population is becoming less mobile; fewer families than formerly migrate with the crops.

Kindergartens in the schools give the Spanish-speaking child a tremendous boost toward the acquisition of enough facility in language to enter a reading program in the first grade. Much has been done also to create a better understanding of Spanish-speaking people by teachers and pupils. In 1951 the schools published the first of a proposed series of books under the general title of *People of Denver*, designed to provide for pupils in the junior high schools information on "what racial and nationality groups settled here, where they came from, why they left their previous homes, why they came here, what they found, how they adjusted themselves to the physical and social conditions, and what share each group has had in the building of our city as we know it today." The first volume deals with *Spanish-Speaking People*. With great sensitivity and evident scholarship, the committee has produced a remarkable volume. The book helps to put the difficulties of the Spanish-speaking people in proper perspective and to show that these people make a real contribution to the community.

The Denver Juvenile Court, of worldwide fame, must be listed as one of the constructive forces for the youth of the entire community. Not only does it help boys and girls who get into trouble, but it gives the community a better understanding of the problems of youth and strengthens the character-building forces of the community.

Denver Boys, Inc., is a unique organization, dating from 1946, formed "as a result of the interest of school people and the Rotary Club of Denver in the problems of boys." It is an example of community effort in which the Rotary Club of Denver, the City Recreation Department, the State Employment Service, and the Denver Public Schools cooperate. It has a trained staff of counselors who give help in finding employment and preparing the boy for the job, in steering boys into recreational activities, and in helping them with health and educational problems. In its "sponsors" program an adult plays the role of a friend to an individual boy who is in need of helpful adult companionship. In the first twelve years of its existence Denver Boys, Inc., made more than seventeen thousand part-time and full-time job placements. During this period it provided counseling for 450 boys. Of 281 closed cases nearly 93 per cent are reported to have made a satisfactory adjustment.

The Denver Commission on Community Relations illustrates a community effort to improve human relations by working specifically toward that objective. The present Commission was established by city ordinance in 1959, but it has a longer history under another name. The Denver Commission on Human Relations began as a committee appointed by the mayor in 1947 and was established by the City Council in 1951. In 1953 a joint city-school project was started with the employment of Lino M. López as consultant in human relations. This project "was designed to demonstrate techniques in securing increased participation by Spanish-speaking citizens in school and community activities, and to improve the understanding of the cultural factors which affect behavior" (Second Annual Report of the Commission, p. 5).

The ordinance creating the present Commission states the need for the Commission in forceful language:

WHEREAS, in the city of Denver, with its great cosmopolitan population consisting of large numbers of people of every race, color, creed, national origin and ancestry, no greater menace threatens the peace, good order, security and welfare of the city and its inhabitants than the existence within it of groups antagonistic to one another and prejudiced against each other because of differences of race, color, creed, national origin or ancestry; and

WHEREAS, it is hereby found that prejudice and discrimination against any individual or group because of race, color, creed, national origin or ancestry is a threat to democracy, the cornerstone of our American tradition, and menaces peace and public welfare. To eliminate such prejudice and discrimination an instrumentality of government should be established through which the citizens of Denver may be kept informed of developments of Community Relations; from which the elected and appointed officials, and the departments of this city may obtain expert advice and assistance in adopting those measures to keep peace and good order and harmony among the citizens of Denver, and to bring about and maintain harmony and avoid inter-group tensions and to promote tolerance and good will, and to insure equality of treatment and of opportunity to all regardless of race, color, creed, national origin or ancestry . . .

There is hereby created a Commission on Community Relations . . .

The ordinances provided that the powers and duties of the Commission should include among others the following:

To receive and investigate complaints and to initiate its own investigation ...

To hold hearings, subpoena witnesses, compel their attendance, administer oaths, take the testimony of any person under oath ...

To issue such publications and such reports of investigations and research as in its judgment will tend to minimize or eliminate prejudice, intolerance, bigotry, disorder and discrimination or tend to promote good will.

To enlist the cooperation of the various racial, religious and ethnic groups, community organizations, labor organizations, fraternal and benevolent associations, and other groups in an educational campaign devoted to teaching the need for eliminating group prejudice, intolerance, bigotry, disorder and discrimination.

To cooperate with federal, state, and city agencies, including the department of education, in developing courses of instruction for presentation in public and private schools, public libraries, museums and other suitable places showing the contributions of the various races, religious and ethnic groups to the culture and traditions of our city and nation, the menace of prejudice, intolerance, bigotry and discrimination, and the need for mutual self-respect.

To promote the establishment of local community organizations, when and where it may deem it desirable, consisting of representatives of different groups in such community, to plan and carry out educational programs in such community.

In 1959 the United Latin-Americans Organization was formed at the suggestion of the mayor and the Commission on Human Relations to provide "a group through which city agencies could work with the Spanish-speaking people." The objectives are: "to work towards the complete civic, economic and political integration of all residents of Hispanic descent, to the end that this group will enjoy all the rights, privileges, and opportunities afforded all other citizens, as well as to share in all responsibility equally with other residents" (Commission, Sixth Annual Report, p. 15).

A State Agency

The Good Neighbor Commission of Texas is a state agency devoted to the promotion of understanding and good will. Beginning as a non-state organization in 1943, it received temporary status as an agency of the state in 1945 and permanent status in 1947. The nine members of the Commission are appointed by the governor, and they in turn appoint an executive director. As suggested by its name, the primary objective of the Commission is to promote good relations with Mexico. One of its concerns is the prevention of discrimination in any phase of community life against Mexican citizens or United States citizens of Mexican ancestry. Education in the broad sense is its chief activity. It helps to create mutual understanding and to bring leaders together in the solution of common problems. Since 1950 the Commission has sponsored the Pan American Student Forum, a Texas organization of students in junior and senior high schools. In 1961 the Forum had some 130 chapters enrolling seven or eight thousand members.

Congress of Parents and Teachers

The Congress of Parents and Teachers, familiarly known as the PTA, is an organization for drawing the home and the school into a closer and more cooperative relationship. Its usefulness appears to vary greatly from place to place. As in all organizations the vision and quality of the leadership are large determining factors in the direction and effectiveness of the work of the organization. In schools where the socioeconomic condition of the families is low, it is usually difficult to enlist the full cooperation of parents and to find adequate leadership. If the school has both Spanish-speaking and English-speaking parents, the building of a single effective PTA is especially difficult. A New Mexico PTA correspondent points to a continuous effort to improve intergroup relations and emphasizes the role of education and understanding:

Education and the ability to understand one another seem to decrease problems between Spanish-speaking and English-speaking people. As in all social problems, when people understand one another . . . in language, customs, culture, etc., the ability to solve all problems increases.

Nonprofessional Teaching Aides

The nonprofessional educational resources of a community are seldom if ever fully realized. On a voluntary basis or with relatively little cost teachers may be provided with extremely valuable assistance by recruiting qualified persons from the community. These teaching aides, with a minimum of orientation, would operate under the direction of the professionally trained staff, performing duties for which they are qualified. Hospitals and various service organizations such as the Red Cross have long known how to supplement their staff through volunteer help. It is time for schools to follow their example more fully and add teaching aides to "homeroom mothers" and "Scout leaders," whose value has long been demonstrated.

The possibility of supplementing the teaching staff with nonprofessional aides is especially attractive in the teaching of English to foreign-language children. At the kindergarten and primary levels, for example, the children need much more contact with good patterns of English speech and much more practice in using English than the teacher alone can provide. Teaching aides can enormously increase the opportunities to hear and use English. At the higher levels these aides can assist in correcting written work so that a child may know where his mistakes lie and may have a reinforcement of his correct responses before it is too late for reinforcement to be effective.

It should be emphasized that all nonprofessional assistance will require careful planning and careful control to give it direction and to make it effective. The work of the teaching aides should be an integral part of the teaching program provided for the children, not an extracurricular project.

Organizations of Spanish-Speaking People

The educational opportunities of Spanish-speaking children have been improved by the activities of organizations within the Spanish-speaking group. The improvement is at times a result of the improvement of social and economic conditions and at times the result of efforts specifically directed toward education. The Alianza Hispano-Americana is an organization dating from 1894, the League of United Latin-American Citizens (LULAC) from 1929, and the American GI Forum from 1948. The latter two are probably most widely known. The Latin-American Educational Foundation of Denver illustrates a type of local effort which may be quite helpful. Its purpose is to provide funds on a loan or scholarship basis for students who need help in order to attend college.

The Alianza Hispano-Americana has its home office in Tucson, Arizona, and has local units (Logias or Lodges) in each of the five states of the Southwest. As both a fraternal society and an insurance organization, it works to advance the welfare of Spanish-speaking people generally. It publishes a journal, *Alianza,* and actively supports a scholarship program for students of "Mexican-American descent" through a subsidiary known as "Alianza Scholarship Foundation." In the June-August-September, 1960, number of *Alianza* an editorial proposes a national organization for united Latins. The following paragraph suggests that there may be some difficulties in forming such an organization:

Yet many questions must be answered before Mexican-Americans can realize an effective unity, dedicated to serving the interests of the many instead of the few. Is the Mexican-American enough of an intellectual to appreciate the value of a proposed Congress of United Latins? More important, is he as emotionally mature as he should be to ignore petty jealousies and trivial bickerings which have materially impeded his progress?

In an undated pamphlet, "Toward the Education of a People," education is said to be the key to a change in culture patterns, to a situation in which the two great peoples of the Southwest recognize the values of the other—a "looking across" rather than a "looking up" and "looking down" relationship. The need is pointed out for a greater number of the Spanish-speaking people "to reach the level of the professional man, the educator or the entrepreneur." In the work of Alianza Hispano-Americana may be seen the same apparent contradiction which is seen elsewhere—the attempt to build a strong organization *of* Spanish-speaking people *for* Spanish-speaking people, but along with it the expressed desire to have their people participate as full members of a community composed of "one people" rather than of two separately operating groups. Perhaps a strong unilateral organization is regarded as a necessary step toward eventual civic unity.

The League of United Latin American Citizens, a national organization with officers in many states, has as its motto "All for one, and one for all." As previously noted, summer schools for Texas preschool children were supported by LULAC. A New Mexico officer of the League lists the following among the activities of the organization in that state: (1) sponsorship of scholarships and student exchange programs, (2) protection of the education of the Spanish-speaking people, (3) placement of "deserving Spanish-American individuals in permanent and important positions," (4) support of Spanish programs in the public schools, (5) support of city athletic leagues to aid youth in general and to create good relationships between Spanish-speaking individuals and others, (6) participation in community services to the needy, (7) publicizing the names of Spanish-speaking persons who perform meritorious activities, (8) encouragement of behavior in accordance with best philosophies of life.

Information on the activities of the American GI Forum was obtained from an officer of the Texas organization. The GI Forum was organized in 1948 following World War II and is primarily but not exclusively a veterans' organization. It has been active in attempts to promote the general welfare of Spanish-speaking people. For example, it has opposed the importation of agricultural laborers from Mexico on the ground that such importation tends to depress the wages and living conditions of domestic migrant labor. In 1953 it sponsored with the American Federation of Labor a study of illegal entrants from Mexico, and has opposed discrimination in public employment. Although the organization is forbidden by its constitution to endorse any party or candidate for public office, it takes a lively interest in government. On both the state and the national levels the Forum supports legislation thought to favor the lower economic classes.

The GI Forum has opposed the segregation of Spanish-speaking children in the schools, and it has petitioned the schools for preschool work for teaching English to Spanish-speaking children before they enter the first grade. The organization encourages "back-to-school" drives and attempts to get migrant families to let their children stay at home to attend school through the entire year. It sponsors scholarships, particularly to help high school students remain in school. It is interested in the teaching of Spanish as a means of improving intergroup relations.

Difficulties of Leadership

Various writers have commented on a lack of strong and effective leadership within the Spanish-speaking population of the Southwest. Writing in the *Southwestern Political and Social Science Quarterly* in 1929 on the League of United Latin-American Citizens, O. Douglas Weeks raised the question of adequate leadership in relation to the future of the organization. He remarked, "It is commonly thought to be a Latin, and particularly a Mexican, trait to make dramatic beginnings amidst a great show of idealism, enthusiasm, and unanimity, and then to lie back and let the undertaking thus launched go on for itself."

Watson and Samora, analyzing conditions in a bicultural Colorado community, state that "disunity is a large factor in the lack of po-

litical power of the Spanish" (*American Sociological Review*, 1954).
They suggest that the inadequacy of leadership results largely from
four conditions: (1) the traditional pattern of leadership based upon
the authoritarian relationship of *patrón* and *peón* is not adapted to
present conditions; (2) many of the Spanish goals and values (for
example, better jobs, more material things, and learning English) are
similar to those of the Anglo culture and for that reason leaders need
to be well adjusted to and familiar with the Anglo culture; (3) persons of Spanish background who are qualified for success in Anglo
culture are regarded with suspicion by their fellows, and there is some
feeling that their positions have come from "selling out to the Anglo";
(4) potential leaders are relatively well adapted to the Anglo system
and are absorbed to a degree into the larger social structure.

There is no doubt that the number of potential leaders among
Spanish-speaking people is increasing rapidly. The general level of
education is rising, more persons are acquiring an adequate mastery
of English, and a greater number are entering the professions. If
Watson and Samora's opinion is accepted that qualifications for
leadership in the larger community make Spanish-speaking persons
less acceptable to their own people, the outlook for building rapidly
a united community seems a bit discouraging. Perhaps slow progress
is inevitable, but certainly there will be progress as the economic,
cultural, and educational levels of the people rise.

Unity or Isolation in Community Effort

Examples of organizations and activities related to the education
of Spanish-speaking children could be increased indefinitely, but
those which have been discussed will serve the purpose of this book.
There remains to be added only an emphasis upon the need for unity
rather than isolation in both organization and activity.

Recalling again that one assumed objective is a unified community, the organization of groups and the initiation of activities which
are essentially unilateral should be viewed with concern. There is a
real danger that the effort of a Spanish-speaking group to help itself
or the effort of an English-speaking group to help the Spanish-speaking people alone will operate to continue rather than to overcome the
isolation of the Spanish-speaking people. When groups such as these
work separately they tend to continue to work separately and thus to
defeat the goal of a united community. At some point, if the two

peoples are to become one, there must be a transition from unilateral organization and unilateral effort to a united program. As long as the major divisions within the community are based on membership in a Spanish-speaking or an English-speaking group, the people will remain divided.

17. The Case in Brief

The population of the five states of the Southwest consists primarily of two intermingling groups, Spanish-speaking and English-speaking, with smaller but significant numbers in other groups. Together they face the task of building and maintaining a democratic society with benefits and responsibilities which are shared by all. The task is not easy anywhere, but it is especially difficult in the Southwest because of differences in language, culture, and economic status, and because of antagonisms deeply rooted in the past.

As a matter of both individual rights and public welfare, the people are committed to a policy of education for all children. The democratic process demands educated citizens. Even actual survival as a great nation requires careful attention to human resources. Education is equally vital for individual welfare, for only through education can latent possibilities be realized. The primary concern in this book has been the problem of educating Spanish-speaking children.

The Heavy Hand of the Past

Until recently, as history goes, the English-speaking people and the Spanish-speaking people of the world have been rivals in the strife for economic welfare and political power and at times even enemies in battle. The struggle for position in the New World at the time of its discovery and colonization continued in one form or another for centuries. The Spanish-speaking people were the first of the two groups in the territory which became the Southwestern states, coming into this area from what is now Mexico. In time the spread of the English-speaking people from the north and east reached the Southwest, and they rapidly became the majority group in the region as a whole. First the Texas Revolution, then the annexation of Texas, then the war between the United States and Mexico, and finally the purchase of a small strip of land changed the Southwest from being a part of Mexico, with its Spanish language and Spanish-Indian culture, to being a part of the United States, with its English language and North European culture. But the transfer of national sovereignty did not change the nature of the populations. The problem of building the two groups into a united community remained. Only the direction of the movement was changed. The task had been to assimilate English-speaking people into a Spanish-speaking, Mexican community. With the change in national sovereignty the Spanish-speaking people had to become part of an English-speaking nation. More than a century has passed and the people of the Southwest, both English-speaking and Spanish-speaking, are still struggling with the problem.

The solution to the problem of building and maintaining a democratic society in the Southwest cannot be found in a kind of federation of Spanish-speaking and English-speaking states. The representatives of the two cultures live together, not in districts from which separate states can be carved. To be sure, in some communities and subcommunities there are concentrations of population which are almost wholly either English-speaking or Spanish-speaking, but in larger units the peoples are inextricably mixed. Even in smaller sections segregation is breaking down, though not nearly as fast as would serve the common welfare.

Difficulties of Spanish-Speaking Children

Cultural differences and enmities inherited from the past tend to keep the two peoples divided, but the most serious handicaps to building one society out of these diverse elements and the most troublesome problems in the education of Spanish-speaking children are those of language and of low economic level, with its accompanying cultural deficiencies.

There are extreme differences in the Spanish-speaking population as the term is used in this report. Some members speak only English and some speak both English and Spanish, but for most of the group, English is still to be learned as a second language. Again, some Spanish-speaking people are wealthy, and many are of the middle class economically. Likewise, many are of superior cultural level. The great majority, however, are of the lower economic levels, and a large number have the cultural traits associated with long-continued poverty. Additions to the original population by immigration from

Mexico in this century have in overwhelming proportion been persons of relatively low economic status and cultural level. Spanish continues to be the home language of most families because of the nearness to Spanish-speaking Mexico, because of constant migration across the border, because of social pressures exerted by the older members of the population, and because of the inherent difficulties of establishing new language habits.

In general, Spanish-speaking children at school entrance have more to learn: a second language and also the knowledge and skills of which they have been deprived by poor home opportunities. They cannot start their schooling at the level already reached by English-speaking children. Starting behind and facing greater handicaps, the Spanish-speaking children tend to fall farther and farther behind with advance in grade. The progress of many is hindered by poor attendance resulting from the poverty of the home and the ignorance of their parents. Many find the going too hard, in part because the school program is not adapted to their needs, and drop out when age permits them to do so. There are exceptions to this trend; many make satisfactory progress, and a large number are even outstanding.

The difficulties of Spanish-speaking children extend beyond the learning of a second language and the acquisition of knowledge. It is difficult also for them to develop normal interests, healthy emotional habits, and helpful patterns of action. Some observers would refer to this problem as one of emotional and social adjustment. Every child faces hazards to his mental health, but the hazards of large numbers of Spanish-speaking children are almost overwhelming. They are caught in the conflict of two groups and two cultures in the same community. As they try to find a place in the larger community, they are often criticized by their own people and rejected to some extent by others. If not rejected, at least they have no easy way to establish the associations which would lead to acceptance. Many of them have no adequate mastery of either the Spanish or the English language. The Spanish of their culture-deprived homes is adequate for little more than basic community associations, and their English lags behind, often far behind, that of others of their age level. Large numbers of these children are unable to compete on an equal basis with other children in material possessions, in the social status of their families, and in that part of their school work which depends heavily upon experience and mastery of English. The poor quality of their spoken English handicaps them in securing employment. Even those who rise above these handicaps and those who have never been so handicapped are sometimes confronted by an attitude which tends to overlook individual merit. This of course is unjust, but it is a reality. Finally, the Spanish-speaking child shares the historical antagonisms and attitudes of his family.

Personality Development

These difficulties tend to produce abnormalities of personality and behavior which are in themselves undesirable and which interfere with learning. For one thing there is a feeling of insecurity. The child is not comfortable, and he cannot give his full attention to learning activities. Then there is frustration and disappointment, often resentment. Sometimes a child who cannot face his real deficiencies finds an escape in blaming the other group, developing a chip-on-the-shoulder attitude which may continue through adult life. In his thinking, it is the prejudice of others, not his own deficiencies, which seems to stand in his way. Another child becomes submissive, overwhelmed by failure. He gives up and quits struggling. He *assumes* the inferior position which the less fortunate of his group seem to occupy, and he accepts the inferiority which others unjustly ascribe to him. In his own thought, feeling, and behavior he puts himself in an inferior position. He feels that there is nothing much ahead for him; and because of this feeling, not because of actual inferiority, there probably is not anything very inspiring in his future. One of the great problems of the school and the community is to prevent discouragement, to inspire hope, and to stimulate the development of normal traits of personality.

The tendency of many to think too much of their own misfortunes rather than to give undivided attention to the situations with which they must deal leads toward defeat. A vicious circle is created: a person's attitudes work against accomplishment, and resulting failures increase his maladjustment. Participation in the larger community is hindered by antagonisms developed in his home and nourished by his own experiences. Sometimes the maladjustment takes the form of antisocial behavior and in extreme cases, of actual delinquency.

Helping Children with Their Problems

The solution is easy in principle: remove as far as possible the conditions which handicap the children, provide educational opportunities adapted to their needs, and help them develop normal personal and social traits in spite of the extreme difficulties with which they must deal. In practice, none of these is easy, but there are definite things which can be done. Many of them in fact are being done in various places—slowly to be sure, but, in the testimony of educators and other observers, progress is being made.

First and foremost as a prerequisite to progress is a dedication to the principles of democracy and a firm will to educate all children. Despite our ready affirmation of democratic principles, there are still many who give consideration to very little beyond the welfare of their immediate group. They are almost totally blind to the fact that even their own welfare is intimately tied to the welfare of all. Many also do not realize that the world is changing. They cling tenaciously to the old familiar ways and resist even constructive change. To meet this situation powerful leaders are needed within the subgroups, leaders to help the people see their problems more clearly and to move ahead more rapidly.

Compulsion may enforce legal rights, and sometimes it challenges people to new ways of thinking, but much more is needed. To bring about fundamental changes of thought and feeling, to inspire a new consciousness of the brotherhood of man, to create an awareness of how the democratic ideal may be realized—all of these call for the aggressive leadership of persons of prestige and vision.

As the Spanish-speaking and English-speaking people of the Southwest continue to intermingle and to live under the same environmental influences their cultural differences will become less and less. People will become more tolerant of the differences which remain, and it is to be hoped that in the conflict of cultures the best aspects of each will survive. Historical antagonisms will diminish with increased understanding and with participation in common tasks.

The improvement of general economic conditions will be a long-term process, depending on many factors and requiring the cooperation of agriculture, industry, and government. Fortunately, there are enough materials and human resources to support the population at a high level. The economy in the United States is clearly moving upward, and it is moving upward also in Mexico. But progress should be speeded up and adjustments made which will achieve a better distribution of the fruits of common effort. Here again leadership is needed.

Although language is becoming less of a problem as more and more children learn English at home, it is still a major difficulty with thousands of children. Because of migration and because of nearness to a Spanish-speaking nation, there is no likelihood that the language problem will disappear at any time which can be foreseen. The tragedy is that the Spanish-speaking group handicaps its own children to the extent that it refuses or neglects to help teach them English. Hearing only Spanish at home, the children enter school with a handicap, and continuing to hear only Spanish at home they fall farther behind in their unequal struggle with an English-speaking environment.

Educational Adjustments

One of the greatest single steps which the public can authorize the school to take—a step which many schools have already taken—is to extend its work downward to the five-year-old child, with a program skillfully directed, in the case of Spanish-speaking children, toward the teaching of English, and toward building up basic experiences and concepts for those who come from culture-deprived homes. A summer program preceding enrollment in the first grade helps, but it is not enough. Five hundred English words are better than none, but they are not equivalent to two or three thousand. Three months can add something to a child's experience, but they cannot make up for six years of privation. For that matter, neither can nine!

The Spanish language is an asset of Spanish-speaking children which should not be wasted through neglect. At some point in their lives these children should have an opportunity to become literate in their spoken language. To provide such an opportunity requires careful and realistic planning. It should be realized that only the more able and those with unusually favorable opportunities to learn the two languages in a natural setting may be expected to develop a high level of ability in both English and Spanish. For most children there simply is not enough time in the school day and in the years which will be spent in school to learn two languages to a high level of efficiency and at the same time learn the other things which life in the modern world demands.

It is possible for overanxiety about learning a language to hinder the learning process itself by robbing it of content. Language grows out of the need for communication, and drill which is normal and necessary can easily be dull and barren when it has no other motive than learning forms which are said to be correct.

The general objectives and problems in the education of Spanish-speaking children are precisely the same as they are for all children. All need an opportunity to develop their capacities and to become useful and productive citizens. Like other children, Spanish-speaking children are widely different among themselves. The special problems of the schools they attend arise from the large numbers who must learn English as a second language and who must be instructed in other fields of study in this second language, from the large numbers who are of low economic level with its accompanying deprivations, from certain differences in cultural traits, and from the fact that the Spanish-speaking and English-speaking people are as yet imperfectly united in a single cooperating community. It is to meet these conditions that the schools need to mould their policies and programs.

Schools need all the devices which can be accumulated to give children who are learning English more contacts with spoken and written English than the teacher can provide in the class period. Filmstrips, tape recorders, television, interesting reading material suitable for different degrees of learning are of inestimable value. Television programs skillfully designed, presented with the help of children, and broadcast at out-of-school hours could help a whole community.

Many children need help in securing adequate food, clothing, and school supplies. In a well-organized community, various agencies can share this responsibility, but in some places the school itself must become a relief agency as well as an educational institution. Whatever the source of aid, one of the central problems is to give it in such a way that it will not damage the child's self-respect or tend to perpetuate and increase his dependency.

The satisfaction of material needs is only part of the problem. The school must adjust its program to large numbers of children who have had less than normal opportunity to learn outside of school. At the same time it must make provision for extreme differences in capacity. The ideal in the development of human resources is to provide such opportunities that the only factor limiting the development of a child will be his capacity. At every level of ability obstacles to progress must be removed, opportunities for learning provided, and children guided in making the most of these opportunities. Efforts to help the slow learner should be balanced by a "Project Talent" which will rescue gifted children whose progress is now hindered by unusual difficulties and by discouragement.

The education of the migrant child presents special problems which can be met only by the cooperation of school, home, employer, and related community agencies. Although there is hope for a lessening of the need of migratory labor through automation and the development of opportunities for year-round employment in a given community, the migration of agricultural laborers to and from areas of peak employment will continue to create major social and educational problems for many years.

Modern Schools for a Modern World

So much is at stake in the education of children that no one should be satisfied with less opportunity than a modern world can provide. "Opportunity" implies buildings, equipment, and materials of the kind which will make educational effort most productive. It is not enough that children be enrolled, housed, and taught without prejudice. Equal treatment may also be inferior treatment for all.

Even more important in the educative process is the professional staff: those who administer, supervise, teach, or engage in the special services which modern education requires. The devotion and professional competence of the staff determine in large measure the kind of school which a community will have. It is a heavy responsibility to interpret the needs of children, to provide appropriate learning opportunities for them, to help them overcome difficulties, to inspire them to do their best, to lead them toward happy and effective living, and to prepare them for citizenship.

Community Support

The kind of schools which a community has is a responsibility of the whole community—local, state, and national. The community must provide the material support and the climate in which superior schools can flourish. Since a child learns from his total environment, the community owes it to its children not only to provide excellent schools but to maintain out-of-school conditions which will be favorable to growth in intellect and character. All the institutions and agencies of a community are part of the teaching environment and thus influence what children learn. In addition to this incidental teaching, many give direct assistance to the schools or conduct educational activities of their own.

The home occupies a unique place in relation to the school and is an educational agency in itself. There the child gets his start in language and in knowledge of the world. There he develops his basic emotional trends. There he is given support or denied it as he makes his way through the school. There his future is profoundly influenced in many ways. Whatever makes the home a better place for children contributes to education.

The church shares with the home the primary responsibility for religious education. Often also it conducts a significant program in general education. Its ministry to physical and economic needs improves the educational opportunity of many children. Its teaching of the brotherhood of man is a powerful influence toward friendship, sympathy, and cooperation.

The government of a community is responsible for the organization and support of public schools as well as for many other activities which serve the general welfare. These activities may include, as in Denver, a definite program for the promotion of understanding and cooperation among the people of different groups.

Parent-Teacher Associations, luncheon clubs, and other voluntary organizations add to the educational resources of a community. Their contribution includes cooperation with schools, promotion of interest in education, cultivation of understanding and good will, and assistance to individuals who need help. Such organizations can make one of their best contributions to education and to the community by including both English-speaking and Spanish-speaking persons in their membership and demonstrating effective cooperation in their own activities. The climate of understanding and good will developed in this way will spread to the larger community and will be reflected in the relations of children in and out of school.

The school itself can be a laboratory in which children prepare for a better community. In such a laboratory both the activities in which the children engage and the climate in which they work are significant factors in such preparation. The fifth grade of a semi-rural school which was visited in California provided an impressive illustration of this point. Of the thirty pupils enrolled, seven were from Spanish-speaking families. The class was working on a unit of study dealing with the colonists of New England. "These people," the memorandum which was given to the visitor recorded, "came with an ideal of personal freedom, both social and religious. As such an ideal inspired and nurtured a concept of complete democracy, it will also develop a deep appreciation and understanding of our democratic way of life." The class was engaged in varied "laboratory" activities, some of which obviously were designed to give a background of experience for their study. A few of the children were dipping candles and in that group was a little girl who seemed to express the spirit of all. It was near Christmas, and as she was dipping her candle she was singing softly "Silent night, holy night."

A Final Word

The education of Spanish-speaking children is a problem of concern to all, English-speaking and Spanish-speaking alike, and all share the responsibility for dealing with it effectively. It is partly a technical problem for the educator who must find and apply better ways of dealing with children handicapped by differences in language, culture, and socioeconomic status. It is partly a problem of obtaining support for research and for the practical work of the schools. It is partly a problem of strengthening the constructive forces of the community. It is partly a problem of developing a better economy.

But it is more than these. The education of Spanish-speaking children is part of the problem of building and maintaining the democratic society to which the nation aspires. It is part of the worldwide problem of building communities, nations, and international organizations in which persons and groups of different origin, language, and culture will participate on an equal basis for the common welfare. The isolation of many centuries developed group differences which tend to keep peoples of different heritage apart, but migration has brought them together, and modern transportation has made all the world neighbors. The problems of living together must be solved or our civilization will perish. There is no choice.

APPENDIX

Number of White Persons with Spanish Surname and
Number of Nonwhite Persons in 421 Counties of the Southwest
(Census of 1960)

	Spanish Surname, White		Nonwhite Total	
	Number	Percentage of Total Population	Number	Percentage of Total Population
ARIZONA	194,356	14.9	132,644	10.2
County				
Apache	960	3.2	23,603	86.4
Cochise	13,764	25.0	1,974	3.6
Coconino	4,341	10.4	12,969	31.0
Gila	5,633	21.9	3,658	14.2
Graham	2,433	17.3	1,658	11.8
Greenlee	5,238	45.5	237	2.1
Maricopa	78,996	11.9	36,430	5.4
Mohave	565	7.3	763	9.9
Navajo	2,604	6.9	20,176	53.1
Pima	44,481	16.7	16,607	6.3
Pinal	17,343	27.7	9,631	15.4
Santa Cruz	6,222	57.6	145	1.3
Yavapai	2,463	8.5	955	3.3
Yuma	9,313	20.1	3,840	8.3
CALIFORNIA	1,426,538	9.1	1,261,974	8.0
County				
Alameda	67,866	7.4	139,213	15.3
Alpine	none		188	47.4

	Spanish Surname, White		Nonwhite Total	
	Number	Percentage of Total Population	Number	Percentage of Total Population
Amador	612	6.1	328	3.3
Butte	2,179	2.7	1,697	2.1
Calaveras	468	4.5	238	2.3
Colusa	1,152	9.5	388	3.2
Contra Costa	24,854	6.1	30,142	7.4
Del Norte	245	1.4	759	4.3
El Dorado	696	2.4	215	0.7
Fresno	61,418	16.8	27,565	7.5
Glenn	1,128	6.5	197	1.1
Humboldt	2,268	2.2	3,031	2.9
Imperial	23,850	33.1	5,730	7.9
Inyo	414	3.5	1,064	9.1
Kern	29,219	10.0	20,407	7.0
Kings	11,656	23.3	3,255	6.5
Lake	358	2.6	479	3.5
Lassen	1,009	7.4	749	5.5
Los Angeles	576,716	9.6	584,905	9.7
Madera	6,225	15.4	3,692	9.1
Marin	5,634	3.8	5,518	3.8
Mariposa	116	2.3	143	2.8
Mendocino	1,201	2.4	1,741	3.4
Merced	13,429	14.8	6,750	7.5
Modoc	166	2.0	325	3.9
Mono	32	1.4	129	5.8
Monterey	23,118	11.7	17,784	9.0
Napa	2,715	4.1	1,275	1.9
Nevada	508	2.4	151	0.7
Orange	52,576	7.4	9,571	1.4
Placer	3,729	6.5	2,133	3.7
Plumas	305	2.6	498	4.3
Riverside	36,224	11.8	16,819	5.4
Sacramento	30,078	6.0	37,952	7.5
San Benito	4,642	30.2	559	3.6
San Bernardino	60,177	11.9	21,396	4.2
San Diego	64,810	6.3	56,940	5.5
San Francisco	51,602	7.0	135,913	18.4
San Joaquin	30,585	12.2	24,747	9.9
San Luis Obispo	5,788	7.1	3,013	3.7
San Mateo	19,722	4.4	19,174	4.3
Santa Barbara	22,267	13.2	6,175	3.7
Santa Clara	77,755	12.1	20,690	3.2

	Spanish Surname, White		Nonwhite Total	
	Number	Percentage of Total Population	Number	Percentage of Total Population
Santa Cruz	5,774	6.9	3,233	3.8
Shasta	1,202	2.0	1,299	2.2
Sierra	125	5.6	79	3.5
Siskiyou	1,363	4.1	1,397	4.3
Solano	7,561	5.6	16,734	12.4
Sonoma	5,196	3.5	3,265	2.2
Stanislaus	11,866	7.5	2,254	1.4
Sutter	1,747	5.2	1,665	5.0
Tehama	931	3.7	285	1.1
Trinity	48	0.5	204	2.1
Tulare	27,387	16.3	6,873	4.1
Tuolumne	766	5.3	254	1.8
Ventura	33,980	17.1	6,574	3.3
Yolo	7,757	11.8	2,397	3.6
Yuba	1,323	3.9	1,821	5.4
COLORADO	157,173	9.0	53,247	3.0
County				
Adams	8,542	7.1	1,995	1.7
Alamosa	2,494	24.9	165	1.7
Arapahoe	2,987	2.6	829	0.7
Archuleta	953	36.2	26	1.0
Baca	172	2.7	55	0.9
Bent	1,454	19.6	71	1.0
Boulder	3,103	4.2	570	0.8
Chaffee	732	8.8	39	0.5
Cheyenne	8	0.3	2	0.1
Clear Creek	17	0.6	4	0.1
Conejos	4,476	53.1	32	0.4
Costilla	3,065	72.6	84	2.0
Crowley	1,023	25.7	40	1.0
Custer	93	7.1	none	
Delta	1,173	7.5	4.	0.3
Denver	43,147	8.7	35,261	7.1
Dolores	3	0.1	137	6.3
Douglas	191	4.0	8	0.2
Eagle	1,187	25.4	29	0.6
Elbert	62	1.7	16	0.4
El Paso	6,135	4.3	6,035	4.2
Fremont	1,798	8.9	214	1.1
Garfield	285	2.4	22	0.2

	Spanish Surname, White		Nonwhite Total	
	Number	Percentage of Total Population	Number	Percentage of Total Population
Gilpin	75	10.9	2	0.3
Grand	91	2.6	8	0.2
Gunnison	142	2.6	36	0.7
Hinsdale	3	1.4	none	
Huerfano	3,608	45.9	57	0.7
Jackson	58	3.3	5	0.3
Jefferson	2,515	2.0	500	0.4
Kiowa	17	0.7	13	0.5
Kit Carson	69	1.0	6	0.1
Lake	901	12.7	48	0.7
La Plata	2,346	12.2	713	3.7
Larimer	2,160	4.0	303	0.6
Las Animas	7,443	37.2	97	0.5
Lincoln	58	1.1	3	0.1
Logan	839	4.1	69	0.3
Mesa	2,612	5.2	231	0.5
Mineral	3	0.7	1	0.2
Moffat	207	2.9	9	0.1
Montezuma	901	6.4	803	5.7
Montrose	1,291	7.1	138	0.8
Morgan	1,642	7.7	72	0.3
Otero	5,328	22.1	295	1.2
Ouray	217	13.6	8	0.5
Park	39	2.1	1	0.1
Phillips	31	0.7	3	0.1
Pitkin	4	0.2	17	0.7
Prowers	1,424	10.7	50	0.4
Pueblo	25,437	21.4	2,622	2.2
Rio Blanco	32	0.6	20	0.4
Rio Grande	3,477	31.2	36	0.3
Routt	99	1.7	27	0.5
Saguache	1,411	31.5	6	0.1
San Juan	145	17.1	1	0.1
San Miguel	132	4.5	354	12.0
Sedgwick	322	7.6	102	2.4
Summit	22	1.1	5	0.2
Teller	20	0.8	none	
Washington	46	0.7	8	0.1
Weld	8,831	12.2	896	1.2
Yuma	75	0.8	7	0.1
NEW MEXICO	269,122	28.3	75,260	7.9
County				
Bernalillo	68,101	26.0	8,751	3.3

	Spanish Surname, White		Nonwhite Total	
	Number	Percentage of Total Population	Number	Percentage of Total Population
Catron	755	27.2	67	2.4
Chavez	7,784	13.5	2,324	4.0
Colfax	5,535	40.1	102	0.7
Curry	3,676	11.2	2,001	6.1
De Baca	748	25.0	3	0.1
Dona Ana	25,214	42.1	1,674	2.8
Eddy	11,224	22.1	1,100	2.2
Grant	8,820	47.2	157	0.8
Guadalupe	4,068	72.5	13	0.2
Harding	497	26.5	2	0.1
Hidalgo	2,013	40.6	24	0.5
Lea	2,555	4.8	2,736	5.1
Lincoln	2,240	28.9	75	1.0
Los Alamos	1,463	11.2	90	0.7
Luna	3,388	34.4	196	2.0
McKinley	4,521	12.2	21,546	57.9
Mora	5,148	85.4	3	0.1
Otero	5,891	15.9	2,737	7.4
Quay	3,604	29.4	143	1.2
Rio Arriba	16,835	69.6	2,398	9.9
Roosevelt	1,024	6.3	123	0.8
Sandoval	4,538	32.0	5,959	42.0
San Juan	3,645	6.8	14,690	27.6
San Miguel	16,077	68.5	137	0.6
Santa Fe	24,400	54.3	1,129	2.5
Sierra	1,382	21.6	63	1.0
Socorro	4,761	46.8	695	6.8
Taos	11,015	69.1	1,040	6.5
Torrence	2,710	41.7	28	0.4
Union	1,472	24.3	5	0.1
Valencia	14,018	35.9	5,249	13.4
TEXAS	1,417,811	14.8	1,204,846	12.6
County				
Anderson	397	1.4	8,365	29.7
Andrews	525	3.9	286	2.1
Angelina	530	1.3	7,083	17.8
Aransas	1,368	19.5	287	4.1
Archer	50	0.8	28	0.4
Armstrong	21	1.1	5	0.3
Atascosa	8,545	45.4	188	1.0
Austin	240	1.7	2,958	21.4
Bailey	1,129	12.4	372	4.1

	Spanish Surname, White		Nonwhite Total	
	Number	Percentage of Total Population	Number	Percentage of Total Population
Bandera	262	6.7	19	0.4
Bastrop	1,819	10.7	5,293	31.3
Baylor	132	2.2	233	4.0
Bee	8,580	36.1	639	2.7
Bell	6,332	6.7	11,398	12.1
Bexar	257,090	37.4	47,395	6.9
Blanco	235	6.4	103	2.8
Borden	none		none	
Bosque	235	2.2	368	3.4
Bowie	652	1.1	14,396	24.0
Brazoria	5,172	6.8	9,150	12.0
Brazos	3,572	8.0	9,485	21.1
Brewster	2,743	42.6	49	0.8
Briscoe	396	11.1	194	5.4
Brooks	5,928	68.9	12	0.1
Brown	1,346	5.4	761	3.1
Burleson	765	6.8	3,498	31.3
Burnet	756	8.2	171	1.8
Caldwell	4,905	28.4	2,604	15.1
Calhoun	4,170	25.1	822	5.0
Callahan	190	2.4	8	0.1
Cameron	96,744	64.0	1,225	0.8
Camp	91	1.2	2,986	38.0
Carson	359	4.6	27	0.3
Cass	94	0.4	6,984	29.7
Castro	1,368	15.3	373	4.2
Chambers	185	1.8	2,293	22.1
Cherokee	503	1.5	8,530	25.8
Childress	277	3.3	527	6.3
Clay	110	1.3	83	1.0
Cochran	1,274	19.9	293	4.6
Coke	244	6.8	5	0.1
Coleman	591	4.7	324	2.6
Collin	1,132	2.7	4,461	10.8
Collingsworth	259	4.1	536	8.5
Colorado	1,181	6.4	4,595	24.9
Comal	5,431	27.4	423	2.1
Comanche	239	2.0	17	0.1
Concho	738	20.1	3	0.1
Cooke	429	1.9	861	3.8
Coryell	1,040	4.3	1,454	6.1
Cottle	495	11.8	344	8.2
Crane	119	2.5	227	4.8

	Spanish Surname, White		Nonwhite Total	
	Number	*Percentage of Total Population*	*Number*	*Percentage of Total Population*
Crockett	1,098	26.1	126	3.0
Crosby	2,084	20.1	881	8.5
Culberson	1,075	38.5	14	0.5
Dallam	437	6.9	59	0.9
Dallas	32,741	3.4	140,266	14.7
Dawson	4,569	23.8	1,081	5.6
Deaf Smith	2,468	18.7	266	2.0
Delta	8	0.1	860	14.7
Denton	885	1.9	2,986	6.3
De Witt	3,928	19.0	2,787	13.5
Dickens	383	7.7	261	5.3
Dimmit	6,760	67.0	57	0.6
Donley	42	0.9	221	5.0
Duval	9,788	73.1	7	0.1
Eastland	814	4.2	346	1.8
Ector	7,000	7.7	4,875	5.4
Edwards	764	33.0	8	0.3
Ellis	2,232	5.1	10,268	23.7
El Paso	136,993	43.6	10,515	3.3
Erath	147	0.9	141	0.9
Falls	1,783	8.4	6,957	32.7
Fannin	273	1.1	2,507	10.5
Fayette	423	2.1	2,880	14.1
Fisher	1,138	14.5	377	4.8
Floyd	1,965	15.9	893	7.2
Foard	157	5.0	278	8.9
Fort Bend	9,972	24.6	8,127	20.1
Franklin	11	0.2	395	7.7
Freestone	28	0.2	4,921	39.3
Frio	6,250	61.8	61	0.6
Gaines	1,003	8.2	365	3.0
Galveston	11,872	8.4	30,067	21.4
Garza	907	13.7	321	4.9
Gillespie	379	3.8	18	0.2
Glasscock	100	8.9	13	1.2
Goliad	1,900	35.0	628	11.6
Gonzalez	3,594	20.1	3,257	18.3
Gray	168	0.5	943	3.0
Grayson	1,275	1.7	6,530	8.9
Gregg	258	0.4	15,930	22.9
Grimes	545	4.3	4,850	38.2
Guadalupe	6,871	23.7	3,312	11.4
Hale	6,504	17.7	2,016	5.5

	Spanish Surname, White		Nonwhite Total	
	Number	Percentage of Total Population	Number	Percentage of Total Population
Hall	321	4.4	965	13.2
Hamilton	193	2.3	13	0.2
Hansford	70	1.1	24	0.4
Hardeman	382	4.6	992	12.0
Hardin	256	1.0	4,020	16.3
Harris	75,013	6.0	249,473	20.1
Harrison	250	0.5	19,796	43.4
Hartley	95	4.4	2	0.1
Haskell	1,155	10.3	643	5.8
Hays	7,208	36.2	1,132	5.7
Hemphill	84	2.6	2	0.1
Henderson	67	0.3	4,523	20.8
Hidalgo	129,092	71.4	676	0.4
Hill	843	3.6	3,691	15.6
Hockley	3,537	15.8	1,274	5.7
Hood	96	1.8	52	1.0
Hopkins	282	1.5	2,320	12.5
Houston	526	2.7	7,458	38.5
Howard	4,091	10.2	1,771	4.4
Hudspeth	982	29.4	14	0.4
Hunt	217	0.6	6,465	16.4
Hutchinson	379	1.1	762	2.2
Irion	198	16.7	11	0.9
Jack	59	0.8	86	1.2
Jackson	1,929	13.7	1,693	12.1
Jasper	170	0.8	5,502	24.9
Jeff Davis	887	56.1	2	0.1
Jefferson	6,571	2.7	57,362	23.4
Jim Hogg	3,861	76.9	6	0.1
Jim Wells	18,848	54.6	397	1.1
Johnson	593	1.7	1,688	4.9
Jones	1,644	8.5	1,120	5.8
Karnes	5,595	37.3	425	2.8
Kaufman	323	1.1	8,966	30.0
Kendall	698	11.9	40	0.7
Kenedy	712	80.5	none	
Kent	23	1.3	47	2.7
Kerr	1,920	11.4	716	4.3
Kimble	533	13.5	9	0.2
King	13	2.0	48	7.5
Kinney	1,166	47.6	190	7.7
Kleberg	12,514	41.6	1,134	3.8
Knox	709	9.0	583	7.4

| | Spanish Surname, White | | Nonwhite Total | |
	Number	Percentage of Total Population	Number	Percentage of Total Population
Lamar	66	0.2	6,435	18.8
Lamb	3,562	16.3	1,679	7.7
Lampasas	702	7.5	290	3.1
La Salle	3,832	64.2	7	0.1
Lavaca	933	4.6	2,112	10.5
Lee	247	2.8	2,141	23.9
Leon	52	0.5	3,798	38.2
Liberty	251	0.8	7,413	23.5
Limestone	432	2.1	5,807	28.4
Lipscomb	26	0.8	28	0.8
Live Oak	2,686	34.2	19	0.2
Llano	205	3.9	46	0.9
Loving	none		10	4.4
Lubbock	17,003	10.9	12,469	8.0
Lynn	2,092	19.2	669	6.1
McCullough	1,308	14.8	328	3.7
McLennan	7,801	5.2	24,221	16.1
McMullen	314	28.1	none	
Madison	52	0.8	2,246	33.3
Marion	21	0.3	4,221	52.4
Martin	787	15.5	211	4.2
Mason	323	8.5	23	0.6
Matagorda	3,582	13.9	5,327	20.7
Maverick	11,253	77.6	34	0.2
Medina	6,998	37.0	180	1.0
Menard	694	23.4	38	1.3
Midland	4,423	6.5	6,313	9.3
Milam	1,262	5.7	4,032	18.1
Mills	98	2.2	4	0.1
Mitchell	1,870	16.6	832	7.4
Montague	120	0.8	2	0.0
Montgomery	414	1.5	6,146	22.9
Moore	321	2.2	64	0.4
Morris	136	1.1	3,400	27.0
Motley	142	4.9	266	9.3
Nacogdoches	566	2.0	7,529	26.8
Navarro	584	1.7	8,567	24.9
Newton	50	0.5	3,447	33.2
Nolan	1,726	9.1	752	4.0
Nueces	84,386	38.1	10,393	4.7
Ochiltree	130	1.4	21	0.2
Oldham	10	0.5	4	0.2
Orange	1,548	2.6	6,039	10.0

	Spanish Surname, White		Nonwhite Total	
	Number	Percentage of Total Population	Number	Percentage of Total Population
Palo Pinto	852	4.2	933	4.5
Panola	140	0.8	5,179	30.7
Parker	471	2.1	467	2.0
Parmer	981	10.2	245	2.6
Pecos	3,708	31.0	94	0.8
Polk	157	1.1	4,451	32.1
Potter	3,668	3.2	7,987	6.9
Presidio	2,700	49.4	5	0.1
Rains	none		307	10.3
Randall	336	1.0	72	0.2
Reagan	512	13.5	262	6.9
Real	402	19.3	4	0.2
Red River	34	0.2	3,828	24.4
Reeves	7,128	40.4	634	3.6
Refugio	3,484	31.7	1,032	9.4
Roberts	none		12	1.1
Robertson	1,084	6.7	6,545	40.5
Rockwall	230	3.9	1,415	24.1
Runnels	1,698	11.3	408	2.7
Rusk	125	0.3	10,613	29.1
Sabine	16	0.2	1,898	26.0
San Augustine	26	0.3	3,009	39.0
San Jacinto	32	0.5	3,209	52.2
San Patricio	22,239	49.4	858	1.9
San Saba	582	9.1	50	0.8
Schleicher	579	20.7	80	2.9
Scurry	1,730	8.5	576	2.8
Shackelford	16	0.4	128	3.2
Shelby	none		5,261	25.7
Sherman	52	2.0	1	0.0
Smith	613	0.7	23,384	27.1
Somervell	51	2.0	3	0.1
Starr	15,196	88.7	15	0.1
Stephens	196	2.2	398	4.5
Sterling	154	13.1	10	0.8
Stonewall	22	0.7	119	3.9
Sutton	1,476	39.5	32	0.9
Swisher	999	9.4	434	4.1
Tarrant	19,373	3.6	59,748	11.1
Taylor	5,032	5.0	4,749	4.7
Terrell	1,128	43.4	9	0.3
Terry	2,460	15.1	605	3.7
Throckmorton	86	3.1	28	1.0

	Spanish Surname, White		Nonwhite Total	
	Number	Percentage of Total Population	Number	Percentage of Total Population
Titus	46	0.3	2,942	17.5
Tom Green	8,876	13.7	3,203	5.0
Travis	26,072	12.3	27,224	12.8
Trinity	none		2,035	27.0
Tyler	53	0.5	2,251	21.1
Upshur	20	0.1	5,128	25.9
Upton	776	12.4	272	4.4
Uvalde	8,002	47.6	167	1.0
Val Verde	10,814	44.2	800	3.3
Van Zandt	155	0.8	1,435	7.5
Victoria	10,767	23.2	4,019	8.6
Walker	584	2.7	7,034	32.8
Waller	331	2.7	6,481	53.7
Ward	1,792	12.0	389	2.6
Washington	106	0.6	6,120	32.0
Webb	51,784	79.9	281	0.4
Wharton	5,664	14.8	7,808	20.5
Wheeler	47	0.6	299	3.8
Wichita	3,444	2.8	9,080	7.4
Wilbarger	583	3.3	1,675	9.4
Willacy	13,734	68.4	107	0.5
Williamson	5,284	15.1	4,889	14.0
Wilson	4,911	37.0	260	2.0
Winkler	917	6.7	439	3.2
Wise	237	1.4	145	0.9
Wood	59	0.3	2,745	15.5
Yoakum	360	4.5	84	1.0
Young	208	1.2	279	1.6
Zapata	3,285	74.8	19	0.4
Zavala	9,440	74.4	67	0.5
		Totals		
Arizona	194,356	14.9	132,644	10.2
California	1,426,538	9.1	1,261,974	8.0
Colorado	157,173	9.0	53,247	3.0
New Mexico	269,122	28.3	75,260	7.9
Texas	1,417,811	14.8	1,204,846	12.6
Southwest	3,465,000	11.8	2,727,971	9.3

REFERENCES

This book provides only an introduction to the many and complex problems with which the Southwest must deal in educating children of different languages and cultures. Too, it is an introduction slanted in the selection and treatment of materials by the interests, point of view, and objectives of the author. It is hoped that many readers will want to dig more deeply into the problems and to examine divergent points of view. To assist in extending the study, the following references are listed.

General

The assumption that the objective of the Spanish-speaking and English-speaking people of the Southwest should be a community in which group lines tend to disappear may itself be challenged. It is possible to argue that efforts should be made to develop the two cultures and the two languages in relative independence each of the other. Joshua A. Fishman and associates describe some of the conditions leading to language maintenance and language shift (to some extent also cultural changes) in populations which are in contact with each other:

Language Loyalty in the United States. A three-volume report to the U.S. Office of Education, Language Research Section, under Contract SAE-8729, 1964. Chapter 16, by Jane MacNab Christian and Chester C. Christian, Jr., is a discussion of the "Spanish Language and Culture in the Southwest," including a "historical survey," a discussion of the "contemporary Spanish-speaking Americans," a "sociocultural analysis," and a bibliography of some 160 references.

The quotation from Horace Mann's Annual Report for 1846 may be found in the volume, *Annual Reports of the Secretary of the Board of Education of Massachusetts for the Years 1845–1848.* Boston: Lee and Shepard, 1891.

European Background

Persons who wish to study the European background of the American colonists will find assistance in the following references:

James Truslow Adams (ed.), *Atlas of American History*. New York: Charles Scribner's Sons, 1943. 360 pp.

Herbert E. Bolton and Thomas M. Marshall. *The Colonization of North America, 1492–1783*. New York: The Macmillan Company, 1920. 609 pp.

Dan Clark. *The West in American History*. New York: Thomas Y. Crowell Company, 1937. 682 pp.

Loren C. MacKinney. *The Medieval World*. New York: Rinehart & Company, 1938. 801 pp.

R. R. Palmer. *A History of the Modern World*. New York: Alfred A. Knopf, Inc., 1950. 900 pp.

James W. Thompson and Edgar N. Johnson. *An Introduction to Mediaeval Europe, 300–1500*. New York: W. W. Norton & Company, 1937. 1092 pp.

Mexico and the Southwest

An interesting anthropological view of Mexican history is provided by:

Eric R. Wolf. *Sons of the Shaking Earth*. Chicago: University of Chicago Press, 1959. 302 pp.

The early Maya civilization is discussed in the following:

J. Eric S. Thompson. *The Rise and Fall of Maya Civilization*. Norman: University of Oklahoma Press, 1956. 288 pp.

Sylvanus G. Morley and George W. Brainerd. *The Ancient Maya*. 3d ed. Stanford: Stanford University Press, 1956. 494 pp.

The Indians of the Southwest are discussed by:

Harold S. Gladwin. *A History of the Ancient Southwest*. Portland, Maine: Bond Wheelwright, 1957. 383 pp.

The history of the Southwest may be surveyed with the assistance of such books as these:

American Council of Learned Societies. *Report of the Committee on Linguistic and National Stocks in the Population of the United States*. Washington: U.S. Government Printing Office, 1932. 441 pp.

Herbert E. Bolton. *Spanish Exploration in the Southwest, 1542–1706*. New York: Barnes & Noble, Inc., 1908; reprinted 1959. 487 pp.

Charles F. Coan. *A History of New Mexico*. Vol. 1. New York: American Historical Society, 1925. 586 pp.

"Mexico," *Encyclopedia Britannica*.

George P. Hammond (ed.) *Coronado Cuarto Centennial Publications, 1540–1940*. Vol. 5: "Don Juan de Oñate, Colonizer of New Mexico, 1595–1628."

Hubert C. Herring. *A History of Latin America from the Beginnings to the Present.* New York: Alfred A. Knopf, Inc., 1955. 796 pp.

Carl F. Karaenzel. *The Great Plains in Transition.* Norman: University of Oklahoma Press, 1955. 428 pp.

Woodbury Lowery. *Spanish Settlements within the Present Limits of the United States, 1513–1561.* New York: G. P. Putnam's Sons, 1901. 515 pp.

Rupert N. Richardson and Carl C. Rister. *The Greater Southwest.* Glendale, California: Arthur H. Clark Company, 1934. 506 pp.

Irving B. Richman. *California under Spain and Mexico.* Boston: Houghton Mifflin Company, 1911. 541 pp.

George L. Rives. *The United States and Mexico, 1821–1848.* New York: Charles Scribner's Sons, 1913. Vol. I, 720 pp., Vol. II, 726 pp.

Walter P. Webb. *The Great Plains.* Boston: Houghton Mifflin Company, 1936. 525 pp.

Government Reports on Population

Many characteristics of the population of the Southwest are shown in reports of the United States census. A special census report, *Persons of Spanish Surname,* was issued for the census of 1950 and for the census of 1960. This report gives data on nativity and parentage, age, education, employment, and certain other characteristics of the white population of Spanish surname in the five southwestern states of our study. Annual reports of the Immigration and Naturalization Service provide data on immigration.

The Spanish-Speaking People

Many writers have discussed the people of Mexico and the Spanish-speaking population of the Southwest. The following references provide an introduction to this extensive literature:

Ralph L. Beals and Norman D. Humphrey. *No Frontier to Learning. The Mexican Student in the United States.* Minneapolis: University of Minnesota Press, 1957. 148 pp.

Emory S. Bogardus. *The Mexican in the United States.* Los Angeles: University of Southern California Press, 1934. 126 pp.

John H. Burma. *Spanish-Speaking Groups in the United States.* Durham: Duke University Press, 1954. 214 pp.

Florence Rockwood Kluckhohn and Fred O. Strodtbeck. *Variations in Value Orientations.* Evanston, Illinois: Row, Peterson, & Company, 1961. 437 pp.

Carey McWilliams. *North from Mexico, the Spanish-Speaking People of the United States.* Philadelphia: J. B. Lippincott Company, 1949. 324 pp.

Sister Mary John Murray. *A Socio-Cultural Study of 118 Mexican Families Living in a Low-Rent Public Housing Project in San Antonio, Texas.* Washington: Catholic University of American Press, 1954. 151 pp.

George I. Sánchez. *Forgotten People. A Study of New Mexicans.* Albuquerque: The University of New Mexico Press, 1940. 98 pp.

Lyle Saunders. *Cultural Difference and Medical Care: The Case of the Spanish-Speaking People of the Southwest.* New York: Russell Sage Foundation, 1954. 317 pp.

Ozzie G. Simmons. "Anglo Americans and Mexican Americans in South Texas: A Study in Dominant-Subordinate Group Relations." Unpublished Ph.D. dissertation, Harvard University, 1952. 583 pp.

Lloyd S. Tireman and Mary Watson. *La Comunidad.* Later published as *A Community School in a Spanish-Speaking Village.* Albuquerque: The University of New Mexico Press, 1948. 169 pp.

Ruth D. Tuck. *Not with the Fist: Mexican-Americans in a Southwest City.* New York: Harcourt, Brace and Company, 1946. 234 pp.

Horacio Ulibarri. *The Effect of Cultural Difference in the Education of Spanish Americans.* Unpublished report prepared for the University of New Mexico Research Study: The Adjustment of Indian and Non-Indian Children in the Public Schools of New Mexico. Directed by Miles V. Zintz. Albuquerque: The University of New Mexico College of Education, 1958. 99 pp.

Sister Frances Jerome Woods. *Culture Values of American Ethnic Groups.* New York: Harper & Brothers, 1956. 402 pp.

State Statistics

The statistical reports of state departments of education need no further citation than is given in the text. Among the Texas studies, now valuable chiefly as historical material, are the author's monograph of 1930, cited elsewhere, and the following:

Wilson Little. *Spanish-Speaking Children in Texas.* Austin: University of Texas Press, 1944. 73 pp.

Lyle Saunders. *The Spanish-Speaking Population of Texas.* Austin: University of Texas Press, 1949. 56 pp.

Ruth Ann Fogartie. *Texas-Born Spanish-Name Students in Texas Colleges and Universities (1945–1946).* Austin: University of Texas Press, 1948. 35 pp.

Educational Problems

A good place to start in the study of bilingualism in education is with the articles on "Bilingualism" and "English as a Second Language" in the *Encyclopedia of Educational Research* (3d ed., New York: The Macmillan

Company, 1960). The bibliographies following the articles suggest additional references. Robert Lado's *Linguistics Across Cultures* (Ann Arbor: The University of Michigan, 1957, 141 pp.) provides a good introduction to the problem of comparing languages. His *Annotated Bibliography for Teachers of English as a Foreign Language* (Washington: Office of Education, U.S. Department of Health, Education, and Welfare, Bulletin No. 3, 1955, 224 pp.) lists 730 references. Ralph B. Long has produced a scholarly and helpful grammar, *The Sentence and Its Parts: A Grammar of Contemporary English* (Chicago: University of Chicago Press, 1961, 528 pp.). Lloyd S. Tireman's *Teaching Spanish-Speaking Children* (Albuquerque: The University of New Mexico Press, 1948, 218 pp.) includes an excellent discussion of language. Sirarpi Ohannessian has prepared an annotated *Interim Bibliography on the Teaching of English to Speakers of Other Languages* (Washington: Center for Applied Linguistics of the Modern Language Association of America, 1960, 53 pp.).

A study directed by J. Cayce Morrison, sponsored by the Board of Education of New York City, and supported by the Fund for the Advancement of Education, is of special interest because it deals with another large Spanish-speaking group (*The Puerto Rican Study, 1953–1957*, New York City: Board of Education, 1958, 265 pp.).

George I. Sánchez and Howard Putnam have contributed an annotated bibliography of 882 titles on *Materials Relating to the Education of Spanish-Speaking People in the United States* (Austin: The University of Texas, Institute of Latin American Studies, 1959, 76 pp.).

Migrant Children

The Colorado State Department of Education has completed a Migrant Research Project directed by Alfred M. Potts. Among the Colorado materials are two publications produced by workshops sponsored jointly by the Department and Adams State College: *Learning on the Move, A Guide for Migrant Education* (1960, 220 pp.); *Guide to Organization and Administration of Migrant Education Programs* (1963, 26 pp.).

An additional reference on migrant children was quoted in the text: Helen Cowan Wood, Director of Project, *Teaching Children Who Move with the Crops* (Fresno: Walter G. Martin, Fresno County Superintendent of Schools, 1955, 95 pp.). This is a report of the Fresno, California, project dealing with the educational program for migrant children.

A third reference is *Nomads of the Classroom: Special Helps for Migrant Children in Arizona Classrooms* (Tempe: Arizona State University, College of Education, 1958, 173 pp.).

A Wisconsin study is reported by Donald R. Thomas, *Determining an Effective Educational Program for Children of Migratory Workers in Wisconsin, Phase I* (Madison: The University of Wisconsin, 1961, 58 pp.).

A significant reference from the standpoint of various agencies is the *Report and Recommendations of the Third Annual Conference on Families Who Follow the Crops* (Sacramento: Governor's Advisory Committee on Children and Youth, Subcommittee on the Migrant Child, 1962, 69 pp.).

Bilingual and Sub-Cultural Factors

The Arizona *Investigation of Mental Retardation and Pseudo Mental Retardation in Relation to Bilingual and Sub-Cultural Factors* (Tempe: Arizona State University, College of Education, 1960, 363 pp.) is notable not only for the report of its own study but also for its listing and analysis of related studies. G. D. McGrath was director of the project and Willard Abraham coordinator of research.

Early Studies

For their historical value several references may be of interest:

Herschel T. Manuel. *Education of Mexican and Spanish-Speaking Children in Texas*. Austin: The University of Texas, 1930. 173 pp.

Annie Reynolds. *Education of Spanish-Speaking Children in Five Southwestern States*. Washington: Office of Education, Bulletin 1933, No. 11, 1933. 64 pp.

J. L. Meriam. *Learning English Incidentally: A Study of Bilingual Children*. Washington: Office of Education, Bulletin 1937, No. 15, 1938. 105 pp.

Algernon Coleman and Clara B. King. *English Teaching in the Southwest*. Washington: American Council on Education, 1940. 307 pp.

Elma A. Neal and Ollie P. Storm. *Open Door Primer, First Reader*, and *Second Reader*, prepared especially for teaching Spanish-speaking children. New York: The Macmillan Company, 1927 and 1931.

Separate Educational Facilities

Segregation is discussed in a booklet by George I. Sánchez, *Concerning Segregation of Spanish-Speaking Children in the Public Schools*, Inter-American Education Occasional Papers IX (Austin: The University of Texas, 1951. 75 pp.).

Teaching Manuals

At various times state departments of education have issued manuals dealing with the education of Spanish-speaking children. As early as 1930 Texas issued *Course in English for Non-English-Speaking Pupils, Grades 1–3*; in 1932 California issued *Guide for Teachers of Beginning Non-English-Speaking Children*; and in 1939 Arizona issued *Instruction of Bilingual Children*. Many city schools have issued booklets for their own teachers.

Tests

Tests of special interest to teachers of Spanish-speaking children include the Goodenough-Harris *Drawing Test,* a nonverbal test of mental ability (New York: Harcourt, Brace, and World, 1963) ; Pablo Roca's *Escala de Inteligencia Wechsler para Niños,* 2d ed. (New York: Psychological Corporation, 1959) ; and the Inter-American Series of *Tests of General Ability* and *Tests of Reading,* with parallel Spanish tests *Pruebas de Habilidad General* and *Pruebas de Lectura,* constructed under the supervision of Herschel T. Manuel. Princeton, New Jersey: Educational Testing Service, 1950; Austin, Texas: Guidance Testing Associates, 1962.

Teaching of Spanish

E. E. Mireles of the Corpus Christi, Texas, Public Schools has been a pioneer in the growing movement toward teaching Spanish in the elementary schools. In 1940 he issued a booklet, *Short Course in Spanish,* containing the text of twenty lessons in Spanish broadcast by radio station KCOR.

Illustrations of manuals for teachers of Spanish in the elementary schools are these: *A Guide for the Teaching of Spanish in the Elementary Schools* (Washington: Public Schools of the District of Columbia, 1952, 87 pp., available from the U.S. Government Printing Office) ; *Spanish for Boys and Girls* (Santa Fe: New Mexico Department of Education, 1958, 164 pp.).

Booklets of Special Interest

Colorado Latin American Personalities, 2036 Eliot St., Denver 11, Colorado, is the address of the booklet of the same name compiled under the direction of Lino M. López.

The Department of Classroom Teachers of the National Education Association and the American Educational Research Association have joined in issuing a remarkable series of booklets, edited by Frank W. Hubbard, under the general title *What Research Says to the Teacher.* The booklets provide a helpful summary of the results of research and references to the literature. Two of interest in this discussion are Jean D. Grambs' "Understanding Intergroup Relations" and William C. Kvaraceus' "Juvenile Delinquency." The source is the National Education Association, 1201 Sixteenth Street, N.W., Washington 6, D.C.

Another series of booklets of special interest to laymen is edited by Mrs. Bert Kruger Smith and published by the Hogg Foundation for Mental Health, The University of Texas, Austin. Illustrative of this series is *Office in the Alley, Report on a Project with Gang Youngsters* by Father Harold J. Rahm and J. Robert Weber.

Teachers

A discussion of the qualifications of teachers of Spanish-speaking children may be found in various references listed in the preceding section. The basic references to research on teaching in general are *Characteristics of Teachers: Their Description, Comparison, and Appraisal*, by David G. Ryans (Washington: American Council on Education, 1960, 416 pp.); and *A Handbook of Research on Teaching*, Nathaniel L. Gage (ed.) (Chicago: Rand McNally, 1963, 1218 pp.).

In their "Project Beacon" the Graduate School of Education of Yeshiva University, New York City, has initiated training programs for teachers, administrators, guidance specialists, and other professional workers in "socially disadvantaged community schools." A "report to the profession," *Training Programs in Project Beacon*, was issued in January, 1963.

A Community Program

Those who are interested in the Denver program will find information in the *Annual Reports* of the Denver Commission on Community Relations, issued by the city of Denver, and in publications of the Denver Public Schools (Kenneth E. Oberholtzer, Superintendent) such as *People of Denver: Book One, Spanish-Speaking People*, 1951; and *Human Relations in Action: Pupils, Parents, and Teachers Work Together*, 1952.

The organization and activities of Denver Boys, Inc., directed by Tom W. Ewing, may be found in a pamphlet, *Opportunity for Youth*, and in the annual reports of the organization issued by the Rotary Club of Denver.

INDEX

Adams State College: 150
alcoholism: home and, 171–172
Aldrich, Daniel G., Jr: 142
Alianza Hispano-Americana: 181–182
Alianza Scholarship Foundation: 181–182
American Friends Service Committee: 175
American GI Forum: 181, 183
Annual Conferences on Families Who Follow the Crops: 151–152
Arizona: area of, 10; settlement of, 14; Spanish-surname whites and non-whites in, by county, 197 (table), 207 (table). SEE ALSO Southwest
assistance. SEE welfare
Austin, Stephen F.: 14
authoritarianism: in Mexican culture, 39–40
automation: 4

Bailey, Helen K.: 62, 66
Beals, Ralph L.: 39
behavior: personality and, 154–155; aggressive reactions in, 155–156; conditions affecting, 155–157; antisocial, 158–160, 189
Block, Marvin A.: 171–172
Blossom, Grace: 68

California: area and resources of, 10; settlement of, 14; Spanish-surname whites and nonwhites in, by county, 197–199 (table), 207 (table). SEE ALSO Southwest
Calvinism: 13

Campa, Arthur L.: 32
Canada: occupational level of immigrants from, 45, 46 (table)
Catholics: conflicts of, with Protestants, 13–14; enrollment of, in parochial schools, 54. SEE ALSO religion
church: home and, 171; educational processes and, 171, 172–176, 194; segregation in, 172–175; welfare activities of, 175–176. SEE ALSO religion
clothing: supplying of, 130, 131, 133; importance of, to personality adjustment, 157
Colorado: area and resources of, 10; Denver program for Spanish-speaking groups, 176–179; Spanish-surname whites and nonwhites in, by county, 199–200 (table), 207 (table). SEE ALSO Southwest
community: educational climate of, 3–4, 163, 193–195; educational demands of, 4–6; Spanish-speaking groups' distribution in, 30; child and family services of, 130–131, 192, 194; community school in, 133–135; Spanish-speaking children in life of, 156, 157–158, 184–185; home support by, 171; Denver program and, 177–179; unity in efforts of, 184–185
Congress of Parents and Teachers: 180, 194
Cooperative Inter-American Tests of General Ability: 65–66, 71
counseling. SEE education; school
culture: Southwest heritage of, 10, 12; diversity in, 10, 12, 31–44, 190; of Mexico, 12, 37, 39–40; described, 31–33;